THOMAS CHALMERS AND
THE DISRUPTION

DR. CHALMERS PREACHING
Silhouette by August Edouart

Thomas Chalmers
and the
Disruption

Incorporating the Chalmers Lectures
for 1940–44

by
Hugh Watt

Professor of Church History, New College, Edinburgh University

Thomas Nelson and Sons Ltd
Edinburgh London Paris Melbourne Toronto New York

BOOK
PRODUCTION
WAR ECONOMY
STANDARD

This book is produced in complete conformity
with the authorized economy standards

First published February 1943
Reprinted 1943

92
C 43W

CONTENTS

15597

CONTENTS

NOTE ON THE ILLUSTRATIONS

The frontispiece and the illustration on page 52 are two out of the four known silhouettes of Dr. Chalmers by Monsieur August Edouart, the French genius with the scissors who visited Edinburgh from 1829 to 1832, practising his art. They are specially good specimens of his flair for the characteristic attitudes of his subjects. Detailed information concerning the artist and his work will be found in *Ancestors in Silhouette, cut by August Edouart: Illustrative Notes and Biographical Sketches*, by Mrs. F. Nevill Jackson (London, 1921). The two illustrations are from a set of three gifted to New College in 1941 by R. H. Simpson, Esq., Hermitage, Corstorphine.

FOREWORD

When the Trustees of the Chalmers Lectureship did me the honour of asking me to undertake the lectureship for 1940–44, they conjoined with the invitation the suggestion that, since the centenary of the Disruption fell within the period, the lectures might suitably be devoted to a general consideration of Thomas Chalmers as a churchman with special reference to that great national event. While recognizing that the suggestion was a natural one, I was not at the time attracted by it : indeed, it was only with very great reluctance that I ultimately consented to accept nomination. For I could not claim to have made any special study of the man or of his time. I knew few of the original documents, and though I had read the three classic studies of the conflict by Dr. Buchanan, Dr. Bryce, and Mr. Turner, and some half-dozen of the shorter lives of Chalmers, I had only the slightest acquaintance with Dr. Hanna's four volumes, and could count on the fingers of one hand the pamphlets belonging to the great controversy which I had seriously looked at. But, since the library of my own college was held to possess the fullest collection of Disruption literature, and since it had been lately enriched by a very large Chalmers MS. collection, including his Journals and his voluminous correspondence, it was insisted that it was my manifest duty to undertake the task. So, for three years I have been living in the period, so far as war conditions would permit ; and, with every new vista gained, I have come increasingly to admire and love this greatest of modern Scottish churchmen.

In view of the fact that very few of the relevant writings of Chalmers himself were reprinted in any of the collections of his works, I found it desirable to draw up a list of all his publications, so far as these survive, and this guide-book is being issued separately by the courtesy and generosity of the Chalmers Lectureship Trustees very shortly. All of the many entries have been read, and at least an equal number in support of or in antagonism to their conclusions. I cannot claim to have read all the relevant contemporary literature ; that task would need much longer than three years.

In the Journals and letters I had noted many points, but in what follows there is hardly a single reference to these MSS. The reason is a simple one. I found on a closer reading of Dr. Hanna that he had anticipated me in practically every case. I do not think that any great man had ever a more conscientious official biographer than Thomas Chalmers had. There are few gleanings for later students in the vast material that Dr. Hanna handled, at least on the central issues. And if this study sends any back to Dr. Hanna's volumes, it will have done a useful service.

This book is based on the lectures as they were delivered first of all to students in Edinburgh, and then (in part) publicly in Glasgow and Aberdeen. While the lecture form has been departed from at all points where this could be done easily, some traces of it have been allowed to remain—especially in places where its elimination would have increased the demands on space.

In putting forth this volume I desire to express my thanks to the many who have helped in its preparation, in especial to Miss H. R. Leslie, M.A., who prepared the typescript ; to my revered former Principal, the Very Reverend Alexander Martin, D.D., LL.D., who read it, for wise and salutary advice from his wide knowledge of the period and the issues involved ; and to my fellow-student and friend, the Rev. R. W. Stewart, B.D., B.Sc., for his painstaking and most serviceable scrutiny of the proofs.

H.W.

New College, Edinburgh
    January 1943

THOMAS CHALMERS AND THE DISRUPTION

CHAPTER ONE

THE NATIONAL BACKGROUND

THOUGH Scotland had almost doubled its population in the eighteenth century it was still, when Thomas Chalmers preached and taught and laboured, a thinly peopled country. At the census of 1801 there were only 1,600,000 inhabitants, roughly a third of the present total. The grim poverty which had long been a national heritage had become distinctly less oppressive and obtrusive. Not only had prosperity visited certain definite localities at certain favoured times, but there was a general increase of comfort and well-being. Though the industrial revolution had not yet herded the great mass of the people into a definite Forth-and-Clyde area, the greater towns had thriven and grown. In 1801 Edinburgh (with Leith) was still the largest of these, with a population of over 80,000 ; Glasgow, having increased sixfold during the century, now followed on its heels, with a few thousands less ; Aberdeen with 24,000, and Dundee and Perth with about 20,000, came next on the list.

The primary industry — agriculture — was still the dominant feature in the national economy ; and farming, with all its ups and downs, had been and was enjoying a large measure of prosperity. Many causes had contributed to this result ; the enterprise of not a few farmers and a few landlords had led to a great improvement in methods, alike in cropping, stock-raising, and dairying ; there had, in part owing to the French Revolution and the consequent wars, been a remarkable increase in the prices of farm products ; and, as a result of both, the area of cultivation had been greatly extended, waste land having been reclaimed for grain and fodder crops, and for permanent pasture. Since the land was largely held on yearly tenancies, this prosperity had been reflected immediately in increased rentals. Between the years 1795 and 1815 the proprietors' incomes from their lands had been more than doubled. From the conclusion of peace in the latter year there dates a period of depression, but, with the artificial buttress of the Corn Law, which lasted until 1846, agriculture continued to be the stand-by of national prosperity.

The phenomenon, however, which catches the eye in these years is the spectacular development of industry, manufacture, and commerce. Both in the heavy industries—coal, iron, and steel—and the lighter—textiles and the like—the rate of growth was almost incredible, and in some of them Scotsmen led the world. Facility of transport kept pace with the increased demand made upon it. Roads were improved out of all recognition ; canals were carrying up to full capacity ; the coastal seaways were studded with sails ; the day of the railway was dawning. The first legally authorized Scottish railway was opened in 1826, though it was only in very limited areas that trains for passengers ran during Chalmers' lifetime.

In all this economic change the ordinary citizen was conscious of the stirrings of a new world, undreamt of by his Covenanting or Prelatic forefathers. Many a man whose youthful promise would, in earlier days, have led him inevitably to the universities and to some branch of the Humanities, found outlet for his gifts as a captain or servant of industry. While Chalmers at the age of twenty-six, during his first visit to the English Midlands, spoke of the " grossness of a mercantile age," [1] his own journal reveals an eager inquisitiveness into all its newest and most elaborate technical achievements.

Education had not kept pace with the increased prosperity. The wide-ranging schemes of John Knox had never been fully translated into practice ; and the new elements which entered in through the shift of population had not yet been effectively dealt with. There were parish schools, good and bad ; and there were the four universities, still largely tied to the methods of earlier ages, but not unresponsive to the new demands. These were the backbone of education, almost entirely under the control of the Church. The General Assembly did its best to supply the deficiencies. In 1824 it established its Education Committee, which during the next fifteen years was able by means of " Assembly Schools," " Parliamentary Schools," and " Sessional Schools " to supplement the existing provision ; and under its care Normal Colleges grew up for the training of teachers. It was not, however, until the Education Committee of the Free Church materially increased, not without frequent overlapping, the scholastic equipment of the land, that its educational requirements could again be said to be adequately met.

In the field of literature, the impetus given to Scottish prestige by the Robertsons and Humes and Homes of the mid-eighteenth century was not yet spent. Outside the

---

[1] W. Hanna, *Memoirs of the Life and Writings of Thomas Chalmers*, vol. i, p. 107

circles of the *literati*, Robert Burns had flashed like a brilliant meteor, and the steadier light of Sir Walter Scott had been keeping Scotland and its past in the forefront of the imaginations of Europe, and was fostering the general romantic revival. The *Edinburgh Review*, with its somewhat later rivals the *Quarterly* and *Blackwoods*, was setting up the Scottish capital as the arbiter of literary destinies. At no period in its history had the Scottish periodical press, though its contributors were by no means all native, pontificated with such assurance. At no time had it on its staff so many would-be " lords of public opinion," as Lockhart puts it. The scorpion chastisements of its stinging articles were the dread or the joy of the literary world.

In the realm of politics a quickening had come with the Reform Act of 1832—a quickening already apparent in the acrimonious discussion which preceded it with its ebullition in the " Radical War " of a dozen years earlier. From the Union of the Parliaments in 1707, down through the eighteenth century, Scotland had been, as a whole, acquiescently Tory in its allegiance. The climax had been reached in the virtual dictatorship of Henry Dundas, the first Lord Melville, whom Dr. MacKinnon describes as " the dispenser of patronage, legal and political, and therefore the moulder of Scottish opinion." [1] The attempted repetition of that autocracy by the second Lord Melville was a notable fiasco. There were forty-five Scottish members in a parliament which gave a minimum of attention to Scottish affairs, and though the number was increased to fifty-three by the Reform Act of 1832, the ratio was not thereby improved. Scottish interests were in the hands, not of a Scottish Secretary, but of the Lord Advocate, and few of them

[1] J. MacKinnon, *Social and Industrial History of Scotland*, p. 200

were men of outstanding importance.[1] One of them—
Lord Advocate Rae—narrowly escaped a vote of censure
in 1822 in the House of Commons for overstepping the
prerogatives of his position, and still more narrowly in
the following year. Tampering with the public Press in
the interests of a Radical prosecution was the main
element in the charge against him.[2] Following on this,
an attempt was made to restrict the activities of the
office, but it emerged unscathed for the time being, and
with undiminished power.

From this condensed summary of the social and
political situation, it is fitting that we should proceed
to delineate at greater length the general ecclesiastical
conditions of the time. Since the early eighteenth century there had been two definite groups within the
Church of Scotland which had crystallized by the middle
of the century into two definite parties—the Moderates
and the Evangelicals. During the leadership (1751–80)
of William Robertson, Moderatism had reached the peak
of its success ; and since it not only dominated the General
Assembly and the Presbyteries of the Church, but was all-
powerful with the great majority of patrons, in whose hands
lay all new appointments, it looked as though its opponents
were doomed to extinction or to be driven, like John Wither-
spoon, to seek new spheres of labour across the seas.

While to-day the name Moderate conjures up in most
minds a certain distinctive type of minister and layman,
and the name Evangelical another widely apart, it is hard

---

[1] Lord Cockburn's verdict was sweeping. " Look at those who have
been Lords Advocate since the century began. . . . Of the fourteen
there have only been *at the very most*, four who, but for the office, would
have been dreamt of by any fair and intelligent person as fitted to be
the public manager of the country." *Journal of Henry Cockburn*, vol. ii,
pp. 310–11.

[2] P. Hume Brown, *History of Scotland*, vol. iii, p. 410

to define precisely where the difference lay. Just as there are some people to-day who say that they can infallibly detect the peculiar drone of a German bomber, so there were those in the eighteenth century who asserted that in two minutes' observation and conversation they could infallibly detect the peculiar sough of an Evangelical or spot the indelible marks of a Moderate. And just as the experts are much more cautious to-day about planes, so were they then about men. There were shades of Moderatism and shades of Evangelicalism, and while the irrevocably committed were known and had acquired certain distinctive characteristics, a very large proportion were of an indeterminate shade. Even in the days when the cleavage was most complete, passage from one party to the other was by no means unknown.

Much has been made of the different notes in preaching, Chalmers' own words being the most familiar of all. "A Moderate sermon is like a winter's day, short and clear and cold. The brevity is good ; the clarity is better ; the coldness is fatal. Moonlight preaching ripens no harvest." But there are volumes of sermons of the later eighteenth century that almost defy classification. It may be that, since the urgency of the popular appeal has failed to permeate the printed page of the Evangelical, and its absence is not noted in the more polished periods of the Moderate, the actual hearing of them would have resolved the difficulty at once. To say that the Moderate ignored and omitted the Gospel appeal, and that the Evangelical despised literary form is one of those broad generalizations which, however pertinent and useful, will not fit every case on either side.

Nor will it suffice to say bluntly, as men like Hugh Miller did,[1] that the Moderates were the opponents of

---

[1] *The Two Parties in the Church of Scotland*, etc., 1841

6

Foreign Missions, and the Evangelicals keen supporters of the cause. This is to make the General Assembly of 1796 with its first dramatic debate the determinative factor in our judgment. It must not be forgotten, however, that this debate arose from the rise of missionary societies, and it was against the co-operation involved in such societies, and not against foreign missions in themselves, that the main weight of the Moderate attack was directed. Further, it ignores the fact that when the first Foreign Missionary Committee of the Church of Scotland was constituted in 1829, it was, whatever elements of policy may have entered into the choice, one whom the Moderate party rejoiced to acclaim as a leader—Dr. Inglis —who was nominated and who acted with universal approval as convener. And while he himself admitted that the financial support came mainly from the Evangelicals, there were those of his own party who were by no means inactive in the matter.

Nor can the much debated question of pluralities be regarded as an infallible dividing line, for, though the Moderates in general supported and the Evangelicals uniformly attacked them, and indeed won their very first victory in the Assembly on this issue, there were those among the Moderates who placed an equally high value with the best of the Evangelicals, on the exacting and exclusive demands of the pastoral charge and office.

Still less can the popular impression of the nineteenth century that a Moderate drank to excess and an Evangelical did not be used as a test. Any extensive reading in the relevant documents of the eighteenth century will reveal that, at times, and in certain cases, there was little to choose between them. The type known across the Border as the " two-bottle Orthodox " was a monopoly of neither party.

7

The real dividing line between the two—as parties in the Assembly—appeared in their respective attitudes to the exercise of patronage. From the days of the Robertson manifesto of 1752 there were two planks in the Moderate platform : steady and uniform acquiescence in, and support of, the law of Patronage, against which their fathers had constantly protested ; and a definite concern for the orderliness of Presbyterian Church government, the subordinate courts in all respects to obey the higher. And these two were normally one, for the sole necessity for their insistence on this orderliness arose out of the disorders of the time, and these, in turn, arose, one and all, out of the exercise, or the abuse, of patronage. The Evangelicals, from the beginning, were supporters of popular rights, determined that, in some fashion, effect should be given to the desires of the people as to their future pastor. By the law of the land they had little say in that choice, by the regulations and resolutions of the Church under the Moderate regime they had still less, asserted the Evangelicals. In this sketch of the general background we may pass from this matter, since, in the various abortive attempts at solution, it will come before us again and again.

A further salient feature of the ecclesiastical situation falls here to be noted. The Church of Scotland was no longer the sole Presbyterian body in Scotland claiming to represent the soundest traditions of the past. The religious societies of the south-west, which had refused to enter the Church of the Revolution Settlement, had now multiplied, and were organized as the Reformed Presbyterian Synod. Since this group, however, stood largely outside the coming conflict, it may be thus briefly passed over.

More important was the ecclesiastical offspring of eighteenth-century secessions. The first secession of 1733

8

had already had a most complicated history of divisions and reunions. Fourteen years after the first meeting of the Associate Presbytery it had split into two over the question of a seceder's relation to the burgess oath. Burgher was the name popularly given to the more liberal section, Anti-burgher to the more uncompromising. Then, two generations later, round about the turn of the century, each of these had become sub-divided into New Lights and Old Lights, after a bitter controversy over a proposed change of relation to their subordinate standards and their original testimonies. About 1815 there were four active and growing stems from the original root— in popular parlance, the New Light Burghers, the Old Light Burghers, the New Light Anti-burghers, and the Old Light Anti-burghers. The New Lights were much the larger communions, but there was one outstanding figure among the Old Lights, Dr. Thomas McCrie, the biographer of Knox and Melville. In 1820 the New Lights united to form the United Secession Church, with 262 congregations scattered over Scotland, mainly in the midlands and the south-west. Alongside the various branches of the first Secession, the Relief Church, formed by Thomas Gillespie in 1761, nine years after his deposition by high-handed Moderate action, numbered about 100 congregations.

The inter-relation of these lesser Churches with the parent Church had repercussions that gravely affected the questions at issue. At present it need only be said that these relations had undergone a considerable change on both sides.

The first Secession had called itself the Associate Presbytery—as associated with the like-minded in the Church of Scotland in maintaining and advancing the principles of that Church in its purest days. The two fierce internal controversies and the success attained in independence had, to a great extent, modified this outlook. Dissatisfaction came to be expressed, not merely with the existing state of the Church of Scotland under Moderate rule, but with the very fact of its existence as an establishment. Through a sermon by a younger minister of the United Secession in 1829 was launched one of the most voluminous theological debates in modern history over the merits and defects, the justice or the iniquity, of an Established Church as such. Moderates and Evangelicals alike rallied to the defence of the National Church ; the acrimonious Voluntary Controversy had begun.

But another aspect of this change of relation—from the side of the Church of Scotland—must now be looked at. Its earlier attitude could be summed up in a phrase, " A good riddance of troublesome elements." And in a famous overture of 1761 the ominous word " schism " was given currency. A parlous situation had arisen. It was felt in many quarters that, through the multiplication of these " schismatics " and their meeting-houses, the Church would have to bestir itself to prevent others wandering, and joining them " outside the pale." To go outside was regarded as an unrelieved degradation and calamity. But by 1842 Dr. Cook, speaking in the Assembly as leader of the Moderate party, argued that there was no infringement of religious liberty created by the decisions of the Court of Session in support of intruded ministers, since the aggrieved parishioner was not forced to attend the ministrations of the patron's nominee ; he might " leave that place of worship, and exercise his original and inherent right in the selection of the ministrations of a minister by whom he may profit." [1] That is,

[1] *Proceedings of the General Assembly of 1842*, p. 98

he may join one of the branches of the Secession. No longer is it an unrelieved degradation to do so ; it is, on the contrary, the relief which redeems the ecclesiastical situation in Scotland from the charge of intolerance.

In this brief survey of the ecclesiastical situation it is necessary for us to look for the moment a little further afield, and to review the relation of the Church of Scotland to the Church of England, and to the dissenters therefrom. Despite their diverse histories, and the difficulties of making the basic constitutional principles of the one intelligible to the other, there were many close ties which knit leaders of the one State Church to leaders of the other. It was at the invitation of a society of friends of the Church of England that Chalmers delivered to the most distinguished audience of his life—almost wholly Anglican—his course of lectures in defence of religious establishments. And during the heat of the ' conflict,' at the height of exasperation with what seemed Anglican obtuseness, no sentiment was received with more tumultuous applause by the non-intrusion enthusiasts than that echoed in an article in the *Witness*, " The Newtons and the Scotts [of the Church of England] are more truly our brethren than the Piries and the Bryces [of the Church of Scotland]." [1]

Chalmers, however, had equally close affiliations with the Dissenters. His very first sermon in London was delivered in the Surrey Chapel under the auspices of the London Missionary Society ; his correspondence and his itineraries in England disclose his esteem for their spiritual leaders ; and there is this revealing entry in the ingenuous diary of his daughter Anne, who records that at a tea-party in Bristol she met " the greatest man in Britain,

[1] *Witness*, January 18, 1840

and perhaps in the world," [1] which judgment reflects, with youthful exuberance, her father's admiration[2] for the notable Baptist preacher and essayist, John Foster of Bristol.

So while the pulpits of the Church of Scotland were still closed, by an Act of 1799, to visiting ministers from England, the general relationship of the Church of Scotland with the Churches of England was not markedly different from that in the generations immediately before or after.

But, of course, the main feature of the ecclesiastical situation was the rise to equality and then to supremacy of the Evangelical party. As the champion of popular rights in the affairs of the Church, it profited from the enthusiasm for similar rights in the affairs of the State. In the full flood of a new national advance, the very word " Moderation " lost its appeal ; and the epithet " High-flier," which had been given to the Evangelicals in derision, came into popular favour. A quiet, though real, revival of evangelical religion, the fruit of much faithful preaching and fostered by the uncertainties of the Napoleonic wars, was a more potent factor. More potent still was the emergence of great-minded and great-souled leaders who, by voice and pen, upheld with power the Evangelical case. While Dr. Andrew Thomson with the foundation of the *Edinburgh Christian Instructor* in 1810 marks the definite turning of the tide, it was left to Dr. Thomas Chalmers to direct its full flow, through many channels, for the Christian good of Scotland.

[1] *Letters and Journals of Anne Chalmers*, p. 138
[2] Hanna, vol. ii, pp. 97, 105, etc.

CHAPTER TWO

EARLY LIFE

1780–1803

No corner of the land is more closely packed with royal burghs than the southern seaboard of the ancient Kingdom of Fife. Important enough in earlier days, they had not kept pace in growth with their lesser rivals in other parts. The town of Anstruther, in the late eighteenth century, was possibly as prosperous as it had ever been, but, comparatively speaking, it had fallen behind its competitors. If as many vessels as ever made for its primitive harbour, they seemed fewer over against the growing number that sailed farther up the Forth. It boasted a fair number of substantial townsmen. One of the most prominent was John Chalmers, who, having inherited from his father a general merchant's business which included shipping and dyeing, carried it on with a distinct, though modest, prosperity. Highly esteemed by his fellow-townsmen, he was more than once provost of the burgh. He had come from a landed family long rooted in Fife, a family with strong clerical connections. Not a few were ministers of the Church of Scotland or married to ministers. He himself had married, in 1771, Elizabeth Hall of Crail, the daughter of a wine merchant, and there were fourteen children of the union. Thomas, born on March 17, 1780, was the sixth child. He was brought up, therefore, in a thronged middle-class home, with relatives in similar homes over much of the adjoining countryside. Not a few members of the family fell a prey early in their maturity to the scourge of consumption ; the survivors lived useful and prosperous lives ; Thomas was the only one marked for distinction.

While the impression conveyed by the mere dates of his early life is that of extreme precociousness, dates can be very misleading. He went to the parish school at the age of three, but he himself said afterwards that this was due neither to an eager desire for knowledge, nor even, as one might have guessed, to a reluctance to be parted from a beloved elder brother, but because home had been made a burden through a capricious and malevolent nurse. If learning had been his motive he would not have found much encouragement from his teachers. Senility and blindness and an undue propensity to rely on the " tawse " were the main marks of the first ; kindness, benevolence, and slackness were the most prominent features in the second. No long list of prizes punctuates his school career. It was not hard to keep up with his fellows, and there was no stimulus to do more. His heart, if we can trust the testimony of fellow-pupils, was more in his play than in his work. He seems, however, to have been a voracious reader. Two works, in particular, quickened his imagination. One, almost inevitably, was *The Pilgrim's Progress* ; the other, unexpectedly, was *Gaudentio di Lucca*, that almost forgotten romance of a kingdom in equatorial Africa, whose laws and customs preserved a primitive purity.

It seems that he early announced his intention of being a minister, and even preached in play. He would have been the exception if he hadn't. Most boys similarly brought up, who later contentedly followed the plough or loaded cargo, had acted and spoken in like fashion. While, no doubt, it was seen to at home that he attended church regularly, and learned his Shorter Catechism, and

said his prayers ; and while the influence of his father,
a man of fervent piety, was more profound than the son
imagined at the time, no trace remains of any marked
religious impulse in these days. Nor have I found in all
his correspondence and reminiscences a single mention
of the minister (Rev. James Nairne) in whose church he
sat Sunday after Sunday. It cannot have been through
any boyish adulation of him that he betook himself thus
early to the pulpit.

What precisely led him to St. Andrews to prepare for
the ministry is now undiscoverable. Is there any hint of
autobiography, I wonder, in this sentence from his
earliest published work ? " They [ministers] are taken
out from the great body of the people ; the choice of their
profession depends on the most accidental circumstances,
a whim of infancy, or the capricious destination of
parents." [1] Did Chalmers include himself in either of
these classes, and if so, which ?

The natural result of going to school so early was
that he went equally early to the university. He had
not reached his twelfth birthday when he matriculated.
It seems an impossibly early age, but his most distinguished
contemporary, John Campbell (afterwards Lord Campbell), was a few months younger ; and few of his fellow-
students were appreciably older. The majority being
from twelve to sixteen, the atmosphere of the university
was not unlike that of a secondary school of to-day,
though the mere suggestion that they were schoolboys
would have roused their fury.

Through the first two years of the curriculum he
idled, to his great regret afterwards that he had not then
acquired a firmer hold of the classical languages. But
the play and exercise of these years built up his powerful

[1] *Observations on a Passage in a Letter*, etc., p. 47

frame, and an over-close application to study might have predisposed him to that malady that struck down so many of his family. It was in his third year—at thirteen—that his mind awoke, and he became conscious of intellectual powers. The instrument of his awakening was his first contact with mathematics. Partly it was through the appeal of exact science itself, and partly it was through the teacher to whom that subject was entrusted. He was not a professor ; he was one of the brilliant succession of assistants the invalided professor had the good fortune to employ—Dr. James Brown, whom Chalmers described much later as " a teacher of singularly varied accomplishments," [1] and to whom he wrote in 1833, " Of all my living instructors, I have reckoned first yourself." [2] His first dominating ambition was to be a professor of that subject, and the closing words of his first publication in 1805 were a protest against that way being barred to a minister who was thereby compelled " to drivel out the remainder of his days in insignificance " [3]—a complete contrast to the attitude of stout William Carey, who, when his son, a missionary like himself, left the mission field for the government service, is recorded to have said, " My son Felix has shrivelled from a missionary into an ambassador." [4]

It was a youth mentally aroused through mathematical science who entered the Divinity Hall at fifteen to undergo the four years' training for the ministry. From this time or just before, his reading began to embrace works of philosophy and theology. The progress of the French Revolution gave point and prominence to works of political philosophy, Godwin's *Political Justice* being

---

[1] In 1847, in his Preface to *Sermons by the late Rev. Robert Coutts, Brechin*
[2] Hanna, vol. i, p. 13   [3] *Observations on a Passage*, etc., p. 48
[4] G. Smith, *Life of William Carey*, p. 172

the chief of these ; but it was Jonathan Edwards on *Free Will* that most deeply engrossed and affected him. Teachers and fellow-students have referred to the time when he could scarcely talk of anything else. His own words in his journal, twenty-four years later, give the clearest insight into his mental and spiritual condition. " I remember, when a student of Divinity, and long ere I could relish evangelical sentiment, I spent nearly a twelvemonth in a sort of mental elysium, and the one idea which ministered to my soul all its rapture was the magnificence of the Godhead, and the universal subordination of all things to the one great purpose for which He evolved and was supporting creation." [1] A " mental elysium " produced by reading Jonathan Edwards will seem to some an impossible conjunction. But was not this precisely the frame of mind that produced that best-seller of the early nineteenth century, Robert Pollok's *Course of Time* ? Did not both these young ardent souls see, irradiating the superficially arid and sombre outline of the Calvinist scheme, the authentic glow of the glory of the Infinite and Sovereign God ?

> "The world at dawn, at midday, and decline,
>   Time gone, the righteous saved, the wicked damned,
>   And God's eternal government approved."

What brought him to earth from his flight in this mental elysium we do not know ; but two further features of his student days in St. Andrews must not pass unnoticed. Conscious of a deficiency in expression, for two years he slogged at his English style, acquiring in the process that billowy rhythmic cadence which, in the spoken word, was to prove so moving to the minds and

[1] Hanna, vol. i, p. 17

hearts of his hearers, but which, in cold print, appears cumbrous and lumbering. We are told that townsmen began to come to college prayers drawn by his exalted eloquence ; and it indicates how fully the foundations of his later style were then laid when we learn that he could introduce a long passage of a college essay *verbatim* into the heart of one of his most solemn speeches more than fifty years later without any impression of unworkmanlike carpentry or the remotest suspicion of a geological fault. Of the actual contents of the theological curriculum there is singularly little mention made, either at the time or later. It may be significant that he had to relearn both Greek and Hebrew when, fifteen years later, the Scriptures became to him the living Word of God. The prevailing atmosphere was Moderate. The Principal of St. Mary's (Dr. Hill) was the uncrowned head of the party ; and the teaching would certainly reflect the Moderate emphasis on Natural Theology, in which discipline Chalmers was so well grounded that, to the end of his days, he showed a predilection for it unusual in an Evangelical.

At the age of nineteen he completed his course, high in the esteem of his fellow-students and of some, at least, of his teachers. He immediately applied to be taken on trials for licence as a preacher of the Gospel. The Presbytery of St. Andrews was willing. But there was one barrier in the way. Custom [1] had prescribed twenty-one as the minimum age. Falling back on an ancient law of the Church, which allowed for exceptional cases,[2]

---

[1] Not only custom, but a definite regulation, Act of General Assembly, Session 7, May 30, 1782

[2] Act of General Assembly, Session 7, April 24, 1582. It has to be noted that when discretion was allowed in the case of those of " singular and rare qualities," twenty-five was the minimum age.

it decided to use its discretion. So on the last day of July, 1799, he was licensed to preach the Gospel. Invitations were at once extended to him to supply pulpits within the Presbytery, but none was accepted. There was a projected meeting of four brothers at Liverpool, and the young licentiate went off to England without having made proof of his ministry. It was on this visit that his first sermons were preached—at Wigan and Liverpool. The general acclaim and the qualified approval of his brother James did not prompt him to devote himself forthwith to his life-work.

He was, indeed, in a somewhat strange position. The way to a parish was then through a presentation, and most young ministers, on licence, sought by some form of personal contact or mediated influence, to secure the interest of a patron. In the meantime they employed themselves in teaching, either in the home as tutor, or in the school as master, or were among the fortunate few who could continue their training as assistant to some older minister whose charge was now too heavy for his unaided efforts. As Chalmers was only nineteen, and could not hope to find a presbytery prepared to *ordain* a minor, it was no use to pull wires for a presentation. So, in the ardour of his unquenched thirst for knowledge, he betook himself to Edinburgh University. It may have been the fame of Dugald Stewart that drew him, but it was Professor Black's pioneer work in chemistry and Professor Robison's thorough-going exploration of natural philosophy that held him.

Between his two sessions the first and minor religious crisis of his career took place. It arose through contact with the materialism of Mirabaud. Did not this imposing " system of Nature " cut the ground from under the theistic position ? Was it necessary to posit an all-powerful and all-creating God? Long afterwards he said in a lecture, " I read Mirabaud's *System of Nature* when a very young man. Its magniloquence I then mistook for magnificence, and the gorgeousness of its generalizations on nature and the universe made a tremendous impression on me. I had the curiosity to read it again within these few months, and what in my earlier days had the effect of a sublime and a seducing eloquence, excites now a sensation of utter disgust." [1] The testimony of early friends makes it clear that the crisis was a most disturbing one. He was in deep distress. He saw his apparently solid universe melt away, and the grounds of his intellectual assurance in God, weighed in the balances, were found wanting. Yet we must not exaggerate this crisis. The growing pains of the intellect create distress in every generation. And the process by which Chalmers regained his poise has only an antiquarian interest. Yet the paradoxical advice which he gave to a young friend in like distress is worth recalling as of permanent value. " Under all the difficulties and despondencies of such a state, I would still encourage you to prayer. Cry as you can. With real moral earnestness, and a perseverance in this habit, light will at length arise out of darkness." [2] This is no mere conventional injunction of piety ; it is real autobiography. And it demonstrates that, long before the second and major crisis, Chalmers was no stranger to personal religion. The early training and " the twelvemonth of elysium " had crystallized into habits of devotion.

His life, nevertheless, was still centred in his scientific studies. He had made further progress in mathematics ; he had mastered the elements of chemistry ; he was

[1] Hanna. Supplementary Note in the two-volume edition, 1854, vol. i, p. 29   [2] Hanna, vol. i, p. 44

entering, with equal zest, into the study of botany and geology. His dominating ambition might be usefulness, but it was to be through the medium of scientific reputation and academic distinction. To this a clerical appointment would be no real hindrance. So he became more active in the search for a charge—one preferably within range of a university. There was in all probability to be a vacancy at Kilmany in Fife in the near future, through the transference of its minister to a chair in St. Andrews. This was an opportunity not to be missed, and all lawful means were taken to press his claims.

In the meantime an assistantship at Cavers in Roxburghshire was vacated by a friend, and at his suggestion Chalmers was appointed. Teviotdale was the scene of his first short spell of ministerial work, and it proved a delight both to the parishioners and their pastor. From the midst of it he wrote this brief yet remarkable letter to his father.

" HAWICK, *July* 23, 1802

" DEAR FATHER,—I have been much resorted to of late for my assistance on sacramental occasions. This, in so thinly peopled a country, necessarily subjects me to long journeys, which I find, however, to be a pleasant and healthy relief from the labours of study. I don't think I will ever allow myself to be so carried away with the attractions of science as not to intermingle a sufficient degree of exercise and amusement.

" I am, Yours affectionately,
" THOMAS CHALMERS "[1]

One wonders what his godly father made of this letter. That his son should be sought after may have gratified him ; but the revelation that he was still absorbed in

[1] Hanna, vol. i, p. 57

scientific study, and the hint that he was conjoining in his mind the solemnities of a communion season with exercise and amusement must have pained his fervent soul.

Chalmers would have remained at Cavers until the presentation to Kilmany was made had he not seen and seized an opening for the exercise of his scientific attainments. That very mathematical assistantship at St. Andrews which had proved the main stimulus to his mental awakening was again vacant, and through immediate action he secured it. Before the opening of the session of 1802–3 he had left Cavers for Anstruther and St. Andrews. Some lectures were ready, and the whole course was planned. He threw himself into the work with an infectious vigour which is but rarely associated with that subject. The selections which Dr. Hanna gives from his lectures illustrate both the thrill of the course and its unusual nature. We do not wonder at the enthusiasm of his class, nor at the criticisms levelled by some at the rate of its progress in the intricacies of that discipline. A most popular teacher, he had at the end of the winter achieved notable success in the way of inspiring his pupils with love for the subject ; his enemies said that he had failed to cover all the ground expected of students. Although in full charge of the class, it was not his province to issue certificates, and when the professor proceeded to issue them without consulting him, Chalmers could not keep silence. A public explosion was followed by a decided rupture of relations.

All the necessary steps having been taken, his ordination at Kilmany was fixed for May. It was over the employment of the intervening weeks that he came to open disagreement with his father, who had never ceased to lament his son's preoccupation with scientific pursuits. Surely he would leave them behind him now, and spend the intervening time quietly at Anstruther in spiritual preparation for his life-work. The son would not hear of this. It would be " a painful and unmeaning solemnity." [1] Besides, he had business in Edinburgh. He must see the professors there. He must explain the St. Andrews uproar, " and counteract the artifices to which I feel myself exposed, from the attempts of an envious and unprincipled malignity." [2] The uproar un-explained might bar the way to a Mathematical Chair in the near future.

It was in this mood, preoccupied by dreams of academic distinction, that he entered on his charge at Kilmany. His eloquence made him a most acceptable preacher ; his breezy and friendly personality made him a welcome visitor ; his first months were crowned with more than average success. But his heart was not in Kilmany, it was nine miles away, at St. Andrews. If only the Pro-fessor of Mathematics had retained his services, how easily he could have fulfilled the duties of the office, and how happy he would have been ! The thorn that rankled was the suggestion of inefficiency implied in his dis-continuance. Could he not remove that stigma ? Was there any way of clearing his university reputation, and of demonstrating that he lay under an unjust reproach ? Bit by bit, a scheme took hold of his mind. It might be audacious, it might stir up further strife, but it would be worth a trial. He would go to St. Andrews for the session, he would offer extra-mural classes in mathematics; he would openly take the field as a rival to the professor and his new assistant. By his success with those students whose training he had begun, and with such beginners as would attend, he would prove to the academic world

[1] Hanna, vol. i, p. 68
[2] Ibid., p. 68, from the same letter, printed in full on pp. 67–68

that his efficiency was on a par with his enthusiasm. He saw clearly the commotion the mere announcement would make, and the heats to which it would give rise. He guessed rightly the name that would be given to him, " a firebrand of turbulence and mischief." [1] But he felt that his honour was engaged in clearing his name, and he persisted. Threats thinned his classes, and while he persevered with a few to their great profit, in December he turned to the less turbulent zone of chemistry, where the prohibitions were not so active nor so sweeping.

Did ever a young man of twenty-three spend a busier winter? He had three classes in mathematics and this new course in chemistry; he had a multitude of daily interviews with friends and foes; he rode every week-end to Kilmany, where he preached and paid urgent pastoral visits. But he was on the top of it all. He was enjoying himself thoroughly. He could write to his father at the peak of the session, " I am living just now the life I seem to be formed for—a life of constant and unremitting activity. Deprive me of employment, and you condemn me to a life of misery and disgust." [2] As the session proceeded, the hostility which had met him at the outset largely disappeared; and the *éclat* which attended the success of his class in chemistry evoked the admiration of early opponents. But the stir in St. Andrews had been communicated to the Presbytery of Cupar. Was this young minister fulfilling his duty to his parish? Had he been the regularly appointed assistant to the Professor of Mathematics this question would never have been raised in a presbytery hitherto tolerant of such minor pluralities. This uninvited intruder, however, might be fitly punished for the turmoil he had created in a quiet university seat,

[1] Journal, quoted in Hanna, vol. i, p. 75   [2] Hanna, vol. i, p. 78

by being roundly rebuked for neglect of his cure. The onslaught of his accuser was met by a most vigorous reply, and since the question had not come up for discussion till the St. Andrews situation had eased, the two hours' debate ended in an acquittal.

The following winter Chalmers was again in St. Andrews, but his attention was now limited to chemistry, and his absences from Kilmany were not so prolonged. Having re-established his reputation, he now applied for more than one Chair of Mathematics. It was the commotion created by the sternly contested election for the Edinburgh one that led to his first venture in publication. While it was anonymous, its style, sentiments, and place of publication made its authorship no secret. Here is its title-page :

Observations on a Passage in Mr. Playfair's Letter to the Lord Provost of Edinburgh, relative to the Mathematical Pretensions of the Scottish Clergy. Cupar-Fife : Printed and sold by R. Tullis, 1805. The author was proud of his first-born at the time, and, from the point of view of the pungency of a polemical pamphlet, he had every right to be. The last ten of its forty-eight pages are models of cogency and pith. But he soon ceased to take delight in it. In his zeal for his thesis he had committed himself to statements that within a few years contradicted completely his new conception of the ministry. In particular there was this : " The author of this pamphlet can assert, from what to him is the highest of all authority, the authority of experience, that after the satisfactory discharge of his parish duties, a minister may enjoy five days in the week of uninterrupted leisure, for the prosecution of any science in which his taste may dispose him to engage." [1] Insignificant as was the circulation

---

[1] *Observations on a Passage,* etc., p. 11

of this pamphlet, no words of its author are more widely known. This is due to the fact that many years afterwards, in the General Assembly, after a speech on the evil of pluralities, he was suddenly confronted with these earlier words of his ; he acknowledged having penned them, but he had done so, he added, in the days of his spiritual blindness. The chair involved was a Chair of Mathematics, he continued. " What, sir," he asked, " are the objects of mathematical science ? Magnitude and the proportions of magnitude. But *then*, sir, I had forgotten *two magnitudes*. I thought not of the littleness of time. I recklessly thought not of the greatness of eternity ! " [1]

His second venture in publication belongs also to the early Kilmany days. This time it was more ambitious— a volume of 365 pages—the product of a deep interest in economic science, coupled with the economic uncertainties of the great Napoleonic struggle. It was entitled, *An Enquiry into the Extent and Stability of National Resources*. It makes heartening reading to-day, and, however deeply orthodox economists then and now dissent from its main contention, it reveals a most penetrating mind, and many of its most novel proposals are now accepted practice.

The impression left by the full record that we have of his early ministry is that of a vigorous and inquiring intellect, capable of taking the routine of his office in his stride, determined to leave no field of human knowledge unexplored, supremely bent on achieving what to him was the most desirable of all goals, literary distinction and the plaudits of the learned. He seemed on the way to become a prodigious polymath, when the second and major religious crisis altered the whole current of his life.

[1] *Report of the Debate in the General Assembly of the Church of Scotland as to the Overtures anent the Union of Offices*, May 1825, p. 191

CHAPTER THREE

AWAKENING AT KILMANY

1803-15

It was during his twelve years' ministry at Kilmany (1803-15) that Chalmers passed through what I have called his second and major religious crisis. In the earlier years, though he was assiduous in all his parochial duties during the small fraction of his time that he allotted to them and counted adequate for their due performance, it was extra-parochial pursuits, scientific inquiries, and academic reputation that engrossed his interests and his time. Had he been translated from Kilmany after six or seven years, he would have left behind him the memory of a ministry by no means colourless, but also in no sense a landmark in the spiritual history of the district. But, just after that interval, he was seized by such a new conception of the Christian ministry, and such a new insight into the Christian Gospel that his work was radically transformed, and Kilmany became the scene of one of the most memorable ministries in the whole history of the Church of Scotland.

The materials for the study of this change are extremely abundant. First place must be given to that private journal (now in New College Library),[1] the essential parts of which were transcribed by Dr. Hanna for his memoir. Next in importance are the numerous references to the change in his own correspondence and in those later addresses and sermons which directly refer

---

[1] Gifted by Mr. W. G. C. Hanna, his great-grandson, in 1939

to it.[1] Then there are the correspondence and the comments of men and women who knew him before, during, and after the change, including some of his own parishioners. And finally, there are many—more or less understanding—appreciations and criticisms from contemporaries, clerical and lay.

From all of these it should be possible, even for one who has not shared the precise experience, to reconstruct, interpret, and follow the stages and the decisive moments of the change. For it had stages, though to some it seemed as sudden and as shattering as the conversion of Saul of Tarsus. Dr. Balfour of Glasgow, who paid a holiday visit to Kilmany from St. Andrews in 1814, reported thus to a friend in the West. " I never saw nor heard him till I came here, but report made him *great* and *good*. I went, therefore, to his parish church with very high expectations indeed. They were not disappointed : his talents are of the first order, and now distinguished grace adorns them. He has long been known as a celebrated philosopher and scorner of the peculiar doctrines of Christianity ; now, from conviction and with a warm heart, he preaches the faith which once he destroyed. I have had serious conversation with him, and am astonished at a man of such superior powers so modest and humble. He is indeed converted, and like a little child." [2]

There is more than a suggestion here that good Dr. Balfour was seeking to make the case conform to a Scripture pattern, and, in consequence, exaggerated both the offence of Chalmers and the cataclysmic nature of the

---

[1] Much the most important of the sermons is that on " The Living Water," preached at the summer Communion in Kilmany in June 1812, and published in *Posthumous Works*, vol. vi, pp. 107–142.

[2] Hanna, vol. i, pp. 437–38

change. This was a not infrequent distortion by some who professed themselves altogether his friends. A brand plucked from the burning ! An unconscious blasphemer transformed in a moment into a triumph of grace ! The currency of the misunderstanding grieved Chalmers greatly. For example, when he preached in Anstruther —in his home church—in November 1811, it shocked him on the following day to hear it accepted among old acquaintances that he had in the pulpit made a formal recantation of his old errors, had declared his conversion publicly, and had astonished the people with an account of his own history and his own experiences. Recording this in his journal, he adds, " The days were when all this would have galled me to the quick, and still it is unpleasant." [1]

The best point at which to begin our study will be found in that *Address to the Inhabitants of the Parish of Kilmany*, which he found time to pen in 1815 during his much-occupied first year in Glasgow. The most relevant part runs thus :

" Here I cannot but record the effect of an actual though undesigned experiment, which I prosecuted for upwards of twelve years among you. For the greater part of that time I could expatiate on the meanness of dishonesty, on the villainy of falsehood, on the despicable arts of calumny ; in a word, upon all those deformities of character which awaken the natural indignation of the human heart against the pests and the disturbers of human society. Now could I, upon the strength of these warm expostulations, have got the thief to give up his stealing, and the evil-speaker his censoriousness, and the liar his deviations from the truth, I should have felt all the repose of one who had gotten his ultimate object. It never occurred to me that all this might have been

[1] Hanna, vol. i, p. 228

done, and yet the soul of every hearer have remained in full alienation from God. . . . But the interesting fact is, that during the whole of that period in which I made no attempt against the natural enmity of the mind to God . . . I certainly did press the reformations of honour, truth, and integrity among my people ; but I never once heard of such reformations having been effected amongst them. . . . I am not sensible that all the vehemence with which I urged the virtues and the proprieties of social life had the weight of a feather on the moral habits of my parishioners. And it was not till I got impressed by the utter alienation of the heart in all its desires and affections from God ; it was not till reconciliation to Him became the distinct and the prominent object of my ministerial exertions ; it was not till I took the scriptural way of laying the method of reconciliation before them ; it was not till the free offer of forgiveness through the blood of Christ was urged upon their acceptance, and the Holy Spirit given through the channel of Christ's mediatorship to all who ask Him was set before them as the unceasing object of their dependence and their prayers ; in one word, it was not till the contemplations of my people were turned to these great and essential elements in the business of a soul providing for its interest with God and the concerns of its eternity, that I ever heard of any of those subordinate reformations which I aforetime made . . ., I fear, the ultimate object of my earlier ministrations. . . . You have at least taught me that to preach Christ is the only effective way of preaching morality in all its branches ; and out of your humble cottages have I gathered a lesson, which I pray God I may be enabled to carry with all its simplicity into a wider theatre." [1]

[1] *Address to the Inhabitants of the Parish of Kilmany*, 4th ed., pp. 41–44

This classic passage serves to demonstrate the reality and completeness of the change ; and it illumines one aspect of it, the radical transformation of the content, the objective, and the effectiveness of his preaching. But it sheds no light on the time of the change, and it only dimly reveals the inward crisis that preceded it.

Where is the actual watershed to be found, and what are its earliest manifestations ? Attempts have been made to link it up with the death of his brother George in 1806, and in particular with the fact that in his last illness the latter had drawn his spiritual support and equanimity from contemporary evangelical writings, which Thomas as yet despised. But this is to place it far too early ; the interests and the pre-occupations of the succeeding years remain unchanged. It may have been that this solemn event made him more amenable to his father's constant endeavour to induce him to devote himself more assiduously to his parish and his spiritual duties, but his literary ambitions are in these years at their strongest, and his correspondence is more taken up with the publication and editions of his *Enquiry into National Resources* than with all other subjects put together.

It has been contended that it must have taken place before May 1809, for after his first speech in the General Assembly, Dr. Andrew Thomson, the leader of the Evangelicals, recognized him as a kindred spirit, and was prompt to enrol him as a contributor to the *Edinburgh Christian Instructor* when he began it in the following year. But his main outside activity at the moment was with an extensive article on Trigonometry, commissioned for the *Edinburgh Encyclopædia*. So the suggestion that it was the death of his sister Barbara, in August 1808, that proved the decisive moment must also be departed from. Yet that death was not without its definite impact, since it

31

led him to ask the editor that he might also be entrusted with the article on Christianity. The desire had sprung up within him to explore the evidences for Christianity more fundamentally than he had yet attempted. Premonitions of the crisis are, therefore, to be detected in the years 1806–9. Its pressure and urgency were not far distant.

In the June of 1809, however, the death of a favourite uncle, whose name-child he was, was followed by a long and critical illness. It seemed to him that some fatality hung over the family, and that he was destined to be the next victim. Confronted with what appeared the probability of an early death, he began to review his past life in the light of eternity. Nothing could have been more perverse, he felt, than his scale of values. The former objects of his ambition dwindled into insignificance ; the duties he had despised and neglected rose up and reproached him. Henceforward, if spared, he would devote himself, heart and soul, to his vocation. Every word he spoke and every action he performed would be governed by the sense of his devotion to God and his responsibility to Him alone.

He found encouragement and inspiration in Pascal's *Thoughts* ; in the thoughts themselves, and even more in the example of their author, who had, unhesitatingly, left his towering mathematical fame to dedicate all the talents which had produced it to the more direct service of the God to whom he owed them all—a man who, as Chalmers himself said, " could stop short in the brilliant career of discovery, who could resign all the splendours of literary reputation, who could renounce without a sigh all the distinctions which are conferred upon genius, and resolve to devote every talent and every hour to the defence and illustration of the Gospel." [1] Just as the

[1] Hanna, vol. i, p. 152

story of Victorinus brought Augustine to the door of the kingdom, so did the story of Pascal bring Chalmers.

A period of strenuous self-examination began during his convalescence and his long absence from the pulpit, of which we have intimate details in his private journal. No corner of his life was to escape this scrutiny, for, as he confided to it in his very first entry on his thirtieth birthday, " my whole conduct has been dictated by the rambling impulse of the moment, without any direction from a sense of duty, or any reference to that eternity which should be end and motive of all our actions." [1] Henceforward everything was to be directed by a sense of duty ; life was to be lived *sub specie æternitatis*.

The year 1810 was spent in the most thorough-going self-scrutiny. Every explosion of temper, every fit of impatience, every inattention to the most trivial duty was rigorously noted and repented. Every activity was examined in the light of the will of God for him. In peripheral matters his standards fluctuate. In April he suspends the study of mathematics. In August he feels that its study must be abandoned as too absorbing, though his interest in political economy may be retained, as bearing more directly on religion. In September he records without comment, " Read a good deal of mathematics." But his determination to have done with everything definitely inconsistent with his Christian profession never wavered. He was living in a new atmosphere. In July he could speak of himself as in the infancy of his religious course. But there is none of the spontaneous joy of a new life. He prays constantly for greater vigilance, for more exclusive attention to the " grand concerns of eternity," for more determined " resistance to the temptations of time." He was still in great disquietude. At

[1] Hanna, vol. i, p. 158

33

times he felt himself " coming on in exertion " ; at other times he felt he was slipping back. A typical comment of the darker days is this of 6th July. " I am sensible that I do not feel the same trembling anxiety on the subject of moral discipline that I did at the outset of this journal ; but let me not relax the vigilance of my efforts. Oh what a small share principle has upon our hourly and familiar movements." We are irresistibly reminded of the early struggles of other great Christian leaders. Here is John Wesley of the Holy Club over again. Here is Martin Luther, attempting to storm heaven by monkery. Here is the same fervent zeal ; the same dispeace. He is still within the toils of the crisis. He has not yet emerged into the full noontide of the day. The Chalmers of 1810 is not yet possessed by the Gospel he was to preach with such power.

In what way, then, and when did the final stage of the transition occur ? A letter of his own, written nine years later to his brother Alexander, gives the accepted answer.

Feb. 14, 1820

MY DEAR ALEXANDER,—I stated to you that the effect of a very long confinement, about ten years ago, upon myself, was to inspire me with a set of very strenuous resolutions, under which I wrote a Journal, and made many a laborious effort to elevate my practice to the standard of the Divine requirements. During this course, however, I got little satisfaction, and felt no repose. I remember that somewhere about the year 1811 I had Wilberforce's *View* put into my hands, and as I got on in reading it felt myself on the eve of a great revolution in all my opinions about Christianity. I am now most thoroughly of opinion, and it is an opinion founded on experience, that on the system of Do this and live, no peace, and even no true and worthy obedience, can ever be attained. It is, Believe in the Lord Jesus Christ, and thou shalt be saved. When this belief enters the heart, joy and confidence enter along with it. The righteousness which we try to work out for ourselves eludes our impotent grasp, and never can a soul arrive at true or permanent rest in the pursuit of this object. The righteousness which, by faith, we put on, secures our acceptance with God, and secures our interest in His promises and gives us a part in those sanctifying influences by which we are enabled to do with aid from on high what we never can do without it. We look to God in a new light—we see Him as a reconciled Father ; that love to Him which terror scares away re-enters the heart, and, with a new principle and a new power, we become new creatures in Jesus Christ our Lord." [1]

Many of Professor James Denney's students retain a vivid memory of these incisive words of his, " Gentlemen, there are only two ways of being religious : one way is to try to put God in our debt ; the other is simply to acknowledge the greatness of our debt to God." Chalmers had persevered persistently with the former ; he was now to experience the joy and power of the other.

The letter quoted above was written nine years after the event, and its phrasing may bear the marks of the preaching of the intervening years ; it is worth while, therefore, to append to it this fragment of a letter to his sister Jane, sent very soon after the climax of the crisis.

" Salvation is the gift of God through Jesus Christ our Lord. . . . We are apt to stagger at the greatness of the unmerited offer, and cannot attach faith to it till we

[1] Hanna, vol. i, pp. 185–86

have made up some title of our own. This leads to two mischievous consequences. It keeps alive the presumption of one class of Christians, who will still be thinking that it is something in themselves and of themselves which confers upon them a right to salvation ; and it confirms the melancholy of another class, who look into their own hearts and their own lives, and find that they cannot make out a shadow of a title to the Divine favour. The error of both lies in looking to themselves when they should be looking to the Saviour." [1]

The nature of the revolution in Chalmers' life should be evident from these two letters, and its effect from the *Address* which was cited earlier ; short notes fall to be added here on the time and the instrumentality of the change.

As to the date—somewhere about 1811, and after reading Wilberforce's *View*, is, as we have just seen, Chalmers' own verdict, on looking back. His journal reveals that he was reading that work in the December of 1810, where he says, " I am delighted with Wilberforce." But the same journal suggests a later date. On February 23, 1811, he wrote : " I feel myself upon the eve of some decisive transformation in point of religious sentiment." The book he was absorbing at that time was Scott's *Force of Truth*. On 28th August he wrote to his young friend, James Anderson of Dundee, " Viewed as an experimental Christian, I am still in my infancy." [2] So the change may be dated somewhere between the February and the August of 1811, and, if we press the implications of the language, nearer the former date than the latter. A careful reading of the journal suggests as the most likely moment February 26, 1811, with this

[1] Hanna, vol. i, pp. 348–49   [2] *Ibid.*, p. 237

entry : " The verse, Acts xxvi. 18, has struck me this night as a compendious expression of Christianity—the object of which is to give forgiveness of sins, and inheritance among them that are sanctified by faith that is in Jesus." Yet the inclination to put one's finger definitely on that precise date is weakened by the absence of any further allusion to that unfamiliar verse in his subsequent writings.

As to the instrumentality, we may put aside as un-proved and unlikely the decisive influence of any of those Evangelicals with whom he came into close contact, like the Rev. James Johnston of the Secession Church in Rathillet, who, after his decease, was claimed by some fellow-seceders as the human instrument in the great change, or the Rev. Dr. McCullough of Dairsie, the leader of the Evangelicals in the Church of Scotland Presbytery of St. Andrews, but there is this to be said in this regard, that there is uniformly a fresh confidence reflected in his journal after converse with them and their like. The decisive influence seems to have been the Bible, which he now studied with a new zest, coupled with the interpretation of the Bible that he found in many evangelical works which formerly he had con-temned, in particular three : Wilberforce's *View*, Scott's *Force of Truth*, and finally *The Marrow of Modern Divinity*, of which he writes : " It is a masterly performance, and I feel a greater nearness to God, convincing me that Christ is the way to Him, and an unconditional surrender of ourselves to Christ the first and most essential step to our recovery." [1] No human being can enumerate and catalogue all the converging forces in his life that make at some moment an irresistible impact, but these, it

---

[1] This entry, being later than the date above assigned for the change, suggests that the *Marrow* was rather a final confirmation of an experience already complete.

would appear, are the major ones in driving Chalmers to know personally the power of the Christian Gospel.

From the autumn of 1811 the new note in his preaching made itself felt. The church at Kilmany was attended as never before. Many of his parishioners shared in his change ; others who, nevertheless, were drawn Sunday by Sunday to swell the throng in his church, bluntly called him " mad " ; strangers were drawn from neighbouring parishes through spiritual concern or from sheer curiosity. The fame of his preaching spread into wider and yet wider areas ; and many who came for a new sensation began to set out on their Christian pilgrimage, or, at least, went away with the conviction that there was much more in religion than they had ever dreamt.

It threw Chalmers himself into new circles. New friends gathered round him. Old Evangelicals were puzzled by the new recruit. He had not the accepted vocabulary. They missed their stock phrases. There was something incalculable and elusive about him. They volunteered to instruct him, only to find themselves involved in an argument which ended generally in their acceptance of the fact that they meant precisely the same thing, though the words were novel. Kilmany church and manse became the centre of a mighty spiritual influence.

The preacher's tireless energies had to find some outlet beyond the parish. He continued his work for the *Edinburgh Christian Instructor*. He threw himself, by voice and pen, into the advocacy of foreign missions, defending and promoting the causes of the Baptist Missionary Society and the Moravians. But his main new interest was the British and Foreign Bible Society. Captivated by its programme of spreading the knowledge of the Bible throughout the heathen world, he devoted

himself, heart and soul, to its promotion and support.
He took the lead in the formation of local auxiliaries
throughout Fife and beyond ; he devised means of
utilizing " the power of littles "—a penny a week and
the like—which were to reappear in the Sustentation
Fund of the Free Church a generation later ; from the
pulpits of many churches he pled for its support. His
one publication of these later Kilmany days which must
be mentioned in view of his future activities was one
in which were conjoined the earlier interest in economics
and his new zeal for the Bible Society. It was called
*The Influence of the Bible Societies upon the Temporal Necessities
of the Poor.* It was thrown off at white heat to counter
a current objection to the local auxiliaries, viz. that
they were diverting to other objects the money normally
devoted by the charitable to the support of the poor.
But it went far beyond its thesis. It entered into the
whole question of pauperism, its increase, and the
incidence of that increase. It contended that where
there was a compulsory poor-rate pauperism increased
by leaps and bounds. Characteristic of the thought of
Chalmers throughout life were these judgments. " The
remedy against pauperism does not lie in the liberalities
of the rich : it lies in the hearts and habits of the poor.
Plant in their bosoms a principle of independence . . .
teach them to recoil from pauperism as a degradation."
" Could we reform the improvident habits of the people,
and pour the healthful infusion of Scripture principle
into their hearts, it would reduce the existing poverty
of the land to a very humble fraction of its present
extent." [1] These judgments, modified fortunately by a
new emphasis on Christian friendship, were to form the
basis of his great social experiment in Glasgow.

[1] *The Influence of Bible Societies*, etc., 4th ed., pp. 33 and 18

There had been one other change in his views at Kilmany. In his early years there he was a confirmed bachelor. When the family spoke of marriage he put the idea from him with scorn. Fortunately for his future his resolution did not hold. On August 4, 1812, he married Miss Grace Pratt, the daughter of a retired army captain. " Peace, harmony, and affection reign in my abode," he wrote on 12th August. And so it was destined to reign, through many changes of place and station, until the end.

CHAPTER FOUR

THE CITY PREACHER

1815-19

IN 1814 one of the leading city churches of Glasgow became vacant through the appointment of its minister, Rev. Stevenson MacGill, to the Chair of Divinity in Glasgow University. Though the congregation had no direct voice in the selection of his successor, a few of the leading merchants of the city who belonged to its membership began to make inquiries about likely men in all quarters in which they had business connections. From these it appeared that the minister of Kilmany had a great and growing reputation. Unofficial representatives found their way to his country kirk, and reported most favourably. The appointment being in the hands of the Town Council, the councillors found themselves besieged from many quarters, particularly by enthusiasts for or against Chalmers. Five members of the council made their way to Bendochy in Angus, and having heard him preach there a funeral sermon on a fellow-student, returned full of his praises.

When the day of the nomination came it was found that he had a clear majority over the other names proposed. Though there was a double reluctance in his mind, to leave Kilmany and to undertake a task which involved so many unaccustomed duties, he accepted the presentation, and was duly inducted on the 21st of July 1815.

From his very first sermon his name was made as

a preacher. The Tron Church became packed as it had never been before ; and the years of his ministry there (from the age of thirty-five to thirty-nine) saw Chalmers at the height of his preaching power. This was mainly exercised in his own church, at the ordinary Sunday services, and through the special Thursday sermons. It was a custom of some standing in Glasgow that every Thursday there should be a service for which each of the ministers of the city churches in turn was responsible. At regular intervals of eight weeks it fell to be conducted by the minister of the Tron.

It was on these Thursdays that he began that series of *Astronomical Discourses* which, when preached, were to fill the church to overflowing ; and, when published, were to take rank as an outstanding best-seller of the day. If this volume were the only material for judging his preaching, there would be small reason for reckoning him among the princes of the pulpit. The particular problems with which he dealt have so lost their urgency that one simply cannot recapture the breathless thrill with which the hard-headed merchants of Glasgow, tearing themselves away from office and shop, awaited the preacher's pronouncements. In his own day there were those who said that Chalmers' apologetic was wasted, that he was facing difficulties which had never been seriously raised, that the problems he stated and solved had never been expressed or hinted at by any opponent of the Christian faith. There were others who asserted that it was only the novelty of introducing astronomy into the pulpit—which would never have occurred to anyone who had not these week-day opportunities—that explained their widespread welcome in college studies, west-end drawing-rooms, and country inns.

While the causes of a great popular success are often

mysterious to a degree, it is safe to assert that it has never come to a volume of sermons through novelty of subject alone, nor through any dealing, however brilliant, with non-existent problems. It must have in it some illumination on very real perplexities and puzzlements besetting and troubling the human spirit. Men have always felt, even when the arch of heaven was low and limited, a difficulty in believing that He who made Orion and the Pleiades, whose hand rules sun, and moon, and stars, can be so intimately concerned with the minuter things of His universe that He notes the sparrow's fall, can so love the world of men as to give His only-begotten Son. In the early nineteenth century this feeling was so much augmented by the fuller mapping of the heavens made possible by the great improvement in the telescope, by the sense of the multitudes of remoter worlds, and the vastness of the interstellar spaces, that Chalmers was dealing with a perennial and universal perplexity which had reached a new stage of acuteness precisely in his day and generation.

What troubles those who read those discourses to-day in search of the springs of their popularity, is not any suspicion of the remoteness of the problem, nor of the adequacy of the solutions, but their grandiose periods, and their apparently over-driven eloquence. Later Chalmers himself was to regard them as jejune efforts, much in need of the pruning hook and the scissors. But, at the moment, they set him on the pinnacle of fame, in Scotland and beyond.

He himself set greater store by the series that immediately followed, though they were not published till he was minister of St. John's, the *Commercial Discourses*, or, to give them their full title, *The Application of Christianity to the Commercial and Ordinary Affairs of Life*. And there is

43

not one of these eight discourses which does not reveal a mind, at once powerful and consecrated, at work on the practical problems of a time of great material prosperity in a thriving and growing metropolis.

Neither of these Thursday volumes, however, discloses the secret of Chalmers' power in the pulpit. Fortunately for us he was compelled to publish some of his sermons on special occasions, to which reference has yet to be made, and through the pressure of his publishers he consented to gather into one volume seventeen of his ordinary Sunday sermons as *Sermons preached in the Tron Church, Glasgow.* While he warns the prospective reader in the Preface that the doctrine most frequently insisted upon will be found to be the unpopular one of the depravity of human nature, and while he recognizes that the constancy and the variety of his insistence upon it may seem to have betrayed him into " the fault of redundancy," [1] it is here that we find most clearly sounded the note which profoundly stirred the hearts of his people and radically transformed the lives of many ; the great truths of the Christian redemption pressed home with a fervour born of personal experience of their power and their preciousness. To take an illustration. Sermon IV is entitled " An Estimate of the Morality that is without Godliness." Here is the way it begins :

" To the people of every Christian country the doctrine of a Mediator between God and man is familiarized by long possession ; though to many of them it be nothing more than the familiarity of a name, recognized as a well-known sound by the ear, without sending one fruitful or substantial thought into the understanding. For, let it be observed, that the listless acquiescence of the mind in a doctrine,

[1] *Sermons preached in the Tron Church*, p. x

to the statement or to the explanation of which it has been long habituated, is a very different thing from the actual hold which the mind takes of the doctrine—insomuch that it is very possible for a man to be a lover of orthodoxy, and to sit with complacency under its ministers, and to be revolted by the heresies of those who would either darken or deny any of its articles—and, in a word, to be most tenacious in his preference for that form of words to which he has been accustomed ; while to the meaning of the words themselves, the whole man is in an estate of entire dormancy, and delighted though he really be by the utterance of the truth, exhibits not in his person, or in his history, one evidence of that practical ascendency which Christian truth is sure to exert over the heart and habits of every genuine believer."[1]

If one were asked to deduce, simply from the contents of published sermons, why there was such abounding life in the Tron, while some other churches were almost moribund, it could not be found in any significant, or even insignificant, variation in the scheme of evangelical truth proclaimed from the pulpit, but rather in this, that while these others with longer experience had fallen into what was, to them and their people, a proven but hackneyed vocabulary, the vivid and recent experience of the power of the gospel had set Chalmers searching for fresh and living words to convey the same great truths. This accounts in part for his interminable sentences. It was not a conscious rhetorical device based on Hebrew parallelism, as has been suggested, but a multiplication of freshly minted phrases, one approximation to perfect expression piled on another, each bringing its own ray

[1] *Sermons preached in the Tron Church*, pp. 113–14

of light from its own angle to converge on the illumination of the point at issue.

It always seems as though much midnight oil had been spent in the elaboration of these effects. But we have the story of one special sermon in sufficient fulness to dispel this illusion. When, late in 1817, Chalmers was having a short break, and was due to preach in Kilmany, word came to Glasgow of the sudden death of the Princess Charlotte of Wales. The funeral was fixed for Wednesday, 19th November. The Town Council of Glasgow resolved at once that services would be held simultaneously in Glasgow on that day. An urgent message was sent to Chalmers, summoning him to return. It reached him as he was going to the pulpit in Kilmany. He obeyed at once, setting out on the Sunday afternoon. The next days were spent on the road, the approaching sermon always in his mind. Much of it was written on scraps of paper at halts on the journey, the rest of it in his house in Glasgow in the all too brief evening of Tuesday. Nothing was further from his thought than publication. But part of the sermon was so grievously distorted in the Press that he came to be regarded as having taken advantage of the occasion to inveigh against the policies of the Whig government. He felt that he was compelled, in self-defence, to publish the sermon, and next month it appeared. It went through many editions, though published at 1s. 6d. It has all the marks suggestive of leisure that characterize his discourses on other themes. Here is one representative paragraph. In dealing with the righteousness which alone exalteth a nation, he had been speaking of loyalty as one of its essential constituents :

" But there is a point on which I profess myself to be

altogether at issue with a set of men who composed at one time, whatever they do now, a very numerous class of society. I mean those men who, with all the ostentation and all the intolerance of loyalty, evinced an utter indifference either to their own personal religion or to the religion of the people who were around them—who were satisfied with the single object of keeping the neighbourhood in a state of political tranquillity—who, if they could only get the population to be quiet, cared not for the extent of profaneness or of profligacy that was amongst them—and who, while they thought to signalize themselves in the favour of their earthly king, by keeping down every turbulent or rebellious movement among his subjects, did, in fact, by their own conspicuous example, lead them and cheer them on in their rebellion against the King of Heaven—and, as far as the mischief could be wrought by the contagion of their personal influence, these men of loyalty did what in them lay, to spread a practical contempt for Christianity, and for its ordinances, throughout the land." [1]

Mention should here be made of another sermon preached on a special occasion which gave rise to a similar furore. This was the one preached for the Hibernian Society on " *The Doctrine of Christian Charity applied to the Case of Religious Differences.*" The text was taken from the Sermon on the Mount, the verses about the mote and the beam. And its general line was : " What right have some so-called Protestants to revile Rome ? Do they not themselves exhibit Rome's characteristic vices, without the same excuse ? " This was certainly not traditional Evangelicalism. And a tradi-

[1] *A Sermon delivered in the Tron Church, Glasgow, on Wednesday, November 19, 1817*, etc., pp. 20–21

tional Evangelical at great length set Chalmers right—
to his own satisfaction.[1]

These are the main sermons published during this
period, and while their good and sound qualities may
still be perceived, they do not leave the impression of a
preacher of overwhelming popularity and power. Yet
such is the testimony of all. The scenes in London on
his visit there in May 1817 are almost unbelievable.
Every biography records some of the graphic contemporary pictures. Here is a new one which has recently
come to light. It is from a letter by James Nicol, son
of the minister in Swallow Street, written immediately
after Chalmers' sermon in that church. " We have had
Dr. Chalmers preaching in London, and also [sic] in
Swallow Street. I never witnessed the place so full in
my life, pews, passages, pulpit stairs, windows, etc. etc.,
all crowded to excess ; and some noblemen, members of
Parliament, and even some most beautiful young ladies
of distinction hauled through the vestry window ; ladies
fainting, gentlemen calling out Murder, etc. I do not
think that such a scene was ever before witnessed in a
place of worship. But happily no damage was done
except the breaking of about 30 panes of glass, which
by-the-bye would be of some good to Messrs. Morris.
The carriages stood from the head of Vigo Lane to near
Sackville Street in Piccadilly." [2]

The young man whose ambition was fame and distinction could never have envisaged such fame and distinction
as came to him when he put these ambitions away. He

[1] *A Letter to the Rev. Dr. Chalmers of Glasgow, on the Distinctive Characters
of the Protestant and Roman Catholic Religions*, etc., by the Rev. Robert Burns,
one of the ministers of Paisley. Paisley, 1818

[2] *Journal of the Presbyterian Historical Society of England*, vol. vi, p.
347

did not like it. He wrote of " the insufferable urgency " [1] of London. He spoke with distaste of the " popularity of stare, and pressure, and animal heat." [2] But it was not in London only that he had to endure it. There were similar scenes in the Tron Church itself. He did his utmost to discourage them. There was one Sabbath evening when the doors were rushed. Dr. Wardlaw, an Independent, one of Glasgow's most popular preachers, who happened to be there that night, has given this account of its sequel. " I stepped into the vestry at the dismission of the congregation, and walked home with him. . . . On the way home we talked, *inter alia*, of what had happened. He expressed, in his pithy manner, his great annoyance at such crowds. ' I preached the same sermon,' said he, ' in the morning ; and for the very purpose of preventing the oppressive annoyance of such a densely crowded place, I intimated that I should preach it again in the evening.' And with the most ingenuous guilelessness, he added, ' Have *you* ever tried that plan ? ' I did not smile ; I laughed outright. ' No, no,' I replied, ' my good friend, there are but few of us that are under the necessity of having recourse to the use of means for getting thin audiences.' He enjoyed the joke, and he felt, though he modestly disowned, the compliment." [3]

One further word must be said about his preaching. In reaching this giddy height of popularity and this summit of usefulness, he trampled underfoot practically every accepted canon of pulpit success. His sermons were all written, whether in shorthand or longhand ; and he read them, sometimes, indeed, following the line with his finger. He did what we are advised on all hands —and that soundly—not to do : he obtruded his manu-

[1] Hanna, vol. ii, p. 104   [2] *Ibid.*, p. 164   [3] *Ibid.*, p. 160

script. In the Kilmany days the great English preacher Andrew Fuller had told him how much his effectiveness would be multiplied if he discarded it. He was deeply impressed. He made a persistent and prolonged attempt to do without it, only to give up the method as unsuited to him. Further, he had a most pronounced provincial accent, which made him—outside Fife—almost unintelligible to his audience during the quiet exordium of a discourse.[1] He had no dramatic gestures, save at rare intervals, and generally on days when he laments that he had " exceeded," and had in consequence fallen flat. Most of those who heard him for the first time were repelled at the outset by the heaviness of his face and the dulness of his eyes. But one and all relate that as he warmed to his subject the whole man was transformed.

The most commonly cited description is that of J. G. Lockhart, Sir Walter Scott's son-in-law and biographer. It can be found in full in Hanna [2] and elsewhere. Here, this may be selected from it :

" He commences in a low, drawling key, which has not even the merit of being solemn, and advances from sentence to sentence, and from paragraph to paragraph, while you seek in vain to catch a single echo of that which is to come. . . . But then, with what tenfold richness does this dim preliminary curtain make the glories of his eloquence to shine forth, when the heated spirit shakes from it its chill confining fetters, and bursts out elate and rejoicing in the full splendour of its disimprisoned wings. . . . I have never heard . . . any preacher whose elo-

---

[1] " How on earth his English audiences got over the bruising barbarism of his pronunciation is a mystery." Professor David Masson in *Memories of Two Cities*, p. 57   [2] Hanna, vol. ii, pp. 2–5

quence is capable of producing an effect so strong and irresistible as his."

The case of Chalmers would seem to indicate that the man and the message can triumph, and do triumph occasionally, over any defect of manner and method. But the young men, and they were not few, who tried to ape his manner and apply his method became the bores of their generation.[1]

Though the four years in the Tron saw the heyday of his preaching, it must not be thought that his pulpit preparation absorbed all his energies. Quite on a par with it was the care and attention that he devoted to the pastoral oversight of his people. The Tron Church had many wealthy members who lived in the suburbs. Chalmers practically disclaimed all responsibility for any pastoral oversight of them; he devoted himself to the huge crowds in the closes and wynds of his over-populated parish, making local provision for their religious instruction, enrolling young office-bearers as official helpers, and a multitude of faithful members to whom he committed definite pieces of parochial supervision: experimenting with vigour and resource along the line of making the parochial ministry in the city the effective instrument for social and spiritual uplift that it was in many a quiet rural area, and moving towards that great social experiment that was to make memorable his ministry in his second Glasgow charge, the new parish of St. John's. To exercise an all-pervasive influence on

[1] Two things which may help others, as they have helped the writer, to realize Chalmers' power as a preacher are the paper by Dr. John Brown in *Horæ Subsecivæ*, Second Series, pp. 57–96, and the three silhouettes of Dr. Chalmers preaching, done in 1830 by August Edouart, the French artist, in that year resident in Edinburgh. Two of these are reproduced in this book.

DR. CHALMERS PREACHING
Silhouette by August Edouart

his parish was an aim not second to that of proclaiming the message entrusted to him, to the great congregations, largely from outside the parish, which gathered week by week in the Tron.

Nor did his interests in the world-wide kingdom of God diminish in intensity. His services as preacher were at the disposal of a multitude of pioneer organisations ; and there may be instanced as typical this incident recorded by James Montgomery, the Scottish Moravian hymn-writer, to whom he paid a visit at Sheffield on his way to London in 1817 :

" Our conversation turned principally on the subject of the Moravian Missions in pagan lands . . . hereupon Dr. Chalmers said . . ., ' I mean to raise five hundred pounds for the Brethren's Missions this year.' ' Five hundred pounds for our poor missions ! ' I cried. ' I never heard of such a thing before.' He rejoined, ' I will do it.' But while I heartily thanked him, and implicitly believed in the integrity of his intention, I could only hope that he might be able to fulfil it, and within myself I said, ' I will watch you, Doctor.' I did so, and traced him through sermons, subscriptions, collections, and donations, till these had realized, to the best of my recollection, a sum nearer to six than five hundred pounds." [1]

Although Presbytery and General Assembly heard little from him during these Tron years, he was coming, through the width and intensity of his Evangelical activities, to be looked on as the rising hope of the Evangelical cause and the Evangelical party.

[1] Hanna, vol. ii, pp. 95–96

CHAPTER FIVE

A GREAT SOCIAL EXPERIMENT

1819–23

WHILE Dr. Chalmers in the Tron was at the height of his preaching power, and while his sermons drew great crowds and there was distinct evidence of their effect in changed lives, he was never completely happy in his ministry there. It was not his impatience with packed buildings nor the distraction of so many extraneous duties and unnecessary functions that constituted the main source of his dissatisfaction. It was the state of the parish attached to the Tron ; the church itself crammed with outsiders, the parish largely unprovided for. He felt that what a growing city needed was the same kind of personal contact that was achieved in many a country parish ; and he wanted to experiment so as to discover and show what could be done on parochial lines in a city area. The constitution of the existing city churches put many barriers in the way. For example, though each of these charges had its own Kirk Session, the real governing body to which was entrusted the whole administration of the collections for the poor in all the churches was the General Session of the city, consisting of all the city ministers and all the elders. Cases that were beyond the stage of the necessarily limited sessional relief were under the committee of the town hospital.

To Chalmers this complicated machinery—a survival of Glasgow's less populous days—was a constant source of irritation. It was cumbrous, wasteful, and expensive.

It did nothing to stem the tide of pauperism ; it helped to swell it. But the Tron could not contract out of it. The one way of conducting a crucial experiment was to induce the Town Council to proceed to the erection of a new parish, definitely and decisively liberated, from the beginning, from this antiquated machinery. At his instigation the Council took action ; and out of three overgrown existing parishes there emerged the new parish of St. John's, comprising some ten thousand inhabitants, and these among the very poorest of the population. A church was to be built, a stipend provided, and Dr. Chalmers was to be presented to the new charge as its first minister.

Since it was to be a demonstration to the city fathers, and to the urban areas of Scotland and beyond, of the way in which both poverty and irreligion could be effectively combated through the ministrations and charity of a local congregation, certain antecedent stipulations were made. The first claim on the church sittings was to be assured to *bona fide* residents in the parish, the second to interested helpers and sympathisers, who had indicated their desire to follow him from the Tron. Further, St. John's was to have its own Kirk Session, which would undertake full responsibility for the poor of the parish.

It was impossible that there could be a completely new beginning. Within the bounds of the new parish there were those paupers who had already been on the general sessional roll in connection with one or other of the three parishes from which St. John's had been disjoined, and there were other worse cases already under the care of the town hospital. What Chalmers proposed was briefly this : to relinquish all claim on the funds of the General Session or on the fund raised by assessment, to take over all responsibility for those already on the sessional roll and for every fresh case as it arose, and, provided that the town hospital would continue its support of those already on its list, to free it from any new demand from the area of the parish. He was confident that he could deal so effectively with the roots of poverty that the plate at the church door would suffice for its relief.

To very many in Glasgow and beyond the whole scheme seemed totally unworkable. He had to face an adverse General Session, a reluctant town hospital, and not a few outspoken critics within the Presbytery. As he himself said, reviewing the beginnings more than twenty years after, " The first warfare with the old established notions on the subject of poverty was far more arduous than the second warfare, with the poverty itself." [1] But he was in a very strong position. He had been asked at the crucial moment to let his name go forward for the Chair of Natural Philosophy in Edinburgh, and he had replied that if he " got his arrangements in the parish of St. John, he would not take the professorship ; but if he did not get these arrangements, he would think of it." [2] Glasgow's fear of losing its most illustrious citizen distinctly helped his appeal.

All initial difficulties overcome, he was introduced to his new sphere of labour on August 26, 1819, by Dr. Andrew Thomson of St. George's, Edinburgh. He could now claim that he had attained the object of his desire, " my own parish in my own way." [3] Yet had he ? Had he really shaken off every possible encumbrance on his enterprise ? He certainly thought he had. In a letter

[1] " The Sufficiency of a Parochial System," etc., *Collected Works,* vol. xxi, p. 97
[2] Hanna, vol. ii, p. 224   [3] *Ibid.,* p. 225

to the Lord Provost three weeks before his induction he
made it clear that he reckoned three further things
necessary for the success of his enterprise. The first was,
that while he was prepared to cope with all normal
poverty out of congregational resources, it should be
understood that, should there be any catastrophic
increase in unemployment, for which the city judged it
necessary to raise an emergency fund, St. John's was not
to be reckoned out of the scope of its operation. The
second was, that the law of residence should be strictly
adhered to, all the other parishes being thus protected
from having to support migrants from St. John's, and
St. John's similarly protected from an influx of paupers
from outside. The third was that, should there be a
surplus of provision over needs (and even at that stage
he conceived it would be large), *that* surplus might be
diverted to the erection and endowment of parochial
schools.

Years after, Chalmers was to claim that there was a
fourth stipulation, " That when those paupers of St.
John's who at the outset of our enterprise received direct
supplies from the town hospital, should have either died
off or ceased in any other way to be chargeable on that
institution, our parish when thus no longer burden-
some on the compulsory fund should be exempted from
the assessment ; or, in other words, should cease contributing to what it ceased to draw from." [1] Although
this is not contained in his letter, there were so many
unrecorded conversations and negotiations, that Chalmers
may well have been led to believe that he had secured
this reasonable request. He was careful to explain in
1841 that these were " understandings rather than con-

---

[1] " Sufficiency of a Parochial System," etc., *Collected Works*, vol. xxi,
pp. 101–102

ditions," [1] and to add in a note that he had not thought it necessary at the time to include the fourth point in his letter to the Lord Provost because of its obvious equity.

In the full scheme which Chalmers now proceeded to put into operation there were, in addition to the normal religious exercises of the Church, four main instruments for securing the Christian well-being of a city parish out of its own resources. This needs to be emphasized, for many of those who have described the St. John's experiment have dealt too exclusively with the fourth, which bears directly on poor relief.

The first was sub-division. The whole parish was divided into twenty-five " proportions " of about equal size, each containing approximately four hundred people. It was quite within the compass of the average zealous worker to get to know intimately the circumstances of every single household in a " proportion," and the needs of its members. It was possible thus to maintain effective Christian contact between home and church with the minimum of overlapping. And further, since a minister and one assistant could not hope to visit pastorally, with any effectiveness, ten thousand people at brief intervals, this sub-division gave an opportunity for informal group gatherings, through which the pastoral link could be established and maintained. A warm atmosphere of Christian friendship was impossible without sub-division.

The second was that an elder was assigned to each " proportion," whose charge was the spiritual oversight, not of the members of St. John's alone, but of every household that was not effectively connected with some other congregation, Secession or Roman Catholic, within the city. With him were conjoined in his religious work Sabbath School teachers. There was a local Sabbath

[1] *Collected Works*, vol. xxi, p. 102

School, sometimes two, and even on occasion three, in each " proportion." Chalmers had no faith in large Sabbath Schools which drew their membership from far and near as a means of overtaking the religious needs of a district in spiritual destitution. These small schools led, not infrequently, to sewing classes which had a marked influence on the appearance and conditions of the homes. The elder and his helpers were the parish agents for seeing that the religious provision was all that it should be.

The third instrument was that by local or parochial day schools a sound education should be placed within the reach of all. The expected surplus duly appeared, and was applied to this purpose. Here he had many critics. Education only produced demagogues, they said, and demogogues bred discontent. But Chalmers made a sounder diagnosis. In a letter to Wilberforce he wrote, " Demagogues are far more formidable when operating on the soil of general ignorance among the population. The true way of disarming them of their influence is to educate the people up to them." [1] And by way of proof he pointed to the statistics of the time of the " Radical Rising." The cotton spinners, despite their higher wages, were more easily influenced than the weavers. The former were drawn from education at an early age to earn their living in the mills, and had no opportunity later of making up their deficiencies. Weavers were longer at school ; they did have opportunities later ; and their standard of literary attainment was much higher. Education was, therefore, one element in countering the schemes of agitators. Further, it had saddened Chalmers greatly to find, in his early Sabbath Schools in the Tron, that there were so many who could not

[1] Hanna, vol. ii, p. 265

read their Bibles, and so many more who could only stumble through them. Such a reproach was to be banished from St. John's, and no glimpses that we have of the great man are more attractive than those frequent visits of his to his parochial schools, beaming over and rejoicing at the marked progress being made by his humble parishioners. This education placed within the reach of all was to be cheap, but not free. For Chalmers strongly felt that what was obtained without cost was rated as of no value. His parishioners paid, like all the other children of the city, but they paid less. His surplus revenue provided an endowment.

Immediate contact with spiritual influences and a good elementary education were indispensable to the working of his social scheme.

It was the fourth element that was the greatest novelty. To each " proportion " there was to be assigned a deacon of the church. Now, the office of deacon had fallen entirely, or almost entirely, into abeyance until Chalmers revived it. He felt that it continually clogged the spiritual work if the minister or elder were also the almoner. He would have to listen to long accounts of spiritual difficulties which proved to be entirely imaginary, concocted by the ingenious as a prelude to a request for money. Few stories of Chalmers are better known than this, which appeared first thus in a note of Dr. Hanna's : [1]

" While Dr. Chalmers was busily engaged one forenoon in his study a man entered, who at once propitiated him under the provocation of an unexpected interruption, by telling him that he called under great distress of mind. ' Sit down, sir ; be good enough to be seated,' said Dr. Chalmers, turning eagerly and full of interest from his

[1] Hanna, vol. ii, p. 191 (note)

writing-table. The visitor explained to him that he was troubled with doubts about the Divine origin of the Christian religion ; and being kindly questioned as to what these were, he gave, among others, what is said in the Bible about Melchisedek, being without father or mother, etc. Patiently and anxiously Dr. Chalmers sought to clear away each successive difficulty as it was stated. Expressing himself as if greatly relieved in mind, and imagining that he had gained his end, ' Doctor,' said the visitor, ' I am in great want of a little money at present, and perhaps you could help me in that way.' At once the object of his visit was seen. A perfect tornado of indignation burst upon the deceiver, driving him in very quick retreat from the study to the street door, these words escaping, among others, ' Not a penny, sir ! not a penny ! It's too bad ! It's too bad ! And to haul in your hypocrisy upon the shoulders of Melchisedek.' "

The channels of spiritual direction must somehow be disentangled from those of material help ; and how could this be better effected than by re-establishing the ancient order of deacons whose duty it would be to care directly for the material well-being of the people in the " proportion " allotted to them. They were very busy men at first, for the whisper had gone around St. John's that now that Dr. Chalmers had come, the golden age had arrived ; money would be lavished on all who asked it. What were these deacons for if not to relieve the necessities of the poor ?

On the first contact with the deacons the dream of an easy direct way of making money vanished into thin air. For they had been drilled in their procedure, and they had written instructions as to what was expected of them.

They were not to hide the fact that they were set apart to deal with cases of hardship and distress. But their first duty was to cultivate acquaintance with each household, till they had at least some knowledge of the nature of the folk with whom they were to deal. Then, when they received applications, they had to conduct a full investigation. They were directed to inquire, first, as to the possibility of the applicant's undertaking some employment which might be found for him ; next, failing such, if he was a legitimate charge on any other kirk session through membership of that church, or on any other parish authority through former residence within its bounds. Only then, when the need was proven, would the deacon begin to consider the possible claim on the funds of St. John's ; and even then he would have to inquire whether the applicant needed to be put on the roll for a regular allowance, or whether temporary aid would meet the case. If a regular allowance was deemed necessary the case was reported by the deacon to the deacons' court, which fixed the rate of the allowance. The intention was not to give temporary relief to poverty by indiscriminate doles, but to banish poverty by calling on the instincts of independence and self-help, the generosity of relatives, and the kindly feelings of neighbours. The deacon was to exhaust every possible alternative before he took the step of recommending that the applicant for relief be put on the regular pauper roll.

With these stringent precautions it was practically impossible for an impostor to get relief ; and experience proved that it was equally impossible for anyone in the parish to sink into a state of extreme destitution ; and the whole of the new cases taken on was far from exhausting the available resources. In addition, before two years were over, St. John's was able to take out of the hands of the town hospital all belonging to the parish who remained on its books.

In point of fact the scheme proved a success even beyond anything that Chalmers himself had predicted or anticipated. He had demonstrated that, by the thorough application of the normal parochial care of the Church, with adequate organization, the problem of poverty could be coped with, even in a populous city parish of the poorest classes.

Why, then, was this scheme not universally adopted? Partly, it must be acknowledged, because of the inertia of many who might well have followed the lead, but partly because of the attribution of that success to adventitious circumstances, and not to the inherent merits of the scheme itself. This attribution, whatever form it took, always awakened Chalmers' indignation as almost no other allegation in the whole course of his career. He has himself classified the false explanations given by its opponents.

It was asserted, first of all, that the success achieved was due to the huge collections which were the inevitable accompaniment of his ministry, and that these were drawn largely from strangers outside the parish. To answer this Chalmers published a complete financial statement of the scheme, and showed that it was the local collections alone—not the much larger morning and afternoon ones—that had proved more than sufficient for all new local needs.

Next, it was alleged that the scheme needed a very large number of men who were ready to give practically their whole time to this business, " that it required a management which no man in ordinary business could possibly have time for." [1] In answer Chalmers produced

[1] " Sufficiency of a Parochial System, etc.," *Collected Works*, vol. xxi, p. 114

the testimony of his deacons individually, which united in showing that, after the heavy spate of applications in the first few weeks, the demands on their time were almost incredibly small.

Further, the insinuation was widely spread that St. John's starved its poor and drove them out of the parish to seek easier and more abundant relief elsewhere. By quoting the actual figures of egress and ingress, and by pointing to his preliminary stipulation as to the law of residence being enforced, Chalmers was able to answer this triumphantly.

Then it was openly asserted that the St. John's deacons were all men of substance, who gave freely of their wealth privately to prevent the appearance of new names on the roll, and thus to ensure the apparent success of the scheme. Here Chalmers' answer was less complete, though he did prove that many of his deacons did not answer this description, and that the occasional charities of the wealthier had been much exaggerated. He admitted, however, that the districts under poor deacons were in the more quiescent and satisfied state.[1]

Last of all those critics who most strongly roused the wrath of Chalmers were those who said that any scheme would have been successful with such a man at its head. " When it did succeed," he complained, " they managed to keep up its discredit by ascribing the whole success to the marvellous and preternatural strength of the projector." [2] They imputed it all to " a sort of wizard power which they were pleased to ascribe to the great Katterfelto or wonder-worker that had come among them from the East." [3] In later years Dr. Chalmers was accustomed to give as one of his reasons for leaving Glasgow when he did the desire to dispel this illusion

[1] *Collected Works*, vol. xxi, p. 122   [2] *Ibid.*, p. 124.   [3] *Ibid.*, p. 125.

He had set the scheme agoing ; men would be able to see how it fared after his departure. And he claimed, and rightly claimed, that during the days of his immediate successors, and even during two prolonged vacancies, the scheme had continued with no diminution of success.

This has always been and still remains a favourite criticism of the scheme. It could only work were there a Chalmers in every parish. There is at least this modicum of truth in it, that if Chalmers had been irresistibly drawn to a very different and less adequate scheme, he could have put it into operation, and could so have communicated something of his own enthusiasm to such a body of the citizens of Glasgow as would have made even it a demonstrable working economy. But naturally, Chalmers refused to believe that there was even a modicum of truth in it. He taught the system to all his students, confident that any one of them could carry it into execution, in any parish to which he might be presented or called. For some reason, however, it did fail to kindle the emulation of his compeers. " I was disappointed," he says, " and make open avowal of it— not in the result of the experiment itself, which was all I could have wished, but in its utter powerlessness of effect on the minds of the public functionaries in Glasgow —men who denounced it *as theory* at the first, and who, after it had become *experience*, would not receive, would not even read, the lesson which had been so palpably set before their eyes." [1]

The reasons for St. John's ceasing to be an enclave in the administrative system of Glasgow, and its return to the general system of parochial relief, are outwith the scope of this review ; but the fruitful experiment there

[1] *Collected Works*, vol. xxi, p. 129

made and faithfully pursued for many years has been an inspiration to reformers in every generation since ; and were it the only achievement to Chalmers' credit, would stamp him as one of the very greatest of all the Christian social pioneers.

Before we take our leave of this subject, there is one effect which it left on Chalmers himself that calls for mention. A parochial ministry fully and rightly exercised had been his ideal for the rural areas. He had now, through his Glasgow experience, an even deeper impression of the benefit that would accrue to the whole land through an adequate territorial ministry. The following sentence from a letter to Wilberforce is characteristic, and, incidentally, it foreshadows things to come. " Nothing but the multiplication of our Established Churches, with the subdivision of parishes and the allocation of each parish to its own church, together with a pure and popular exercise of the right of patronage, will ever bring us back again to a sound and wholesome state of the body politic." [1] " The multiplication of our Established Churches," " the pure and popular exercise of the right of patronage," these two were to be his lodestars in the days ahead, and were to bring him into the conflicts which led to the Disruption.

But lest the great distinctive feature of his St. John's ministry blot out all the rest, it is well to recall the extent and variety of his spiritual ministrations. With four services each Sunday for which he and his assistant were jointly responsible, Chalmers, even when the assistant was as distinguished as Edward Irving, had a formidable preaching programme, and though he not infrequently fell back on old material, his regular Sunday sermons were as powerful and almost as popular as they ever had

[1] Hanna, vol. ii, p. 264

been in the Tron. Yet some of his elders said that their minister was at his best in the short, informal addresses that he delivered to gatherings in the various " proportions." There, in the midst of a small company of working-folk, he showed a tenderness, an intimacy, and a directness of appeal that moved both heart and conscience. And when, in the height of summer, his wife and family went on holiday, he was accustomed to betake himself to a room in a working-class home that he might spend his days and nights in the midst of his people. His prayers reveal the urgency of his desire that the gospel might come with power into their hearts and lives. The " proportions " might respectfully receive the deacons as just and generous benefactors : they welcomed and honoured Dr. Chalmers as evangelist, pastor, and friend. Very touching were the narratives that Dr. Chalmers told in after days out of their simple lives. Equally numerous and affecting were the anecdotes they told of him.

At the very height of his success, the parish and the city were stunned by the news that he was about to leave them for the Chair of Moral Philosophy in St. Andrews. It was to them incredible that one who was born, they felt, to be a preacher and evangelist should leave his mighty work in Scotland's second city for a handful of students in its smallest university. Recovering from the first shock of the blow, they rallied round him to bid him God-speed. The tumultuous concourse that gathered to hear his farewell sermon (a contemporary record states that the congregation took nearly half an hour to pass out at the front door, three thousand, it was calculated, having heard the sermon) ; the elaborate nature and wild enthusiasm of the farewell civic banquet, alike testify to the city's sense that, as the Lord Provost said on that occasion, it was "losing its brightest ornament." [1]

Two questions suggest themselves at this point. One is, "What had Glasgow done for Dr. Chalmers?" It had given him an insight into all the problems that confronted the Church of Scotland ; it had taught him that neither the richest merchant nor the poorest operative was incapable of receiving the gospel and having his life reshaped by it ; it had assured him that there was a potential wealth of Christian enterprise in the secluded suburban mansion and the over-crowded wynd waiting only to be tapped ; that the forces which make for degeneration could be met on their own ground and overcome by the gathered might of believing men ; that not Glasgow alone, but every other great city, could and might flourish by the preaching of the Word. A wide experience had reinforced his initial conviction that the one hope of the world was in the gospel.

The other is, "What had Dr. Chalmers done for Glasgow?" The penetrating answer of Lord Rosebery is, "He had warmed it." [2] There was a new atmosphere in the city now, of social zeal and civic responsibility. The men trained in his "agency" were fervent souls, and they stirred up kindred spirits to new avenues of social service. Nowhere, in the days that followed, did any appeal to relieve material or spiritual destitution find more active supporters or more open-handed contributors than in Glasgow. Very definite was the change in the attitude of its leaders towards Evangelicalism. Despite some notable Evangelical ministries, the cause they represented had been despised. They were regarded as men who relied on some magical power in phrases ;

---

[1] *Farewell Memorial of Dr. Chalmers*, p. 16
[2] Lord Rosebery, *Chalmers*, p. 5

who could harp only on one string ; whose only strength lay in reiteration ; who despised general culture ; whose interest was only in souls ; who were totally apart from the main currents of thought. But through Chalmers these despisers had learned that Evangelicalism and culture were not necessarily divorced, that there was more in the distinctive truths of the gospel than they had dreamed, and even though they themselves had not experienced its power, they ceased to speak of it with disrespect. Some of those least attracted personally had become convinced that it was the one effective barrier to revolution. The whole tone of their utterance altered. High-brow contempt was no longer in vogue. Chalmers had put Evangelicalism on their map, as at least a force to be reckoned with, if not as yet a cause into which they must throw the weight of their influence. Evangelical ministers found many more ears open to their message, and while one cannot speak of any general revival of religion, the soil for such a revival was prepared. Apart from the many who had been directly converted by his ministries, or stirred up into new Christian activities, Chalmers might well have looked back on the total achievement of these eight years with no small measure of satisfaction. He had changed the prevailing tone of a city.

Chapter Six

THE MORAL PHILOSOPHY CHAIR AT
ST. ANDREWS

1823–28

On Friday, November 14, 1823, Dr. Chalmers entered upon his new duties as professor of Moral Philosophy in the university of St. Andrews by delivering his inaugural lecture. This brings us face to face with what is, to many, the most puzzling personal problem of his whole career. What were the motives which led him into this comparative backwater ? He was in no sense an applicant for the chair. Its offer came without a hint of solicitation. But it could not have been made without some ground for believing that it would not be summarily rejected.

Was there anything, therefore, in Dr. Chalmers' circumstances which could lead St. Andrews to make hopefully even tentative approaches, especially when it was widely known that he had turned down other apparently more attractive spheres offered to him almost immediately before ? There were no rumours of trouble in St. John's ; he was at the zenith of his usefulness ; he was in process of piloting with success the initial stages of what promised to be a definite further improvement, the erection of a chapel of ease within his parish to house his reclaimed parishioners—a chapel whose arrangements for its poor were to be equally free from the General Session of Glasgow. Had St. Andrews heard a whisper of a letter that he had written to the Town Council of Edinburgh, refusing a city parish there, but hinting at the same time that if a suitable chair within their patronage fell vacant, he might not prove so unresponsive ? Or did it trust simply to that haunting spell with which St. Andrews seems to bind so many of its old students ? Or did it feel that Chalmers might well desire greater leisure now to devote to nation-wide propaganda on behalf of a general adoption of the schemes he had put into operation and thoroughly tested ?

For the first two suggestions there is no documentary evidence ; for the third there is this. The principal's letter of invitation contained the sentence : " By coming amongst us, your plans of public usefulness will not be upon the whole impeded, for though you will be completely occupied during session time with your duty as a Moral Philosophy Professor, you will have six months entirely to yourself unfettered by College rules." [1]

While it is difficult to disentangle the sources of hope in the St. Andrews' invitation, no similar difficulty besets the path of the student who seeks to lay bare the reasons for Chalmers' acceptance. For he himself was deeply conscious that he would have to justify the step in the eyes of his parishioners, and in the eyes of the people of Scotland. He took, therefore, the first opportunity in a letter to his " agency " of stating them plainly and unequivocally. Mrs. Oliphant has said that " we cannot but feel something apologetic, even something sophistical, in these reasons for the change," [2] and she adds, " the step remains unaccountable." If she had weighed them more carefully, and studied alongside them certain other utterances of his, both earlier and later, she would hardly have ventured on the word " sophistical," nor would she have found the step unaccountable.

His first reason, which he called " a reason of neces-

[1] Hanna, vol. ii, p. 372   [2] Mrs. Oliphant, *Thomas Chalmers*, p. 149

sity," concerned his health. His robust frame was being put to an undue strain. He had found himself at times, incapacitated for any full and continued mental exertion. Body and mind needed a change. It is all very well to say, with Mrs. Oliphant, that, being in the prime of life, with no definite attack of illness, and " with all the vigour of a sturdy and unexhausted race," [1] he must have been aware that this was a mere excuse. Even the strongest man may overtax his energies to the point of mental barrenness, and this is what Chalmers felt he was rapidly doing.

His second reason, which he styled one of conscience, was more complicated. While he might have looked forward, had he stayed in Glasgow, to being relieved of some of his responsibilities by the new chapel of ease, a fresh burden had been laid upon him by his success, and one that he could not lay down. It had become increasingly his concern to defend his scheme of operations, which entailed making elaborate comparisons with the machinery for Poor Relief prevailing elsewhere. His last break during his ministry in St. John's—seven weeks in all—had been spent in a most strenuous tour through England, devoted to one end alone, an elaborate investigation of the variations adopted in the English system of compulsory assessment in every significant locality, south of the Tweed, together with their whole financial and social implications. During this inquiry he had accumulated a huge mass of statistics and relevant verdicts which he felt bound to digest, assess, and co-ordinate. It was his manifest Christian duty to explore these data to the full. If he did justice to this call, would he not necessarily be forced to neglect his parish ; would he not be " to all intents and purposes, a pluralist " ? [2] Whereas,

---

[1] Mrs. Oliphant, *Thomas Chalmers*, p. 148   [2] Hanna, vol. ii, p. 375

were he set apart to teach a subject which was closely connected with, and indeed in the practice of St. Andrews
University included, political economy, could he not with
a clear conscience develop the views to which his wide
experience had led him, and give them forth to the world
in the setting of other competing theories and practices ?
It is true that his literary production along this line did
not prove to be either so important or so voluminous as
he planned, but this does not affect the sincerity of his
intention.

Further, his severance from St. John's need not be
so complete as would be entailed by the acceptance of
another pastoral charge. He would have time, he
declared, to " renew for months together, my converse
with Glasgow, and so perpetuate my intimacy with
yourselves." [1] And so it proved. His Journal bears
witness to the eagerness with which he devoted part of
each long vacation to preaching in the new chapel, and
to contacts with old friends and members.

Still further, he acknowledged the spell of St. Andrews
itself and the attraction of being once more " among the
fondest remembrances of my boyhood." [2]

But at the basis of it all was an ineradicable persuasion of the high calling of the professoriate. At the
outset of his career he had coveted a chair as the
recognized highroad to literary distinction. Now it was
his conviction of its practical Christian usefulness that
moved him. " Some of you," he wrote, " have long
known what I think of the great worth and importance
of a professorship, and that I have even held a literary
office in a university, through which the future ministers
of the parishes pass in numerous succession every year,
to be a higher station in the vineyard, even of Christian

---

[1] Hanna, vol. ii, p. 377   [2] Ibid., p. 375

usefulness, than the office of a single minister of a single congregation." [1]

That this was no mere passing fancy is apparent in all his later actions. The prospect of a call to any parish —even so great an opportunity as the succession to the Rev. Sir Henry Moncrieff in St. Cuthbert's, Edinburgh —created for him no problem. He lost no night's sleep over it. He simply set it aside. But the invitations that came to other academic posts perturbed him profoundly. Even when one entailed severance from his beloved Scotland, he could not bring himself to decline it till he had examined it in all its bearings as a competing sphere of Christian usefulness. [2]

His actions, however, do not stand alone ; they are reinforced by many pronouncements on the subject, two of which will serve adequately to indicate his point of view.

The first is this. Four years before, at the very moment when he was embarking on the experiment of St. John's, he had written in the first volume of his *Christian and Civic Economy of Large Towns* : " To produce a steam-engine, which sets one hundred looms going, is a far larger contribution to the goods of a country than to work a single loom. . . . He who does the work is not so productively employed as he who multiplies the doers. . . . A professorship is a higher condition of usefulness than an ordinary parish." [3] And he added, in words that anticipated the incessant murmur that it was an Arts professorship that he had undertaken, " Some of you may think that this holds only of a theological professorship ; but this is your mistake." [4] Than a

---

[1] Hanna, vol. ii, pp. 375–76   [2] *Ibid.*, vol. iii, pp. 155–57
[3] *Christian and Civic Economy of Large Towns* (in the original first number of 1819, which, being so local and personal, was not reprinted in the three volumes), pp. 22–23.   [4] *Ibid.*, p. 23

Christianized university no mightier accession to the Christian good of a country could be conceived.

The other was made after some years' experience of the chair. " In giving up the direct work of a Christian minister I cannot regret the station into which Providence has translated me, one of the fountain-heads of the Christian ministry in our land." [1]

There were to be times of despondency, when the financial disputes of a provincial university proved as detrimental to intellectual concentration and spiritual work as the insistent outside calls of a great city ; and alienation from colleagues created as painful a situation as the obstructionist tactics of vested interests in Glasgow ; but his conviction never faltered that he had been justified in his decision to move, and that he was occupying a strategic centre from which his deepest convictions of evangelical truth and his plans for their full operation might spread throughout the whole Church of Scotland and even beyond the limits of the nation.

There is no need to say much of Chalmers as an academic lecturer. While it cannot be claimed that he made any distinctive contribution to the advance of his subject, he did succeed in crowding his classrooms with students from far and near, and evoking from them demonstrations of appreciation. More than once he had to beseech them to be more active with their heads than their heels. Not a few of them in later life bore testimony to the permanence of the intellectual stimulus there received. If he had "warmed" Glasgow he was to do the same service for St. Andrews. On his return there, while by no means disappointed in his welcome, he was disheartened in his early closer contacts with the community, both gownsmen and townsmen. " Perhaps,"

[1] Hanna, vol. iii, p. 189

he wrote after a few months in residence, " there is no town in Scotland more cold and meagre and moderate in its theology than St. Andrews." [1] The most congenial preaching was that provided in the Independent chapel; but while he allowed his family to frequent it, he could not bring himself to desert the Church of Scotland Sunday services, though on a weekday he might be found in the chapel pews—a silent criticism of Moderate preaching which did not pass unnoticed or unrebuked.

His ardent spirit had to find some outlet for Christian activities. His first venture was a Sabbath School in his own home, modelled on the local Sabbath Schools of his Glasgow ministries. Through door-to-door visitation of a poor area in the neighbourhood he gathered in a number of children for Sunday evening instruction, devoting himself as closely to preparation for that class as for any academic lecture.

A new field was found, however, among the students. Some parents had committed their sons to Dr. Chalmers' pastoral care. From that nucleus developed his Sunday Bible Classes, whose members, in turn, with their friends became responsible for the original local Sabbath School, and many similar schools in private houses, as well as for district meetings of adults. From the house of the Professor of Moral Philosophy there radiated a whole host of minor evangelical activities.

Then an almost moribund Foreign Missionary Society enlisted his services as president. Immediately it woke into new life, and in a short space of time had to seek out larger premises, which speedily became filled to overflowing, though its programme continued to be merely the reading of reports, interspersed by brief comments and elucidations from the chair. This zeal of the citizens

[1] Hanna, vol. iii, p. 80

nfected the students of the Arts Faculty in the university, and a second society was formed among them. Frowned on at first by the authorities, it came to be taken under their wing and encouraged.

Few things are more noteworthy in those five years at St. Andrews than the number of students who received the impulse to volunteer for foreign mission service. The most distinguished of the company was Alexander Duff, who could never speak of his St. Andrews days except in terms approaching sheer rhapsody. One of the lower lights may be given as a sample :

" Altogether, what a change in the course of two or three years ! Whatever may have been the *extent* of *inward* spiritual renovation, no-one could question the extent of the *outward* visible amelioration in the religious aspect of things. Religion, which had long settled down at zero, or many degrees below it, was sensibly raised in its temperature, and in some instances kindled into an inextinguishable flame. . . . Those who compare what St. Andrews was immediately before Dr. Chalmers' residence there with what it was two or three years after his arrival were constrained to feel that no language could more appropriately express *the greatness of the change* than that of the Prophet Isaiah, ' The wilderness and the solitary place shall be glad for them ; and the desert shall rejoice and blossom as the rose.' " [1]

In reviewing the St. Andrews days some notice must be taken of the two controversies with the majority of his colleagues in which he found himself involved.

It might prove a fascinating parenthesis to deal at length with one of these, over the matter of the Candlemas

[1] Hanna, vol. iii, pp. 200–201

dividend, to show the heartiness with which Dr. Chalmer
could belabour a Royal Commission he had welcomed
and how he could pillory its report before all Scotlan
as, in one respect, a masterpiece of insincerity and in
consistency. At no time in his career did he write
more pungent pamphlet than his *Letter to the Roya*
Commissioners. His dissentient colleagues joined in th
general acclamation.

The other arose out of the compulsory attendance a
St. Leonard's Church prescribed for all students of th
United College belonging to the Church of Scotland. I
was a change in its ministry that gave rise to a deman
for greater freedom. Dr. Chalmers supported th
suggestion. He was at great pains to make it clear tha
he was animated by no hostility or disloyalty to th
Church of Scotland. There are two sentences from hi
utterances in the heat of the controversy which shoul
here be recorded as another foreshadowing of things t
come.

" I have no veneration for the Church of Scotlan
merely *quasi* an Establishment, but I have the utmos
veneration for it, *quasi* an instrument of Christian good
and I do think that, with the means and resources of a
Establishment, she can do more, and does more, for th
religious interests of Scotland than is done by the activit
of all the Dissenters put together. I think it a hig
object to uphold the Church of Scotland, but only becaus
of its subserviency to the still higher object of upholdin
the Christianity of our land." [1]

Fully to appreciate, however, the significance of thes
four and a half years, attention must not be confine

[1] Hanna, vol. iii, p. 109

to St. Andrews itself. The yearly months of freedom, dangled before his eyes by the Principal, had been utilized to their utmost. The demands on his services as special preacher were continuous and far-extended. A visit to London, opening Edward Irving's new church, and one to Belfast, inaugurating a new venture there, were amongst the notable occasions ; but in Edinburgh, Glasgow, and the rural districts we find him preaching for more than one missionary society and many a different charity. There is a naïve touch in the pleasure with which he records the various collections, but no trace of any delight in crowds, in themselves or as a symptom of personal popularity. Going from one scene of enthusiasm to another, he betrays no sense of elation, except in the continuous stream of liberality.

The feature of these years most significant for the future is his intense and sustained interest in the activities of the General Assembly. He had certainly attended it before, when he was duly elected as a representative minister by his presbytery, and he had more than once intervened with powerful effect in its discussions on subjects that directly interested him. Now he found himself beyond the caprice or the rotation system of a Presbytery, being nominated annually as the representative elder of the Royal Burgh of Anstruther, his native town being proud to have such a distinguished delegate. Year by year he went to Edinburgh in advance of the opening, and welcomed into the Evangelical counsels by Dr. Andrew Thomson and the Rev. Sir Henry Moncrieff, he began to be a most effective spokesman for their general policy, and a brilliant advocate in the cases in which they were committed to intervene.

With special zest he fought in the final engagements against the remaining pluralities, in one of which he

made the dramatic retraction already referred to ; [1] and
with dogged persistence he carried his point as to the
reform of the Divinity curriculum. Up to this date it
had been singularly fluid. There was a normal course
it is true ; he himself had taken it ; but to meet the
cases of men who, for financial reasons, went directly
from their Arts course to some paid employment as tutor
or as schoolmaster in the country, it had been allowed
that such a student, without attending a single term
could by occasional visits to his university seat, and by
complying with some not too onerous conditions, at the
end of six years (*i.e.* six years after the close of his Art
curriculum) acquire a certificate which enabled him to
proceed to licence. The amendment suggested by
Chalmers which would have been dropped but for his
own perseverance was simple, and was intended only as
a first step. It was that no such certificate should for
the future be issued to any student whatever who had
not satisfied his professors by attendance and diligence
during one complete session.

In the eighteenth and early nineteenth centuries the
Assembly was far more exclusively the final court of appeal
than it is to-day. Many of its most exciting debates
were over local disputes which had already attained a
wide publicity through the earlier discussions in Presbytery
and Synod. Of all the cases in the consideration of which
he addressed the Assembly in these years, only one need
be resurrected. It concerned the extent and the limit
of a patron's power. To the parish of Little Dunkeld
within the Highland area, the Crown, as patron, had
presented a licentiate who knew no Gaelic. While both
Presbytery and Synod had refused to sustain the pre
sentation, it was feared that the General Assembly would

[1] 1825, *v.* p. 26

adhere to its traditional reluctance to bar the way to a patron's nominee. The Evangelical party felt that here they had an excellent opportunity for loosening the hold of that evil tradition, and threw their whole weight on the side of the Presbytery and Synod. Dr. Andrew Thomson moved, and Dr. Chalmers seconded, that the presentation be not sustained, and after one of the most keenly contested pitched battles for many years, they carried their point by a majority of eighteen votes. It was the result of this trial of strength, on ground singularly favourable to the Evangelicals, that helped to deepen the growing impression in Chalmers' mind that there was a field of usefulness for him in the Assembly which he could not neglect or ignore. He had taken his place unmistakably among the protagonists.

In the end of 1827 the Chair of Divinity in Edinburgh fell vacant, and within a few weeks Chalmers was unanimously elected. His duties, however, were not to commence till the winter session of 1828. He spent, therefore, the session already begun in St. Andrews in the full knowledge that it was to be his last.

CHAPTER SEVEN

FIRST YEARS IN EDINBURGH

1828–32

WHILE there were not a few in the Scotland of his day who deplored Dr. Chalmers' acceptance of an Arts chair in St. Andrews, his removal to the Divinity chair in Edinburgh called forth a chorus of approval. There were, however, some dissentients who thought that his distinctive gifts were wasted on a chair, and ought to be devoted to a parish. One of these was Sir Michael Shaw Stewart, who, when the important and highly endowed West Parish of Greenock fell vacant, offered it in 1831 to Professor Chalmers. Consideration of this competing claim only confirmed him in his conviction as to his proper sphere of labour, as appears from his letter of reply, which opened thus :

" DEAR SIR MICHAEL,—I deeply feel the whole force of the compliment you have done me in offering to my acceptance the most lucrative ecclesiastical living in Scotland, and whose endowments, I believe, are nearly double those of the one which I now occupy. You may well believe that nothing could induce me to decline the honour and the advantage of such a proposal, but a firm conviction of the superior importance of a theological chair to any church whatever, along with the rooted preference which I have ever felt for the professorial over the ministerial life." [1]

With the chair of Divinity in Edinburgh, therefore,

[1] Hanna, vol. iii, p. 310

Chalmers was entirely satisfied ; to it he had been called, there he would remain ; and there he would have remained until the end had it continued possible for him to hold it with a clear conscience. He was parting from a great deal when he signed the Deed of Demission in 1843.

From the very beginning his work in the university was attended with extraordinary success. When I had the privilege for a year or two of teaching in his old classroom, the repainted walls still showed traces of the gallery that had to be erected to accommodate the numbers of the general public who were drawn to his regular lectures. While it has been not infrequently asserted that his lectures were too declamatory to be effective instruments of education, it was not the outside visitors alone who responded to their eloquence and point. They, indeed, might compass him about with gifts, but his real reward was in a succession of student generations inspired by an enthusiasm for the subject, and constrained to seek, in parishes at home and mission stations abroad, through the fresh exposition of gospel truth and its implications, the Christian good of the people committed to their charge.

He certainly did not tie himself down to the recognized sub-division of his subject, to the schematism currently accepted as scientific ; he had an approach of his own. When his lectures were being issued later as the *Institutes of Theology*, he acknowledged that he had left the ground-lines of the system hitherto taught through the medium of Marck's *Medulla*, and inherited from Calvin and Turretin. He admitted that his own looked bare and unsystematic alongside theirs, and even over against the custom of Anglican divines of following the course of the Apostles' Creed.[1]

[1] *Institutes of Theology*, vol. i, p. 10

But his method is quite defensible. Indeed, it was almost inevitable for one with strong Evangelical convictions approaching the subject afresh after five years of teaching moral philosophy. He began with a survey of the relevant branches of ethics, natural theology, and the evidences of Christianity, and then, plunging into Christian dogmatics proper, he felt that he had first to deal with man in his weakness and sinfulness, in the state in which he finds himself apart from the revelation of the grace of God in Jesus Christ. Thus he came to his three main heads : " the disease for which a gospel remedy is provided," " the nature of the gospel remedy," and " the extent of the gospel remedy." [1] It is partly this novel layout of his subject, and partly his rhetorical style, that have kept Chalmers from being regarded as a great systematic theologian, and have allowed his works on pure theology to gather dust on the shelves, while the works of lesser men are more frequently referred to and discussed. Had they been less orthodox in content, or more orthodox in system, their lasting vogue would have been greater. But no-one can deny the evidence of the immediate effectiveness of the lectures, nor the lasting impression they made on the minds of his students.

Among the men who most profoundly influenced Chalmers at this time two should be mentioned. One was Dr. Thomas Brown, Professor of Moral Philosophy in Edinburgh, " the last of the Scottish school of metaphysicians," who had died eight years before Chalmers came to Edinburgh, but whose *Lectures*, later to be severely castigated by Sir William Hamilton, still stood very high in popular esteem. Admiration for Dr. Brown took him on a summer excursion to Galloway, to see the

[1] *Institutes of Theology*, vol. i, p. 317

manse of Kirkmabreck where he was born, and to visit the graveyard in which he was interred with, as Chalmers lamented, " not a stone to tell where the great philosopher lies." [1] This same admiration led him on to the manse of Crossmichael to meet the Rev. David Welsh, Brown's biographer and the editor of his *Lectures*. At the end of this visit he was to record in his journal, " Mr. Welsh is the most congenial person that I have met with in this country." [2] The result of this meeting was that when in 1831 the chair of Church History in Edinburgh fell vacant the government of the day, at the suggestion of Dr. Chalmers, appointed Mr. Welsh. From that day forward Chalmers' delight in his work was increased by the knowledge that there was alongside him a brilliant and like-minded colleague.

The other notable influence was that of Dr. Andrew Thomson, minister of St. George's and leader of the Evangelical party, the man who, far more than any other, had succeeded in rehabilitating Evangelicalism in the eyes of the cultured of Edinburgh, and in reinvigorating it as a force in the councils of the Church. He had encouraged Chalmers from the beginning. From the outset of his St. Andrews professorship he had welcomed him as a junior colleague and possible successor. He had been the main mover in the transference to Edinburgh where he became " a joyous, hearty, gallant, honourable and out-and-out trustworthy friend." [3] With tragic suddenness he died on his own doorstep in 1831. A dreadful sense of loss seized hold of Edinburgh, for as Chalmers said in the funeral sermon, " there was none who moved with greater acceptance or wielded a greater ascendant over so wide a circle of living society." [4] The

[1] Hanna, vol. iii, p. 132   [2] *Ibid.*, p. 132
[3] *Collected Works*, vol. xi, p. 218   [4] Hanna, vol. iii, p. 296

Evangelicals were for the moment stunned ; but it was speedily apparent that the mantle of Andrew Thomson had fallen on Thomas Chalmers, that the colleague had become the successor, a successor who in the three years of intimate converse had imbibed much of the sound yet cautious strategy and the tactical wisdom of his predecessor.

Chalmers did not, however, throw himself immediately headlong into schemes for the betterment of the Church. One long-meditated project had a prior claim. He must put forth to the world his mature views on political economy. Two related entries from his journal will serve to indicate his preoccupation with this project.

" Old things are not wholly passed away ; the love of literature for *itself*, and the love of literary distinction have not passed away. Let me love literature as one of those creatures of God which is not to be refused but received with thanksgiving. Let me desire literary distinction, but let my desire for it be altogether that I may add to my Christian usefulness, and promote the glory of God ; then, even with these, I would be a new creature." [1]

" My chief earthly ambition is to finish a treatise in Political Economy, as the commencement of a series of future publications on Moral Philosophy and Theology. Consecrate this ambition, and purge it of all sin and selfishness, O God." [2]

In nothing was Chalmers more grievously disappointed than in the reception accorded to his *magnum opus.*

[1] Journal for October 1, 1826, transcribed in Hanna, vol. iii, p. 104
[2] Journal for January 1, 1827, transcribed in Hanna, vol. iii, p. 298

Reviews, ignoring its basic contentions, fastened on some subsidiary generalizations and dismissed them as the product of an incompetent amateur, an intruder into a discipline he had not mastered. It fitted in with the fashionable theories of no school, and most of them joined in the almost universal condemnation. In the preface he had said, " We are not sanguine either of a general, or of an instant, reception for the doctrines of this work. Its novelties may long be disregarded or derided as paradoxes." [1] But he had hoped against hope for a better reception than this ; and his confident expectation that later ages would turn to it as to a ray of light has not been justified.

As a theoretical economist Chalmers has never been reckoned in the front rank, though some later masters like John Stuart Mill have spoken in the very highest terms of parts of his exposition. But as a practical economist, who had achieved something of quite first-rate importance in dealing with the problems of pauperism, his reputation did not wane. No relevant Commission of Inquiry could afford to do without his evidence, and not infrequently it is to this part of the report alone that the student of to-day turns with any hope or expectation.

A most revealing verdict on this lengthy treatise is implicit in the fact that when in 1900 Mr. N. Masterman published his volume on *Chalmers on Charity*, he quoted largely from all the shorter works in which Chalmers had delineated and defended his Glasgow scheme, but hardly took a single citation from the *Political Economy*.

Another major work during the same period, to which he devoted the summer vacation of 1832, met with a much greater acclaim alike from the general public

[1] *Political Economy in Connection with the Moral State and Moral Prospects of Society*, p. v.

and from the experts. This was one of the series of Bridge-water treatises. The Bishop of London, in his invitation, gave him a choice of subjects within the original scope of the endowment, " a treatise to be written in proof of the wisdom and benevolence of the Deity as manifested in the works of creation." [1] His previous studies in Natural Theology made this an easy task, and a very few months' labour sufficed to produce his work, *On the Adaptation of External Nature to the Moral and Intellectual Constitution of Man*, which after three editions was incorporated in, and continued to be sold as part of, his *Collected Works*, the publication of which began in 1836. In contributions to literature outside the realm of ecclesiastical controversy, the early years in Edinburgh were indeed rich and fruitful.

These same years saw far-reaching changes in the constitution of the United Kingdom, and it is of great interest to observe his public and private reactions to them.

The first of them came after his appointment, but before his removal, to Edinburgh. This was the repeal (partial) of two old Acts of the reign of Charles II, the Corporation and Test Acts. These had required all holders of office, national or municipal, in England, to receive the Communion according to the form of the Church of England. Regarded by most in England as a bulwark of the Established Church, these Acts with this obligation had come to be viewed in the same light in Scotland by not a few leaders of its Church. In its address to the throne, the General Assembly of 1828 made no reference to this repeal. Dr. Chalmers felt that this was a grave omission. So he moved that in a Special Address to His Majesty the Assembly should express its

[1] Chalmers, *Bridgewater Treatise*, p. ix.

gratification that this disability had now been removed, and that Dissenters, aspiring to serve city or nation in office, were no longer called upon to take Holy Communion according to the rites of the Church of England. His memorable and moving speech contained these passages which fully explain his attitude :

" In walking through a street, the eye is sometimes arrested by the sight of large wooden props leaning obliquely on the walls of one of the houses, and obviously placed there for the purpose of upholding it. Is it possible, Sir, to resist the impression of that being the craziest edifice along the whole pavement ? The fabric of the English Church, with her Test and Corporation Acts, incurred the whole discredit of such an appearance ; and she has inconceivably strengthened herself, both in reality and in public estimation, by the taking of them down." [1]

He rejoiced in the reform, he continued, not because it was a blow at the Establishment, but because he believed it would strengthen its usefulness.

" It does not follow because there should be a full equality between Churchmen and sectarians in every civil and political right, that therefore a Church and an Establishment are uncalled for. Believing, as we do, that without the maintenance of a national clergy, all the zeal and effort and activity of Dissenters could not save our land from lapsing into a tenfold grosser heathenism than it otherwise would do . . . we are all the more imperiously called upon to distinguish between the things which differ." [2]

[1] Hanna, vol. iii, p. 217   [2] *Ibid.*, p. 218

Dr. Chalmers lost his motion, but he gained an expression of the Assembly's general approval of the repeal.

No speech of Dr. Chalmers is more frequently alluded to in contemporary writings than one delivered at a great public meeting in Edinburgh in favour of Roman Catholic Emancipation.[1] Since he was known as a supporter of that reform, he was urged from London to stir up public feeling in its favour by some published pronouncement. This he consistently refused to do. He had already published all he meant to ; and his mind on the matter was fully known. But when a public meeting of the citizens was organized to petition the Government in favour of the Bill, he accepted an invitation to be present and to speak. The speech is a *tour de force*. Its effect was electric. Even the most stolid and unimpressionable were stirred to the depths. Lord Jeffrey has put on record that " never had eloquence produced a greater effect upon a popular assembly, and that he could not believe more had ever been done by the oratory of Demosthenes, Cicero, Burke, or Sheridan." [2]

No speech of his is more closely knit. To select specimens would be to tear them violently from their context, but, with one word of explanation, the passage may be quoted which evoked the most deafening and prolonged applause. The general line of the speech was that religious truth is never helped by coercion ; that Roman Catholics at present are rendered resistant to the claims of Bible truth through their sense of genuine grievance created by the use of coercion ; that it would be all to the good if Protestants and Roman Catholics could meet

[1] For the most interesting generally accessible account of this meeting, see James Dodds, *Thomas Chalmers*, pp. 199ff
[2] Ramsay, *Biographical Notice*, p. 34

on equal terms, as citizens of equal status. " Give the Catholics of Ireland their emancipation ; give them a seat in the Parliament of their country ; give them a free and equal participation in the politics of the realm ; give them a place at the right ear of majesty and a voice in his counsels ; and give me the circulation of the Bible, and with this mighty engine I will overthrow the tyranny of Antichrist, and establish the fair and original form of Christianity on its ruins." [1] This speech ought to be recalled as often as it is asserted that the Protestant Church bitterly opposed Catholic Emancipation. There are statements by some English bishops which can always be brought forward to lend plausibility to this assertion. But it is a hasty generalization which ignores the action of many churchmen like Chalmers who openly worked for it and brilliantly commended it, not for reasons, however, of which Rome would have approved.

The most fiercely contested constitutional change of those eventful years was of course the Reform Act of 1832. It might have been expected that Chalmers, who welcomed these lesser reforms, would rejoice even more whole-heartedly in this belated measure of justice, not only for its abolition of indefensible inequalities in representation—extinct burghs with two members, and great cities with one—but also for its real if somewhat niggardly extension of the franchise. But no, he disliked that extension ; and for two quite different and disconnected reasons.

For one thing, he genuinely believed that there was more political wisdom to be found in the hereditary aristocracy and the old landed interest than in any other class in the community. Before the end of his life, largely as a direct consequence of the barriers put by so many

[1] Hanna, vol. iii, p. 239

of them on the acquiring of sites for Free churches, he had changed his mind, but through most of his life " un-alleviated plebeianism " was a condition to be regarded with horror. It was " wholesome and befitting " that political preponderance should be given to the aristocracy.

The other reason arose out of the general expectations of the time. Extension of the franchise had been trumpeted as a panacea. Let the citizen have a vote, and all his ills will vanish. It was this sort of talk that both depressed and infuriated Chalmers. The roots of man's troubles lay deeper : no political prescription could afford a cure for human misery. When riots in England occurred shortly after the new Act had come into operation, " There," said he, " tak ye that, my friend, as a swatch of your political millenium." [1] That it buoyed men up with false expectations of a golden future was the main reason for the chilly reception the Reform Act received from him.

He was not quite so despondent, however, about its evil results as Sir Hugh Playfair at St. Andrews, of whom it is recorded that round his large garden at St. Leonard's he had a sort of balustrade, on the top flat rail of which he had inscribed the principal events in the world's history since the creation, ending abruptly in 1832 when the Reform Act was passed, and according to this old Conservative " the sun of England set for ever." [2]

It may here be said that Chalmers was not definitely attached to any of the political parties of his day. If he once called himself a Radical it was only to claim that his plan of Christian education was the only radical

---

[1] N. Masterman, *Chalmers on Charity*, p. 374
[2] E. M. Sellar, *Recollections and Impressions*, p. 61

remedy. His closest affiliations certainly were with the Tory party. He had greater faith in its leaders and more confidence in their integrity. He had larger expectations from its policies. The attractive but delusive gilt wrappings of Whig promises were contemptible devices to delude the public.[1] But when the contents unexpectedly proved palatable he did not hesitate to acknowledge the fact. He obeyed no party whip, though he liked best the crack of the Tory one.

There were many occasions in this quiet lull before the storm when Chalmers had occasion to utter fundamental convictions on Church and State. The subject came up in his academic lectures, and there he thus delivered himself : " In Scotland the Church permits no interference whatever by the civil power in things ecclesiastical. Her doctrine, her discipline, her modes of worship are her own." [2] The second French Revolution (1830) drew from him this weighty and characteristic dictum, " I am not one of those who underrate the value of civil and political liberty ; but I am well assured that it is only the principles of Christianity which can impart true security, prosperity, and happiness, either to individuals or to nations. I am prepared to expect that, on the efforts we are now making in the world to regenerate our species, without religion, *God will impress the stamp of a solemn and expressive mockery.*" [3] From this, according to our informant, Mr. Gurney, Dr. Chalmers proceeded to expatiate on the value of religious establishments.

In that same year Dr. Chalmers had consented to open an Independent chapel at Bristol. He found on

---

[1] No political saying of his is better known than the oft-repeated, " I hae a moral loathing o' thae Whugs."
[2] *The Pulpit*, vol. xxiv   [3] J. J. Gurney, *Chalmeriana*, p. 84

his arrival that there was a distinct bitterness in th
attitude of the Independents to the Church of Englan
and to Established Churches in general. He considere
himself bound, in the circumstances, to proclaim his ow
convictions. " I hold the Establishment to be not onl
a great Christian good, but one indispensable to th
upholding of a diffused Christianity throughout the land
. . . In connection with an Establishment we wish eve
to see an able, vigorous, and flourishing dissenterism. . .
Such wholesome dissent is a purifier, and because
purifier, a strengthener of the Church." [1]

In the beginning of 1832 the cholera epidemic wa
threatening Edinburgh. The Presbytery appointed
special fast day for the city to be devoted to prayer
Hardly had it done so when Parliament, which ha
seemed contemptuous of any such action, agreed t
appoint a day for a national fast. Some members o
the Presbytery held that, in view of the Government'
declared intention, it would be disorderly for Edinburg
to proceed with its own. They succeeded in having
a special meeting of Presbytery summoned to deal with
the dilemma. For Chalmers there was no dilemma a
all. The Presbytery must proceed with its own day, fo
which so many arrangements had already been made.
" On this question," he said, " I do feel for the character
and independence of our Church. The inconvenience
of a double fast is a bagatelle when compared with the
permanent stain that we shall inflict by this method of
avoiding it. Did ever the ecclesiastical give way to the
civil in such a manner before ? . . . The men who do
profoundest homage to the Presbyterial fast will do profoundest homage to the national fast also. We shall do
the one, and most assuredly not leave the other undone." [2]

[1] Hanna, vol. iii, pp. 266–67   [2] *Ibid.*, vol. iii, p. 317

The men who desired so to defer to the Government as to postpone the Edinburgh appointment till the undeclared day of the national one were defeated by a two to one majority.

These representative utterances reveal Chalmers, before the breaking of the storm, as a firm believer in an Established Church, an equally firm believer in its independence in spiritual things, and with a generous appreciation of the function of dissenters within the commonwealth.

It will be noted that in this chapter only one mention has been made of Chalmers in the General Assembly, and that one really belongs to the days when he was still officially a professor in St. Andrews. His relation to the Supreme Court changed when he came to Edinburgh. He was now once more a ministerial member of a Presbytery. Anstruther could no longer nominate him as an elder, and Edinburgh Presbytery had no special privileges in the way of nominations. In view of this Assembly inactivity, it is somewhat surprising to find him at the age of fifty-two nominated as Moderator to preside over the General Assembly of 1832. Thus it was as an ex-Moderator that he began really to guide the Assembly and direct the Church's policy.

CHAPTER EIGHT

IN DEFENCE OF THE ESTABLISHMENT

1829–38

ROMAN CATHOLIC Emancipation, for which Chalmers ha‹
so dramatically contended, had one unexpected reper
cussion which was destined to affect gravely the cours‹
of his later ecclesiastical policy and to complicate hi›
task. This was the outbreak of the Voluntary con
troversy. Up till 1829 there had been strong link›
between the Evangelicals within the Church of Scotlan‹
and the Seceders outside. Throughout the eighteentl
century, despite occasional outbursts of hostility, thei›
main rivalry was as to which was to be considered th‹
true custodian of the best traditions of the Church o›
Scotland. The New Light movement, and the subse
quent formation of the United Secession (1820), di‹
nothing to foster any increase of tension. The New Ligh›
emphasis on the spirituality of the Church's weapons, an‹
the repudiation of anything that could be construed a›
approval of persecution in the Westminster Confession
could be no added barrier to men like Chalmers, whos‹
oration on Roman Catholic Emancipation was, in essence
a plea for the removal of all civil compulsions, as both un
christian and inexpedient. There were, it is true, withir
the Secession voices raised here and there suggesting tha›
the mere fact of Establishment implied a departure fron
the high principle of the spirituality of the Church's worl
and warfare, but the range to which their words carrie‹

was very limited and circumscribed. The pamphlets of men like Ballantyne of Stonehaven [1] caused no more than tiny local ripples on the face of the waters.

It was a sermon entitled *Ecclesiastical Establishments Considered*, preached in April 1829 in a Secession church in connection with a Secession society, which precipitated what was to prove one of the most wordy, bitter, and devastating pamphlet wars ever waged in Scotland. The genesis of the sermon was plainly stated by the preacher, the Rev. Andrew Marshall. Would not the Roman Catholics of Ireland, having achieved Emancipation, now begin to clamour for Establishment ? Would it not be hard to reject this plea, in view of their vast preponderance in numbers ? " And what would the consequences be were Popery again connected with the State—were it getting hold of those rich temporalities on which it has so long been casting a covetous eye—were it again erecting its proud hierarchy and again lifting its mitred head in courts and parliaments." [2] The only effective barrier against this calamity is for the nation to repudiate all establishments of religion. Then follows a downright and unadorned attack on establishments—their lack of foundation in Scripture, their impropriety, injustice, and impolicy, their tendency to secularization and their inefficiency. From this the sermon proceeded to commend the just and scriptural principle of Voluntaryism, in obedience to the positive ordinance of our Lord, " that ordinance in which he has appointed the members of the Church to provide, by their free-will offerings, for the support of its institutions." [3] Finally, it claims that this method is adequate, and this further passage should be

[1] J. Ballantyne, *Comparison of Established and Dissenting Churches*, 1824
[2] A. Marshall, *Ecclesiastical Establishments Considered*, p. v
[3] *Ibid.*, p. 35

quoted, for though he is not named, it is directly aimed at a favourite plea of Dr. Chalmers :

" It is said that unless we send the gospel to men, they will never seek it, it is none of the things they naturally desire, none of the things which they are apt to deem essential to their comfort, or which, of their own accord, they will endeavour to provide. Means must therefore be employed to send it to those who have it not, means must be employed to continue it among them ; and what means are so suitable, or promise to be so efficient, as a national Establishment ? To this argument we reply by admitting the premises but denying the conclusion. We admit that the gospel must be sent to men, we admit that the expense of sending it, and in all probability of preserving it among them for a time, must be defrayed ; but we deny that the interposition of the civil power is either necessary for the purpose, or to be desired. We are able to point out " a more excellent way." Let the gospel emanate from those who have been put in trust with the gospel : let it emanate from the Church to which the Lord Jesus has given the commission ; and if the ministers of the Church require assistance in the work, pecuniary assistance, or assistance of any other kind, let them look for that assistance, let them confidently expect it, from their Christian brethren." [1]

The sermon when preached had evoked enthusiasm from the majority of its hearers, while it created misgivings in others. Its publication, three weeks later, intensified both the enthusiasm and the misgivings, and awakened a keen opposition in some of the wider circles into which it now penetrated. It was the *Edinburgh*

[1] *Ecclesiastical Establishments Considered*, pp. 41–42

Christian Instructor, edited by Dr. Andrew Thomson, which in an elaborate review made the first reasoned answer.[1] Pamphlet followed pamphlet in the next three years. Two definite parties began to emerge. The adherents of Mr. Marshall's position organized themselves as the Voluntary Church Association, " for asserting and maintaining the rights of Voluntary churches." This gave rise, within a few months, to the Association for Promoting the Interests of the Church of Scotland. Speedily each side had its own magazine : the *Voluntary Church Magazine* and the *Church of Scotland Magazine*, the one as vitriolic as the other. Whatever could damage the cause of the other was industriously raked up out of the local squabbles of the present and the dubious incidents of the past, until extremists on both sides, fed on one or other of these magazines alone, must have begun to doubt if there was any Christianity at all left in their opponents. Old friendships were shattered. Missionary societies were rent in twain, and even when agreed terms of separation were drawn up, recriminations followed. The struggle led to new affiliations. Within the Church of Scotland Moderates and Evangelicals joined forces to repel the attack ; the classic defence of the Church of Scotland came from a Moderate, Dr. Inglis, in his *Ecclesiastical Establishments Vindicated*. The Seceders were thrown into alliance with the Independents and with the Dissenters of England, the result of which association was to instil into the minds of the Seceders a confusion between the positions and claims of the two Established Churches, parallel to that into which the law lords were later to fall. To a certain extent, also, the two Establishments were themselves brought closer.

[1] *Edinburgh Christian Instructor*, August 1829, pp. 569-95.

Now Dr. Chalmers himself was never drawn into the vortex of this controversy, though he was the object of attack on the one side, and called into the defence on the other. Yet it is against this background of the Voluntary controversy that we have to examine his opinions on the virtues and merits of the Scottish Establishment, and his general doctrine of Church and State, as it found expression before the final conflict of the years 1839–43. The chief materials for our investigation are three in number : his treatise, *On the Use and Abuse of Literary and Ecclesiastical Endowments*, first printed in 1827, two years before the controversy began ; his sermon, *On Ecclesiastical Establishments*, preached in 1829 just after the sermon which kindled the controversy ; his *Lectures on the Establishment and Extension of National Churches*, published in 1838, when the contention had reached its fiercest point.

The motive of the treatise was to make a case against the threat to the university endowments of Scotland. Some of these had come under the stigma of mismanagement, and there were not wanting those who desired to apply the economic principles of Adam Smith to the business of education. Let the demand create the supply, they said ; education, like commerce, will be all the healthier if free from the pernicious system of bounties and endowments. The demand for higher education and for professional qualifications should, in itself, be enough to stimulate the supply of opportunities and to pay a reasonable salary to those who provided them. The spread of this attitude, Chalmers saw, would herald the end of both educational and Church endowments, and he gave his mind to the problem of laying bare its underlying presuppositions. For while it was a calamity when such endowments became excessive, leading through corrupt patronage to the appointment of mere office-seekers, who would inevitably become " lazy priests " and " lazy and luxurious professors," [1] it would prove even more disastrous for a country to withdraw such endowments altogether. Education could never be equated to " an article of ordinary merchandise " [2] ; here was one fundamental difference.

" It is not with the desire of knowledge, as it is with the desire of food. Generally speaking, the more ignorant a man is the more satisfied he is to remain so. But the more hungry a man is, the less satisfied he is to remain so. In the one case, the starvation of the mind is followed up by the apathy of an utter disregard for the food of the mind. In the other case, the starvation of the body is followed up by the agony of an intolerable desire after the food of the body, and to appease which any exertion or sacrifice will be made. There is no such appetite for knowledge as will secure a spontaneous and originating movement towards it on the part of those who need to be instructed. There is such an appetite for food as will secure a spontaneous and originating movement towards it on the part of those who need to be subsisted. In the matter of education, the supply of the article cannot be confided to the operation of demand and supply ; for there is not a sufficiently effective demand." [3]

Any worthy commonwealth will, therefore, take pains and use resources to put the means of education within the reach of all its people. That education need not be free, but it can never hope to be completely self-supporting.

[1] *On the Use and Abuse of Literary and Ecclesiastical Endowments*, p. 22
[2] *Ibid.*, pp. ix, 25, etc.   [3] *Ibid.*, pp. 25–26

It is through the national support of education—in
adequate though it may be—that the national characte
has been built up.

From this he passes to religion. Left to the fre
operation of the law of supply and demand, religio
would be in an even worse case than education. Th
more sunken a community is, the more degraded it
populace, the less is its desire for religion. To supply th
ordinances of religion only where there is an effectiv
and express demand is to leave the neediest areas un
touched. A Christian state which sees in the Christia
faith a necessary element in any general uplift is boun
to provide for every citizen opportunities for Christia
as well as for general education. How is this to be done
A generation brought up in an era of compulsory educa
tion, might incline to give as the logical answer, " Provid
a church and a minister in every locality and compel th
whole population, under penalties, to attend that churc
at its stated services." The possibility of such an answe
never entered Chalmers' mind. Education was voluntar
in his day. The mere provision of the school and th
presence of the schoolmaster stimulated the demand fo
education until, at least in parts of Scotland, it was almos
universal, and people were ashamed to be totally illiterate
A similar local provision for religion would always have a
similar result, as the history of Scotland had proved up
to the time of the great shift of population. This, however
had created a vast practical problem which neither th
enormously swollen original parishes, nor the quit
remarkable enterprise of dissenters, nor both together
could cope with. A territorial ministry, with a manage
able population, say, two thousand people, allocated to
each—that is to say, the readjustment of the existing
machinery—was the only solution. This is " the good o

an establishment." [1]   It secures " over the whole length
and breadth of the land such a juxtaposition between the
gospel and every human creature as never will be accomplished in any other way." [2]   The many, who need them
most, least recognize their need of the ordinances of
religion.   They must be provided in their midst, yes,
even " obtruded upon them." [3]   A church close at hand
and a minister going out and in among them must
be provided.   " His week-day attentions and their
Sabbath attendance go hand-in-hand.   A house-going
minister wins for himself a church-going people." [4]
While it is admitted that many men have abused, and
do abuse, their position as parish ministers, nevertheless the machinery is sound if universally installed
and adequately manned.

It will be obvious from this that two things have
determined Chalmers' approach to the subject.   One
is, the necessity of finding an answer to the challenge of
those who would refuse or withdraw endowments from
both education and religion, which has drawn forth his
characteristic economic argument.   The other is, his
experience during eight years among the working folk
of Glasgow, both in the Tron and in St. John's, which,
though it is not explicitly adduced, has supplied the
grounds of his generalizations.   His main concern is that
the gospel so essential to temporal and eternal well-being,
but for which the natural man has no innate desire, shall
be allowed to effect its blessed work in every corner of the
land.   His most striking general analogy is that of the
irrigation system of Egypt :

" Should the Nile cease from its overflows there

[1] *On the Use and Abuse of Literary and Ecclesiastical Endowments*, p. 113
      [2] *Ibid.*, p. 114   [3] *Ibid.*, p. 113   [4] *Ibid.*, p. 121

would no fertilizing influence be conveyed over the land through the dry and deserted channels by which it was intersected. And should the Spirit of God withdraw the showers of his grace from our nation, we have no such blind confidence in the existence of frameworks as to look for a sanctifying influence from the mechanism of pulpits and parishes. Nevertheless, it is good to uphold the sluices and reservoirs and aqueducts of Egypt ; for when the Nile shall again rise above its banks, that is the apparatus by which its water shall be most beneficially dispersed over the fields of the territory. And, nevertheless, it good to uphold the churches, the parsonages, and the livings of our establishment ; for when the celestial influence shall again come down upon us, that is the terrestrial apparatus for the most beneficial dispersion of it among the families of our population." [1]

The second main public declaration of Dr. Chalmers was made in a sermon preached in St. George's Church Edinburgh, before the Society for the Daughters of the Clergy, in May 1829. No reference is made in it to Mr. Marshall's sermon preached in Glasgow in the preceding month, but some report of it must have reached Dr. Chalmers, even if the printed discourse was not already in his hands. For it is directed largely against two of the objections to an Establishment which found expression in that sermon. One was, that nothing is heard in the early heroic days of the Church of a religious Establishment, no hint at all until Constantine, and that with it came the beginning of the Church's corruption and decay. The other was, that Establishment inevitably implies State control, which in turn entails a secularising of the Church and a smothering of its witness. These

[1] *On the Use and Abuse of Literary and Ecclesiastical Endowments*, pp. 117–18

re answered together in a closely knit argument which
roceeded from a common enough current analogy. A
roup or society of Christian men impressed with the
mportance of Foreign Missionary work, and equally
npressed with the results achieved by the Moravians,
and themselves together to equip and support an
xpedition of the *Unitas Fratrum*. In this enterprise the
missionaries, while deriving their subsistence from outside,
re left in full control of the gospel to be preached, and
he methods to be employed in commending it, in full
ontrol of faith, order, discipline, and policy. Step by
tep the argument advances from this, through Con-
tantine's problem, to the situation in Scotland at the
moment. " The State may pay the Church ; yet with-
ut conceding to it one particle of temporal sovereignty.
'he Church may serve the State ; yet without the sur-
ender of one spiritual prerogative." [1] " For the sake of an
bundant gospel dispensation we are upheld in things tem-
oral by the State. For the sake of a pure gospel dispen-
ation we are left in things spiritual to ourselves." [2]
t culminates in a most passionate assertion of this spiritual
utonomy, which, however, is best left over till a sur-
ey has been made of the very important third exposition.

By 1837, the year of the accession of Queen Victoria,
he Voluntary controversy in Scotland had reached its
maximum of intensity, but in England the heats and
passions of a similar debate were even fiercer. Parliament
ad already dealt with the Church of Ireland, " over
eniently," said the Dissenters ; " to the point of mutila-
ion," asserted English Churchmen. The Church of
England itself was most gravely threatened. It was said
hat a majority of the House of Commons were bound
by election pledges to its overthrow, and that the Prime

---

[1] *Collected Works*, vol. xi, p. 450   [2] *Ibid.*, p. 451

Minister himself was not unwilling to introduce a measure
of Disestablishment and Disendowment. It was this
situation that gave birth to the Oxford Movement; it
gave rise also to a less permanent but more immediately
useful body, the Christian Influence Society, whose
programme united purification and defence of the exist
ing Establishment. This society besought Dr. Chalmers
to come south and deliver, under its auspices, a course
of lectures to the *élite* of London. Having kept, as we
have seen, as clear as he could of the controversy raging
in Scotland, it seemed to him that here was an oppor
tunity to deliver himself at length of his mature thought
on the subject, away from the din of the local conflict
He agreed, therefore, to give six lectures in the spring
of 1838. In view of his great fame as an orator, the
Society made what it thought to be abundant provision
for a distinguished audience, which would be sure, it
was confident, to include a few peers of the realm and
not a few members of the House of Commons. But the
overcrowding with which Chalmers associated London
continued to beset him ; and it was to uncomfort
ably packed audiences of England's most distinguished
citizens, totally unaccustomed to such close proximity
with their fellows, that the lectures were delivered. A
vivid picture comes from the pen of Dr. Begg, who
accompanied him on the trip.

" Nothing could exceed the enthusiasm which pre
vailed in London. The great city seemed stirred to its
very depths. The Doctor sat while delivering his lectures
behind a small table ; the hall in front being crowded
with one of the most brilliant audiences that ever
assembled in Britain. It was supposed that at least five
hundred of those present were peers and members of the

House of Commons. Sir James Graham was a very constant attender. The sitting attitude of Dr. Chalmers seemed at first irreconcilable with much energy or effect. But such an anticipation was at once dispelled by the enthusiasm of the speaker, responded to by the still more intense enthusiasm of the audience ; and occasionally the effect was even greatly increased by the eloquent man springing unconsciously to his feet, and delivering with overwhelming power the most magnificent passages —a movement which, on one occasion at least, was imitated by the audience when the words, ' The King cannot—the King dare not ' were uttered in accents of prophetic vehemence that must still ring in the ears of all who heard them, and were responded to by a whirlwind of enthusiasm which was probably never exceeded in the history of eloquence." [1]

[1] Hanna, vol. iv, p. 39

Mr. Begg's description sent me in search of these words. I had already read the lectures in the *Collected Works* (vol. xvii) and had not seen them there. But I had noted the words in the sermon of 1829. So I began to wonder if Dr. Begg had not been guilty of some confusion. I went over the lectures carefully again, and I found a hiatus in the argument where they might have fitted in. This sent me to the original edition ; and there I found the passage not in the text but in a footnote, with this appended to the note—Sermon XV, vol. xi, of Dr. Chalmers' works. Now there are only thirteen sermons in that volume, and the reference ought to be to Sermon XIII. So the history of the passage as in the text is this. It was written in 1829 for the sermon we have just been looking at ; it was incorporated in an improved form in the actual lectures, but printed only in the notes. When the lectures were published in the collected works, Dr. Chalmers, averse to anything of his appearing twice (with only slight variations), suppressed the note in the original edition, leaving an obvious hiatus, however, in his argument. This type of omission is not infrequent in his *Collected Works*. For he began early the practice of incorporating favourite passages in new contexts, *e.g.* there is this entry in his journal for October 14, 1821 : " Have begun a sermon on Psalm xli. 1, for the Destitute Sick Society, Edinburgh, and I am collecting passages out of former discourses for it." Hanna, vol. i, p. 303

The full context was this :

" In respect of this ecclesiastical independence, I am not aware of any serious practical obstacle to the exercise of it in England ; and, at all events, we know of nothing more perfect in this respect than the constitution of the Church of Scotland. There is, to each of its members, an independent voice from within ; and from without, there is no power or authority whatever in matters ecclesiastical. They who feel dislike to an establishment do so, because of their recoil from all contact and communication with the State. We have no other communication with the State than that of being maintained by it, after which we are left to regulate the proceedings of our great home mission with all the purity, and the piety, and the independence of any missionary board. We are exposed to nothing from without which can violate the sanctity of the apostolical character, if ourselves do not violate it. And neither are we exposed to aught which can trench on the authority of the apostolical office, if ourselves make no surrender of it. In things ecclesiastical we decide all. Some of these things may be done wrong, but still they are our majorities which do it. They are not, they cannot, be forced upon us from without. We own no head of the Church but the Lord Jesus Christ. Whatever is done ecclesiastically is done by our ministers acting in His name, and in perfect submission to His authority. Implicated as the Church and the State are imagined to be, they are not so implicated as that, without the concurrence of the ecclesiastical courts, a full and final effect can be given to any proceeding by which the good of Christianity and the religion of our people may be affected. There is not a clerical appointment which can take place in any one of our parishes till we have sustained it. Even the law of patronage, right or wrong, in force, not by the power of the State, but by the permission of the Church, and with all its fancied omnipotence has no other basis than that of our majorities to rest upon. It should never be forgotten that, in things ecclesiastical, the highest power of our Church is amenable to no higher power on earth for its decisions. It can exclude, it can deprive, it can depose at pleasure. External force might make an obnoxious individual the holder of a benefice ; but there is no external force in these realms that could make him a minister of the Church of Scotland. There is not one thing which the State can do to our independent and indestructible Church but strip her of her temporalities. *Nec tamen consumebatur*, she would remain a Church notwithstanding —as strong as ever in the props of her own moral and inherent greatness ; and, though shrivelled in all her dimensions by the moral injury inflicted on many thousands of families, she would be at least as strong as ever in the reverence of her country's population. She was as much a Church in her days of sufferings as in her days of outward security and triumph ; when a wandering outcast, with nought but the mountain breezes to play around her, and nought but the caves of the earth to shelter her, as now, when admitted to the bowers of an establishment. The magistrate might withdraw his protection—and she cease to be an establishment any longer—but in all the high matters of sacred and spiritual jurisdiction she would be the same as before. With or without an establishment, she, in these, is the unfettered mistress of her doings. The King by himself, or by his representative, might be the spectator of our proceedings ; but what Lord Chatham said of the poor man's house is true in all its parts of the Church to which I have the honour to belong—' In England every man's house is his

castle—not that it is surrounded with walls and battle
ments. It may be a straw-built shed. Every wind
of heaven may whistle round it ; every element o
heaven may enter, but the King cannot—the King dar
not.' " [1]

But we must turn from these celebrations and speci
mens of his eloquence to the general argument of th
lectures. It is simply an ˙expansion and elaboration o
the sermon of 1829. It starts from an improved form o
the same basic example, improved, because it is n
longer a society or group that sends the Moravia
missionary ; it is a magnate who calls him in to do wor
among his dependents. " When a West India plante
sends for a Moravian missionary, and maintains him i
the work of instructing the labourers on his estate, w
have here the little model of an Establishment. Th
planter maintains the missionary ; and the missionary
in return, teaches on the estate of the planter, yet teache
nothing there but his own Christianity." [2]   It is th
State's duty to provide a perfect framework within whic
the Church may freely operate. An organized provisio
for an adequate local ministry is all that is contended fo
It is such a definitely localized Christian ministry tha
alone can secure and preserve the Christianity of th
land in every corner. For the minister's task is not t
fill his church anyhow, but to fill it out of his distric
The Voluntary churches, despite their manifest service
as auxiliaries, can never meet the total situation. Pur
Voluntaryism (Voluntaryism *ab intra*) can never win
foothold in an area completely lapsed : Voluntaryism a
it is (*i.e.* assisted by Voluntaryism *ab extra*) has, with al

[1] *Lectures on the Establishment and Extension of National Churches*, pp. 38–9
(note)   [2] *Ibid.*, p. 13

its missionary spirit, proved itself unequal to the task. Concurrent endowment is not possible with the territorial allocations which are necessary ; one village will be Presbyterian, its neighbour to the east Baptist, and to the west Independent, the town to the north Episcopalian, the hamlet to the south Methodist. The problem can only be met by the adequate endowment of one Church. Neither in Scotland nor in England are there reasonable grounds for supplanting the one in possession ; and no wise government will infringe the independence of either Church in the pursuit of its supreme task of winning the land for Christ.

In these lectures, therefore, Chalmers merely vindicates the simpler statements of his earlier writings with an amazing command of language and fertility of illustration. He operates throughout all his teaching with a very few fundamental ideas and convictions. The one new element is the direct dealing with the Voluntaries ; and they had the right to complain that what Chalmers called pure Voluntaryism (*ab intra*) was precisely what he had condemned earlier as the doctrine of the economists, and that what he called Voluntaryism (*ab extra*) was the specific teaching of those who claimed the name, as the first quotation in this chapter serves to show. But certainly the two were confused in the current thoughts and activities of their English compeers.

The lectures when published in the daily Press and in book form met with tremendous acclaim and exercised a widespread influence in England. Indeed, it would be possible to defend the thesis that Dr. Chalmers saved the Church of England.

It was currently reported that a great many copies of the various London editions were bought up by clergymen of the Church of England to send to their members of Parliament. It should be noted, however, lest the applause of London should be interpreted as a general acceptance of his views, that one of his hearers, the young rising politician, W. E. Gladstone, had grave misgivings. He had already met Dr. Chalmers in Edinburgh, and had conceived a profound respect for him. As one of his audience in London, his admiration for the man deepened. "He has a mind keenly susceptible of what is beautiful and great and good." But, wrestling as he was with his own first book on *Church and State*, and seeing the only deliverance from sheer Erastianism in the tenets of the Tractarian movement, Gladstone was so deeply pained by the lecturer's assault on these positions —in particular, his " flogging " of the Apostolical Succession—that he wrote in a letter to Manning, " Such a jumble of church, non-church, and anti-church principles as that excellent and eloquent man Dr. Chalmers has given us in his recent lectures, no human being has ever heard." [1]

In Scotland, the reception was even more mixed. To many who were in the thick of the Voluntary controversy, they seemed irrelevant to the stage the discussion had reached, and even friends complained that there was no new light in them ; they had heard the same doctrine in almost the same words from the same man on Church Extension platforms.

It is interesting to contrast the reception they met with in the two rival magazines. The *Church of Scotland Magazine* in its July number contained a very long and solid review, consisting largely of quotations, and while speaking of the vast genius, keen discernment, extensive range, lofty conception, graphic power, resistless energy,

[1] Morley, *Life of Gladstone*, vol. i, p. 171

untiring perseverance, and so on, of the author, ventures to correct him on two points of Church history. But it had to preface this with a reference to the angry buzz created in the Voluntary hive, and to perpetrate this gem of vituperation. " Even the beggar of Derrynane [1] did homage to the great genius who delivered them, by pouring upon him his ribaldry, not so much for the gratification of his own malignity, or brutality, but as his offering of garbage to the coarse and vitiated maw of the Radical, Infidel, Popish, and Voluntary multitude, on whose degraded shoulders he marches to power, and plants the hoof of the beast on the back of Great Britain, sorely humbled by such base contact."

It was not until October that the *Voluntary Church Magazine* made its pronouncement. It confined its attention to the first lecture. Its general line was that Chalmers was well guided in confining himself to the " idea " of an Establishment ; how little it corresponded to actualities no one knew better than himself, whereupon it proceeded to deal trenchantly, in the approved controversial manner, with these actualities. But its prelude matched that of its rival.

" Our readers, perhaps, may think that some attention is due to these lectures, from the name of their author. Of the living defenders of church establishments, Dr. Chalmers is unquestionably the most celebrated, though he is also by far the most absurd and wrong-headed. . . . When we open a book of controversy, we expect to be entertained not with poetry, but with reason ; not with the glitter of words, or the building of mighty periods, but with some grains of intellect. If a man undertakes to discuss an argu-

[1] Daniel O'Connell

mentative subject before an enlightened public, he should be prepared to handle other tools than those of the rhetorician. He should have a mind disciplined by the rules of an accurate logic . . . above all, he should have a reasonable portion of that moral integrity, that superiority to partisanship, that freedom from gross and vulgar prejudice, which will enable him to meet difficulties fairly. . . . How far Dr. Chalmers possesses these qualifications we need not say. The public know, and have long known, that few men possess them in a lower degree."

Though to a certain extent outside the ranks of those engaged in the Scottish battle, Chalmers could not escape being the target of expert snipers. His interest, however, in the questions in dispute was neither biblical, nor historical, nor inquisitorial (*i.e.* prying into the failings of the other side) ; he was solely concerned to preserve, expand, and improve the existing machinery in order that a self-determining Church, such as he believed the Church of Scotland to be, might operate that machinery to its full capacity for the Christian good of Scotland, a goal which no other instrument could reach. It is quite clear, even at this date, that in no way was he prepared to accept outside endowments at the cost of outside control. It was as a free Church that the Church of Scotland held his allegiance, and drew forth the wealth of his personal service.

CHAPTER NINE

PATRONAGE AND THE CALL

1832-33

THE Assembly of 1832, over which Professor Chalmers presided as Moderator, was noteworthy in that it witnessed the beginnings of concerted action to get rid of the evils which had grown up in connection with the exercise of patronage,[1] action which was to lead to a clash between the ecclesiastical and civil courts, culminating in the Disruption of 1843. The particular evil complained of was that during the long Moderate ascendency the General Assembly had practically ignored one particular element in the settlement of a minister, viz. the concurrence or assent of the congregation which he was to shepherd, and had reduced their call to a meaningless formality. It will be well, therefore, to review the various steps taken at that date in the settlement of any minister.

The first step, after the vacancy had been officially intimated to him, was taken by the patron who normally presented one of the licentiates of the Church. The presentee then lodged his deed of presentation with the local Presbytery. The document followed a set form; it desired the Presbytery to " take trials of the qualifications of the presentee, his literature, good life, and conversation,

[1] Patronage, that *fons malorum* of the Scottish Church, abolished at the Revolution Settlement, had been re-imposed in 1712 " as a means of political control in the interests of the Jacobites." H. W. Meikle, *Scotland and the French Revolution*, p. 35

and of his fitness and qualifications for the functions of the ministry at the church to which he is presented." [1] The Presbytery thereupon appointed him to preach on one, two, or three Sundays in this church " that the people may have trial of his gifts unto edification." [2] Then, on the day, or the final day, of his preaching, a meeting was summoned by the Presbytery that a call might be moderated in. At this meeting, after public worship, the form of a call was produced which, even in the days when it was least regarded ran in some such terms as these : " We whose names are subscribed, heritors, elders, and others of the parish of X being destitute of a fixed pastor through . . . and being well assured of the ministerial abilities, piety, and prudence of you, the said A.B., have agreed, with the concurrence of the reverend Presbytery of C to invite and Call, like as we, by these presents, do invite and Call, you to undertake the office of pastor among us, and we promise, on your accepting this our Call, to give you all suitable respect and obedience in the Lord." [3]

In current practice, the scarcity of signatures was no bar to its being accepted as a call to be moderated in. The Presbytery then proceeded to take the presentee on trials for ordination, which, with all the local variations, were of much the same general nature as the earlier trials for licence. These being sustained, a day was fixed for his ordination. On this day one of the questions appointed to be put by the presiding minister was, " Do you accept of, and close with, the Call to be

---

[1] *Reports of the Debate, etc., on May 23, 1833,* p. 3   [2] *Ibid.,* p. 3

[3] *Ibid.,* p. 3. The form given in the *Styles of Writs* issued by the Church Law Society in 1838 (p. 81) lays even greater stress on the Call of the people. The disputed call to Auchterarder actually contained the phrase, " having heard you preach to our satisfaction and edification." Robertson's *Report of the Auchterarder Case,* vol. ii, Appendix vi.

astor of this parish ? " [1] Only after a satisfactory nswer to the array of questions of which this was one, ould his ordination to the ministry and induction to he parish take place.

It is obvious from the mere outline of the current procedure that the Church had at one time laid great tress on the call ; and the records of the Assembly for a eneration after the re-introduction of patronage in 712 bear witness to this fact. Indeed, in 1736, in order o prevent more ministers and congregations hiving off o the Seceders it was enacted by the General Assembly : ' The General Assembly, considering . . . that it is, and aas been since the Reformation, the principle of this Church—that no minister shall be intruded into any parish contrary to the will of the congregation—do, herefore, seriously recommend to all judicatories of this Church to have a due regard to the said principle in planting vacant congregations ; and that all Presbyteries pe at pains to bring about harmony and unanimity in congregations, and to avoid anything that may excite or encourage unreasonable exceptions in people against a worthy person that may be proposed to be their minister, in the present situation and circumstances of he Church, so as none be intruded into such parishes, as they regard the glory of God, and edification of the pody of Christ." [2]

Bit by bit, however, through decision after decision of the General Assembly, the call came to be denuded of meaning. In 1782 there was a movement to abolish it altogether. Overtures were before the Assembly to discard from the established procedure the formality of

[1] Alex Hill, *The Practice of the Several Judicatories of the Church of Scotland*, p. 62

[2] *Acts of the General Assembly of the Church of Scotland, 1638–1842*, p. 641

moderation in a call. But even in that high noon of Moderatism the Assembly shrank from this step. It declared instead that " the moderation in a call, in the settlement of ministers, is agreeable to the immemorial and constitutional practice of this Church, and ought to be continued." [1] Continued it therefore was, but merely as an opportunity to give some sort of a welcome to a minister they could not escape having placed over them. Indeed, one of the current manuals of Church law said explicitly, " Whether the number of signatures attached to it was such as to make it a good and sufficient call was long a difficult and an agitating question. But there is much less ceremony upon this point at present ; and provided there are signatures attached to a call, a presbytery does not hesitate to concur with it." [2] And one of the venerable fathers of the Church, Dr. Hugh Laird of Portmoak, said in the 1833 debate, " I was witness to the sustaining of a call in this House, which was not signed by a single free individual in the parish. It was signed by the Patron's factor, who did not reside in the parish, by a labouring man from another parish, and by the kirk officer—and yet, upon the call of a single individual belonging to the parish [i.e. the beadle], the presentee was forced upon it." [3] Is it too strong to say, as one minister did in the 1832 debate, that this was reducing the call to a " solemn mockery " ? [4]

It had always been one of the aims of the Evangelical party to restore the call to its former place, and even when they formed an insignificant minority, they fought against every tendency to ignore the rights of the local

[1] *Acts of the General Assembly of the Church of Scotland, 1638–1842*, p. 811
[2] Alexander Hill, *The Practice in the Several Judicatories of the Church of Scotland*, pp. 57–58   [3] *Report of the Debate, etc., May 23, 1833*, p. 51
[4] *Report of the Debate, etc., 1832*, p. 31

congregation. It was not to be wondered at, that as their numbers grew nearer to parity, they should raise this question, and that overtures from eight Presbyteries and three Synods should be laid upon the table of the 1832 General Assembly with this end in view.

Before looking, however, at these overtures and their fate, it will be well to consider whether there were not elements in the political and ecclesiastical situation which contributed to the raising of the question with special urgency. Were there any co-operating forces which conspired to inspire the Evangelical party with fresh zeal at this precise moment ?

The overtures were being prepared when the first Reform Bill was on the way to become an Act. Citizens were now to have, in vastly increased numbers, a vote in the election of their representatives to Parliament. It was only to be expected that members of Christian congregations should be demanding a restoration of their standing in the election of their ministers. One of the great troubles that beset the Evangelical leaders was that many of them were demanding much more than a mere restoration. They were beginning to re-assert as a a just right the whole voice in the choice of their pastors.[1] What right had a patron to interfere at any point in their proceedings ? Why attempt to mend patronage ; why not end it once and for all ? While it was foolish on the part of some heirs of the Moderates to attempt to assess the whole movement as a pandering to popular political theories, it is undeniable that the political situation influenced the ecclesiastical.

Further, there is no doubt that the Voluntary con-

[1] This claim had been most forcibly made within the Church of Scotland a century earlier by Currie of Kinglassie, particularly in his *Jus Populi Divinum*, 1727.

troversy augmented the sense of urgency. On many platforms scornful words were being poured forth about the bondage of the Church of Scotland, about her traditional subservience to patrons, and her constant disregard of her own Christian people. Nothing was calculated to gall an Evangelical more bitterly than when a fellow-Evangelical outside twitted him as one tied to a system in which he had, willy nilly, to accept as his minister the nominee of a patron who might be an expert judge of hunting ponies or Ayrshire cattle, but whose competence and whose motives in selecting the most suitable minister from among the licentiates of the Church might both be exceedingly questionable. On many Church of Scotland platforms the Voluntaries were accused of treating unfairly as of the essence of Establishment abuses in the exercise of patronage which the Church had riveted on herself in the recent past, and which it was in the Church's power to remove as soon as a majority could be persuaded that they were abuses. In the General Assembly debates one country minister spoke out plainly. The Church of Scotland, he said, had many enemies at the moment ready to rejoice in her fall. " They are envious of her prosperity, and jealous of her purification ; and nothing would more gratify their hatred than to find us who are set for the Church's defence tenaciously upholding her corruptions, and with singular infatuation not only striving to perpetuate existing abuses, but to check the progress of all salutary improvements." [1] Beyond question, the effort to make the Church of Scotland less liable to the open sneers of critics outwith her borders was an element in hastening and shaping the course of reformation.

Further, the mere presence of Secession churches, even

[1] *Report of the Debate, etc., May 23, 1833,* p. 53

when they were not unfriendly, within and alongside the old parishes, had a considerable effect. In these churches from the beginning communicant members, or at least the heads of households, chose their own ministers. A large farmer who was perhaps an elder in the parish church with no real voice in the selection of his parish minister, listening eagerly to the talk of a neighbouring crofter about the various candidates for his Secession meeting-house, would come inevitably to the point when he asked why some such privilege was denied to him ; and the growing number of chapels of ease within his own Church of Scotland, which enjoyed similar privileges, increased his restiveness.

These three have long been recognized and accepted as contributing factors helping to explain the keenness of the Evangelical party in their more determined pursuit of what had been a main element in their policy from the beginning, but there is a fourth which has been almost consistently ignored.

There had been a tendency in the eighteenth century to draw a veil over the first beginnings and the early struggles of the Reformed Church in Scotland as belonging to a ruder age which the century of enlightenment had left behind. George Buchanan as an ornament of Scottish scholarship was not without his admirers. It was his Latinity, however, rather than his thought that appealed to the *literati*. The average minister and scholarly layman knew his Scottish Church history back to the Revolution Settlement, and behind that to the Westminster Assembly ; but for him the first beginnings of his Church was a land of shadows and uncertainties. It was Dr. Thomas McCrie who changed the whole perspective. His elaborate biographies of John Knox and Andrew Melville flooded this dim background with light. While packed with erudite annotations, they were eminently readable ; and they drew many to admire and to emulate the earliest contendings of the Scottish Kirk. The policy of Non-intrusion was seen in a wider context, and a new firmness in handling the question of spiritual independence made itself manifest. Chalmers himself was one of McCrie's many warm admirers, and while he was unwilling to follow him in all the practical suggestions to which his studies had led him, he constantly acknowledged the insight he had acquired through these works into the aims, policies, and ideals of those who had moulded the Church in the first two generations of its history. McCrie's publications played no small part in stimulating the courage and shaping the policy of the leaders of his day.

The Assembly of 1832 had before it eleven overtures on the question of intrusion. They were not all framed in the same language, nor did they make the same crave. The most radical one came from the Presbytery of Auchterarder. It asked bluntly that the Assembly should enact that it shall be " out of the power of any presbytery to settle a presentee in a parish or congregation who is opposed by the majority of the heads of families therein, being in full communion with the Church." [1] Since this was to be done " with consent of Presbyteries " it meant a new law under the Barrier Act, but only a new ecclesiastical law, on the ground that the matter of determining what does or does not constitute a call belongs solely to the sphere of the Church's jurisdiction.

Typical of the more cautious was one from the Presbytery of Forfar, which asked that " such measures as may be deemed necessary be adopted, in order to restore the call in the settlement of ministers to its constitutional

[1] *Report of the Debate, etc., on May 24, 1832*, p. vii

and salutary efficiency." [1]   If the overtures had been uniform, and all had taken the shape of the Forfar one, no handle would have been given to the opponents who raised the cry of " innovation," and urged that this was a most unsuitable time to make a new law, and to tamper with the rights of patrons.

An able debate followed, which ranged over the whole history and practice of the call in Scotland, diverging at times into the wider issue of patronage.   During its course there emerged two motions.   The one from the Evangelical side was : " That the General Assembly, having considered and deliberated on these overtures, and finding that they related to a subject of great importance, on which various opinions appear to be entertained, remit the said overtures to a committee with instructions to consider the same, and report to next Assembly." [2]   The other was : " That the Assembly judge it unnecessary and inexpedient to adopt the measures recommended in the overtures now before it." [3]   There was a majority of 42 for the second motion, the figures being 127 to 85.[4]   The plea for the restoration of meaning to the call had been decisively lost.

In the debate it was frequently asserted that the small number of the overtures showed that there was no general sense of grievance in the Church.   The Evangelical party determined that this would be remedied in the next Assembly.   As soon as it was obvious that the increase would be notable, it was felt necessary to take counsel to decide on the policy to be followed when they came up for consideration.   Since it was Dr. Chalmers who eventually submitted the agreed motion of his party, and since his sincerity in so doing

---

[1] *Report of the Debate, etc., May 24, 1832*, p. viii   [2] *Ibid.*, p. 35
[3] *Ibid.*, p. 45   [4] *Ibid.*, p. 93

has been challenged, his actual position at the time must be closely examined.

Dr. Bryce in his survey of the conflict has said : " At the very zenith of his fame and usefulness he was seized upon by a party in the Church as the ostensible leader of a movement which, had his own sagacious and considerate counsels been followed, would never have attained the height to which it proceeded, and in carrying it on to which Dr. Chalmers had more than his share assigned to him ; and to serve the purposes of others, eager to consecrate their acts under the high sanction of his name—that name while he lived, and his memory after his death, have been overlaid with a load of adulation from which his own modesty and good sense would have recoiled." [1]

Has this judgment any foundation in fact ? It has this much, that Dr. Chalmers did suggest another way of achieving the same end than the plan ultimately adopted, and that he accepted that plan in preference to his own only after considerable hesitation. But that is all.

It has been seen how fundamental to his thinking was the self-determination of the Church in all matters pertaining to its province, the most striking part of his London declaration of 1838 having already been printed in a sermon of 1829. Approaching more nearly the specific question one finds that in February 1833, he writes to a member of the Government : " However patronage is to be modified, there is one principle which I think the Church must firmly abide by, and that is its own ultimate power of deciding (even after a presentation is laid upon the table) whether, viewing all the circumstances of the case, it is for the Christian good of the population that that presentation shall be sustained. The

[1] James Bryce, *Ten Years of the Church of Scotland*, vol. i, p. 247

concurrence of the ecclesiastical court has been too much lost sight of for half a century as an indispensable element to the validity of every induction." [1] Now, this does not definitely state the assent or concurrence of the people to be an essential element, but in insisting that the Presbytery shall be entitled to have regard to the Christian good of the whole population, it implies it.

It is even more explicit in the plan which he laid before the Evangelical conclave. How, he asked, had it come about that the call had been reduced to a nullity ? Simply by a series of decisions in disputed cases before the Assembly. Let the Assembly retrace its steps, let it, by a series of new decisions, all based on the fundamental principle of Non-intrusion, gradually increase the proportion of signatures required for a valid call, and so, patiently but surely, restore the call to its rightful place. The scheme was wise, but it was held to have three drawbacks. It would take a long time ; there might be much confusion through lack of uniformity in the action of Presbyteries ; and at any stage in the process there might be protracted litigation. The large majority of the group desired some uniform measure that might come into operation as soon as it was accepted. Let the Assembly itself determine what, in its judgment, fulfilled the requirement of the consent or concurrence of the people, and let it make this into an Act of Assembly. While Chalmers had no doubt whatever as to the right and power of the Church to follow this course, he did urge that, in view of the doubts expressed by others, the consent of the legislature should be concurrently asked. Scottish legal opinion, however, was averse to submitting any Scottish Church matter to Westminster, and equally positive that the determination of what

[1] Hanna, vol. iii, p. 351

constituted a call was entirely within the province of the Church's authority.

But what was to constitute an adequate call? A certain percentage of the parishioners? The circumstances of parishes varied so greatly that no identity of requirement in this was feasible. But if a majority dissented and intimated their dissent, there was unmistakable proof of a lack of concurrence. So the plan of a Veto, already suggested in more than one overture, was the one ultimately adopted by the supporters of the call.

It was the first motion in favour of this that Dr. Chalmers proposed in the Assembly of 1833; and while many capable and indeed brilliant speeches were made in that debate, his is the most balanced and cogent of them all. If he did have, a few weeks before, any hesitation about the specific plan he was putting forward, there is certainly no trace of it in the speech. Having dealt with the disastrous effects of intrusions, and the need of an immediate remedy, and having stated his reluctance to adopt a new law when a declared interpretation of an old one would serve the purpose, he said : " The law of calls places such a facility in our hands ; and, as I feel that I must not take up the time of the Assembly, let me state at once, and without further preamble, *my own preference* [1] as to the best way of restoring significance and effect to this now antiquated, but still venerable, form—and that is, by holding the call a solid one, which lies, not in the expressed consent of the few, and these often the mere driblet of a parish ; but larger than this, which lies in the virtual or implied consent of the majority, and to be gathered from their non-resistance or their silence. In other words, I would

[1] *Italics supplied*

have it that the majority of dissentient voices should lay a veto on every presentation. In this power of a negative on the part of the people there is nothing new in the constitution or practice of the Church of Scotland." [1] While there are parts of the speech which would be distinctly unpalatable to the radicals of his party—for example, his disparagement of popular election and his defence of patronage purely exercised—there is certainly no hint of half-heartedness in commencing the positive policy adopted in conference.

The official counter-motion on this occasion was not a simple " Pass from the Overtures." It was a definite proposal moved by Dr. Cook [2] to define and enlarge the scope of specific dissents on the part of the people, while insisting that they be specific ; that the Presbytery consider not the number of the dissentients, but the grounds of their dissent ; and that revised regulations in harmony with this finding be framed for next General Assembly. The motions this time were nearer each other both in substance and in support. Dr. Cook's motion had a majority of 12, the votes being 149 to 137. It was manifest from this that, should the supporters of the call maintain the same rate of progress, there would be a majority for the Veto in the next Assembly, and 1834 was indeed to prove the crucial year.

Ecclesiastical politics, academic work, and special preaching did not absorb all Chalmers' energies in these testing years. They saw also the beginning of his first experiment in Edinburgh in the aggressive territorial

[1] *Collected Works*, vol. xii, pp. 385–86. In Mr. Simon MacGregor's report there are two variations in the above, " persuasion " for " preference," and " valid " for " solid."

[2] Dr. George Cook, Chalmers' successor in the Moral Philosophy chair at St. Andrews, was throughout the entire conflict the unwearied uninspiring leader of the Moderate party.

work which lay so near to his heart. Living, as he did then, in Forres Street, he looked down daily on the village of the Water of Leith, then, much more than now, a community by itself. It was the home of a considerable population without a church of its own. A survey revealed the fact that out of its 1,356 inhabitants only 143 had sittings in any place of worship. Here was a field of labour to his hand, where he could prepare the way for a territorial church. A beginning having been made by visitations and by local Sabbath Schools, a missionary was appointed for the area in 1833. An old malt granary became the centre of his activities. It was a great joy to Chalmers to assist him, and he seldom preached with greater effect than in these makeshift premises, when the seating accommodation of 400 was taxed to the uttermost. A church, erected by private subscription, was opened by him in May 1836 — a church which he could proudly regard as the first-fruits of his territorial work within the Presbytery of Edinburgh.

CHAPTER TEN

THE CRUCIAL ASSEMBLY

1834

THE General Assembly of 1834 was to prove one of the most determinative in the whole history of the Church of Scotland. The close voting in the preceding Assembly stirred both parties into action to secure the biggest possible representation in the nominations from Presbyteries. Eager eyes scrutinized every list as it appeared with a view to forecasting the probable issue.

When the Assembly met, the preliminary skirmishes over the sustaining of doubtful commissions revealed a distinct Evangelical majority. To their leaders, who had all their lives fought a losing battle, it seemed like the dawning of a new day. The abuses which had grown up in the long night of Moderatism could now be swept away. The Church of Scotland, as an institution, could now be brought into closer harmony with her standards, and regain the mobility and the verve of her best days.

Certain reforms clamoured for immediate enactment. Attention to these had been secured by many overtures sent up from Presbyteries and Synods. Chief among them was the restoration of reality, significance, and emphasis to the call of the congregation. The method which Dr. Chalmers had proposed in vain in the preceding Assembly —that of determining the acceptability of the presentee by the absence of any distinct majority against him—the method of the Veto—had been winning adherents all over the land. The great majority of the overtures incorporated it in some form or other. Apart from the small group who would have done with patronage once and for all, which policy even the most ardent of them recognized was bound to entail a prolonged and embittered parliamentary struggle, there was a whole-hearted concentration on this simplest of all remedies, attainable as it was through the declaratory action of the Church. It was equally free, as one admirer [1] put it in the Assembly, " from the tyranny of the patron on the one hand, and unbridled suffrage [so he designated popular election] on the other." [2] That the Assembly should declare " acceptability to the parishioners " as one of the essential elements to be taken into account when the Presbytery decided on the qualifications of a presentee—an element so essential that, when it was lacking, no further steps were to be taken towards his settlement—was quite within its competence, and in line with the constant contentions of the Church until the days of William Robertson.

It was Lord Moncrieff, one of the Lords of Session and a son of the Rev. Sir Henry Moncrieff, who made the first motion when the overtures on Calls came up for consideration. It ran as follows : " That the General Assembly, having maturely considered the overtures, do declare that it is a fundamental law of this Church that no pastor shall be intruded on any congregation contrary to the will of the people ; and that, in order to carry this principle into full effect, the Presbyteries of the Church shall be instructed, that if at the moderating in a call to a vacant pastoral charge, the major part of the male heads of families, members of the vacant congrega-

---

[1] H. Beveridge, Esq.
[2] *Proceedings of the General Assembly of 1834,* p. 105

tion, and in full communion with the Church, shall disapprove of the person in whose favour the call is proposed
to be moderated in, such disapproval shall be deemed
sufficient ground for the Presbytery rejecting such person,
and that he shall be rejected accordingly, and due notice
thereof forthwith given to all concerned ; but that, if
the major part of the said heads of families shall not
disapprove of such person to be their pastor, the Presbytery shall proceed with the settlement according to
the rules of the Church ; and further declare that no
person shall be held to be entitled to disapprove, as
aforesaid, who shall refuse, if required solemnly, to
declare in presence of the Presbytery, that he is actuated
by no factious or malicious motive, but solely by a
conscientious regard to the spiritual interests of himself
or the congregation ; and resolve, that a Committee
be appointed to report to a future diet of the Assembly
in what manner, and by what particular measures, this
declaration and instruction may be best carried into
full operation." [1]

The opposing motion, proposed by Dr. Mearns, was
even more elaborate. It also made provision for dissents,
but they must be dissents with specific reasons. Its
central part was phrased thus : " If the objections
relate merely to the insufficiency or unfitness of the
presentee for the particular charge to which he has been
appointed, the objectors shall not be compelled to
become libellers, but shall simply deliver in writing their
specific grounds for objecting to the settlement, and shall
have full liberty to substantiate the same ; upon all of
which the presentee shall have an opportunity to be fully
heard, and shall have all competent means of defence." [2]

[1] *Proceedings of the General Assembly of 1834*, pp. 57–58
[2] *Ibid.*, p. 62

It was on this much-narrowed issue that the debate proceeded. One of its central pivots was the interpretation to be put on the Directory of 1649.[1] Could it be claimed as an authority for a dissent without reasons assigned? Sir Henry Moncrieff was three times cited as denying this interpretation. It was with great glee that the father was brought in to counterweigh the son. The son, however, stuck to his point; and his is the sound interpretation. The pronounced antithesis between the "major part" and the "lesser part" is decisive. "But if it happen that the major part of the congregation dissent from the person agreed upon by the session, then the matter shall be brought unto the Presbytery, who shall judge of the same; if they doe not find their dissent to be grounded on causelesse prejudices, they are to appoynt a new election. But if a lesser party of the session or congregation dissent without exceptions relevant and verified to the Presbytery, notwithstanding thereof, the Presbytery shall go on to the trials and ordination of the person elected."[2] The reasons submitted by a minority are to be weighed and sifted, the dissent of the majority has only to be proven conscientious. This Directory of 1649 will be encountered again.

The most frequent argument against the Veto was its unfairness to the presentee, whose opportunities in a second vacancy would be greatly prejudiced by his previous rejection elsewhere. It was going to ruin the career of many a promising licentiate. Strange to say, it was not on the legal points, but in dealing with this stock objection that the speech of Lord Moncrieff reached

[1] This was the Church of Scotland's elaboration of one particular point of the Westminster Directory. *Acts of the General Assembly of the Church of Scotland, 1638–1842*, pp. 212–13

[2] *Acts of General Assembly, 1638–1842*, p. 213

its highest levels. Would such a rejection really mar a good man's usefulness ? Would it not be maimed more disastrously if he was thrust upon a people that did not want him ? " A deserted church—desolation in his heart —the meeting-houses rising around him—Sabbath after Sabbath treading his way to the church door, and there finding none whom he can spiritually edify . . . the total abuse and frustration of his powers—his learning becoming a burthen—his talents utterly useless, because he has not been placed in a sphere where he might employ them." [1]

But many subsidiary arguments, evolved through the previous two years in many a quiet study, were given an airing now, on both sides. One supporter brought forward triumphantly the parallel of the Roman veto, exercised, he claimed, by the tribunes of the plebs in the name of the Roman people ; [2] one opponent adduced the terrible example of the Presbyterian Church of England, the theological degeneration of which into Arianism and Unitarianism he traced to tendencies fostered by the popular election of its ministers. [3]

When, at the close of the debate, the vote was taken it disclosed the unexpectedly large majority of 46 for the Veto. The figures were 184 to 138.

A fortnight later, on the closing day of the Assembly, the Committee appointed in pursuance of this finding submitted its report, consisting of twenty-three regulations for directing the procedure of the Presbyteries. Their new element is contained mainly in Regulations 7–14.
7. " That if it shall happen that, at the meeting for moderating in the call, dissents are tendered by any of the male heads of families, being members of the con-

[1] *Proceedings of the General Assembly of 1834*, p. 57
[2] *Ibid.*, p. 64   [3] *Ibid.*, p. 70

gregation, and in full communion with the Church, their names standing on the roll above referred to, without the assignment of any special objections, such dissents shall either be personally delivered in writing by the person dissenting, or taken down from his oral statement by the moderator or clerk of the Presbytery." Then follows the full detail of the procedure of the Presbytery for testing the sincerity of the dissents, leading up to Regulation 14. " That if the Presbytery shall find that there is at last a major portion of the persons on the roll dissenting, they shall reject the person presented, so far as regards the particular presentation, and the occasion of that vacancy in the parish ; and shall forthwith direct notice of this their determination to be given to the patron, the presentee, and the elders of the parish." [1]

It was the contention of the Moderates that such a grave departure from previous usage as the admission of dissents without reasons assigned could not be enacted unless sent down to the Presbyteries under the Barrier Act, thus delaying its operation for one year at least ; while the Evangelicals asserted that this amendment of regulations involved no constitutional change and thus could be effectively introduced at once without any approbation of Presbyteries. A compromise was arrived at, whereby, although the procedure of the Barrier Act was to be followed, the regulations should be passed as an Interim Act, to regulate presbyterial practice during the ensuing year.

Almost equally important with the Assembly's action in restoring substance to the Call was its dealing with the problem of the status of chapels of ease and their ministers. It is self-evident that an Established Church if it is to retain its national character must not be fettered

[1] *Acts of General Assembly, 1638–1842*, p. 1039

with a rigid framework. Provision must be made some-where for the amalgamation of parishes depleted of their population, and for the erection of new parishes where the inhabitants have multiplied. Up till the year 1707 there had been little difficulty. There had been no rush from the country to the town and no concentration of population in the Forth–Clyde area. With the departure of the Scottish legislators to London, the business of the secular arrangement for the erection of new parishes had been transferred to the Court of Session, which was now to act as a " court of teinds and plantation of kirks." [1] This readjustment of machinery—this transference of authority from an administrative to a judicial body—would have proved no hindrance to a progressive Church had not the Act authorizing it contained the proviso that no process for the erection of a new parish could be entered into, unless with the consent and concurrence, previously obtained, of heritors possessing at least three-fourths of the valued rent of the parish from which the new one was to be disjoined. [2] The Act was devised by legislators who were mostly heritors themselves, to protect their own financial interests. It was only in the rarest cases that concern for the religious welfare of the new-comers who had augmented their incomes outweighed their dread of a raid on the unexhausted teinds. This road, therefore, being barred, the Church had to find another. It succeeded in devising two.

One was the way of parliamentary churches. In one of its spasmodic moods of sympathy with the destitute districts of the Highlands, Parliament had enacted [3] that forty new churches should be built in these areas and endowed sparely. Ministers were settled there but,

[1] Act 1707, c. 9 : In *Styles of Writs* (1838), Appendix, p. 365
[2] *Ibid.*, p. 366   [3] 1823 and 1824

while they had their own Kirk Sessions, they had no parishes allocated as a field of labour and they had no seat in Church courts. They certainly filled a gap in the church provision of Scotland, for they were situated in areas where it was hard for any congregation of the Secession or of the Relief to exist. It was increasingly felt by all parties in the Church that the position of the ministers of these churches, state-erected and state-endowed, was an offence against Presbyterian parity. Hence in the Assembly of 1833 it was moved by Dr. Cook, the leader of the Moderates, and carried—with one dissent recorded, that of the Rev. William Pirie of Dyce, afterwards Principal Pirie of Aberdeen [1]—that the anomaly be ended. This was done simply by a declaratory enactment of the General Assembly, which had two main parts : that the districts which these parliamentary churches supplied shall be disjoined from the parishes of which they form a part, and be erected into separate parishes *quoad sacra*, and that the ministers shall be constituent members of Presbyteries and Synods and be qualified to represent their Presbyteries in the General Assembly.[2]

These parliamentary churches being, one and all, in the vast unprovided tracts of the North, the pressing need of the underchurched areas of the industrial belt had not been touched. It was here that the Church's second method operated—the provision of chapels of ease. These were erected and supported by the liberality of the church's own members. A wealthy member, or a group of such, noting the spiritual destitution of a great new area of workmen's cottages or tenements, would supply a building. Work would be begun in the chapel

[1] *William Robinson Pirie : In Memoriam*, p. 37
[2] *Acts of General Assembly, 1638–1842*, p. 1024

under a licentiate. When a considerable congregation had been gathered, official recognition would be
sought from the General Assembly. In the days of the
Moderate domination, the applications met with no warm
welcome ; and not seldom a refusal meant that the chapel
was handed over by its donor or donors to one of the
dissenting bodies. But even when it was recognized, the
position of its minister was inferior to that of the minister
of one of the parliamentary churches before 1833.
Though trained in the same University Faculty as the
average parish minister, licensed by the same Presbytery,
called by a congregation of considerable numbers, and
regularly ordained to the ministry, he had not only no
defined field of labour, and no seat in any Church court,
he had not even a Kirk Session of his own. So difficult
was it in practice even to found a chapel of ease, and so
depressed its status when founded, that during the one
hundred and twenty-six years since the Union of the
Parliaments, during which the population of Scotland
had more than doubled, only sixty-six chapels of ease
had been added, and this at a time when the various
bodies of Dissenters had erected well over five hundred
places of worship.

Not unnaturally, the springs of generosity for such
chapels had dried up. There were men, many of them,
willing to do their utmost to supply the needed churches,
but only if the ministers of these churches were fully
recognized as having all the rights of a minister of the
Church of Scotland, with a territorial district of their own
—a parish *quoad sacra*. " I know a gentleman in Glasgow,"
said one of its ministers, " who is proprietor of a large
extent of ground in the parish of Gorbals. He assured
me of his readiness to give ground *gratis* for the erection
of parish churches ; but he added that he would give

none for chapels of ease, as their clergymen were in fact no clergymen, and wanted even the power possessed by dissenting ministers." [1]

The general approval accorded to the Declaratory Enactment of 1833 in regard to parliamentary churches increased the hope of a similar enactment for chapels of ease. In consequence, many overtures were presented to the Assembly, and these were supplemented by direct petitions which enabled certain ministers of these chapels to be heard in the Assembly—from the bar. The impression one gathers from two of these speeches—those of the Rev. Andrew Gray, of Woodside Chapel, Aberdeen, and the Rev. C. J. Brown, of Anderston Chapel, Glasgow —is that very few of their brethren in any position in the Church could have opened up the whole question in all its legal and historical bearings so cogently and brilliantly. Their speeches must have predisposed the Assembly to welcome them wholeheartedly. Reference must be made to one section of Mr. Brown's plea, for it concerns Dr. Chalmers. It is evident that Chalmers felt that to admit unendowed chapels at once into the position desired by their friends and supporters would weaken his constant plea for an adequate State endowment for the religious needs of every lapsed area. He had published a pamphlet on the subject, in the course of which he had written : " If we do not make the assimilation ourselves, by transmuting these voluntary chapels into endowed churches, but admit them on their present footing, then the likelihood is that the assimilation will be made for us, in another way, and that is, by the transmutation of the endowed into voluntary." [2] Mr. Brown, it emerges, had a more personal interest in the matter.

[1] *Proceedings of the General Assembly of 1834*, pp. 101–102
[2] *Churches and Chapels*, etc., p. 29

For in this same pamphlet Dr. Chalmers had expressly referred to his chapel in Anderston as an outstanding success as a chapel, but a deplorable failure as a territorial institution, ministering largely to the " grandees of Blythswood Square " who kept it up by their high seat rents. What it needed was an endowment to release the minister " from his present dependence on the patricians at a distance, that he might afford to spend all his strength and his time among the plebeians of his own proper and immediate charge." [1]

It was little wonder, therefore, that the opposition took mainly the line along which it could shelter under Chalmers' name. " Churches unendowed have no stability ; they might be here to-day and away to-morrow. To attach territorial districts to such fleeting and transitory institutions would be to degrade the parochial system." [2] Its leader, Dr. Cook, further insisted that the action was beyond the power of the Assembly. If it was to be done, it must be done through the legislature. The supporters of the plea took the high ground of the necessary conjunction of the teaching and ruling functions of the ministry, appealed to history as witnessing against the novel doctrine of the determination of ecclesiastical status by endowment, claimed that a declaratory enactment in regard to chapels of ease was as demonstrably within the power of the Church as that with regard to parliamentary churches, to which there had only been one single dissentient.

This, however, has led away from Mr. Brown's answer to Dr. Chalmers. " Would your admitting us," he asked, " into Church courts unendowed imply that you thought endowments useless, or that you had altered your judg-

[1] *Churches and Chapels*, p. 12
[2] *Edinburgh Christian Instructor*, August, 1834, pp. 555-56

ment as to their vast importance, nay, indispensable necessity to the full efficiency of the church ? " [1] . . . Are we to stand knocking at the door of a government for endowment while the mass of the people deserts our communion ? Will not the removal of this indefensible anomaly, the righting of this manifest wrong, give us a greater hold of the hearts of the people, and thus, through them, irresistibly induce in the now reluctant civil authorities a more favourable disposition to our claim for financial support ?

The petition of the chapel ministers was approved by a majority of 50 (153–103), and a committee was formed to prepare the enactment. It was much the same as that of the previous year, with this addition : an instruction to Presbyteries " to take the necessary measures for selecting and ordaining, according to the rules of the Church, for each of the said districts so to be erected, a body of Elders, who, with the said Ministers respectively, may exercise sessional jurisdiction within the same." [2]

The majority of the Church felt that, with the incubus of two generations of hampering precedents swept away, the time had come for a great forward movement of Church extension ; and when the opportunity arose through the retirement of the convener of a committee which had accomplished little through the conditions under which it laboured, Dr. Chalmers was made convener of the Church Accommodation Committee, and was thus harnessed to one of the most exacting and rewarding tasks of his life. There was a feeling of spring in the air ; the Church had renewed her youth ; the light of dawn was on her path ; her greatest days were just in front. In the light of the sequel one grim shadow

---

[1] *Proceedings of the General Assembly of 1834*, p. 101
[2] *Acts of the General Assembly of 1834*, p. 28

can be discerned. It was not the fact that there was a considerable number of dissentients to both decisions. That was far from unusual in those days. It was that a solitary elder, Mr. John Hope, the Dean of Faculty, had entered a special additional dissent to the Veto Act on fourteen grounds, of which the first two give the gist : " Because I consider the attempt of the General Assembly thus to impose, practically, a restriction amounting to a veto on the right of Patronage, to be wholly incompetent, and beyond the powers of the Church." " Because I am clearly of opinion, in point of law, that a Presentee, though rejected by a majority of heads of families, yet there being no judgment of the church courts on his qualifications, will, nevertheless, be legally, validly, and effectually presented to the benefice, and will have a clear right to their stipend and all other rights pertaining thereto." [1]

In this, whether intended or not, there was a clear invitation to any vetoed presentee to take legal proceedings to secure his stipend with every prospect of success.

If this particular lone dissent cast any shadow at all, it was soon dispelled by an utterance of Lord Brougham, at that time Lord Chancellor.

" My Lords, I hold in my hand a great number of petitions from a most respectable portion of His Majesty's subjects in the northern parts of this island, all referring to one subject—I mean Church patronage in Scotland, which has greatly and powerfully interested the people of Scotland for many months past, and respecting the expediency of some change in which there is hardly any difference of opinion among them. The late proceedings in the General Assembly (viz. in passing the Veto Law)

[1] *Proceedings of the General Assembly of 1834*, p. 156.

have done more to facilitate the adoption of measures which shall set that important question at rest, upon a footing advantageous to the community, *and that shall be safe and beneficial* to the Establishment, and in every respect desirable than any other course that could have been taken : for it would have been premature if the Legislature had adopted any measure without the acquiescence of that important body, as no good could have resulted from it. I am glad that the wisdom of the General Assembly has been devoted to this subject, and that the result of its deliberations has been these important resolutions (viz. the Veto Act), which were passed at the last meeting." [1]

With the almost unanimous approval of the legal authorities of Scotland, and with the benediction of the Lord Chancellor of the Realm, the Church began joyfully to operate its repaired mechanism, little dreaming that the same Lord Brougham was later, in his judicial capacity, to decide that it was the reverse of " safe and beneficial."

[1] Hanna, vol. iii, p. 362 (*italics supplied*)

CHAPTER ELEVEN

CHALMERS AND CHURCH EXTENSION

1834–40

IT was natural that an Assembly which contemplated a Forward Movement at home should have nominated Dr. Chalmers to assume its leadership. For, gripped as he was by the territorial principle, he had for nearly twenty years been urging the necessity for a more " thickly-set Establishment," with a church and a minister within easy reach of every door. Under his inspiration a notable scheme has already been mooted before the Assembly met. Its sponsor was a Glasgow business man, Mr. Wm. Collins, Dr. Chalmers' publisher and friend. It was a local scheme for Glasgow, which proposed to raise money among its well-to-do citizens for twenty new churches within the city bounds. They were definitely to be parochial churches, and no active steps were to be taken till assurances to that effect had been received. By the Chapel Act the General Assembly removed all obstacles in the way of their ecclesiastical status. Through an Act of Parliament a few weeks later, the legislature freed the new parishes to be disjoined from any possible claim to appointment on the part of the patron of the original parish. Without delay the scheme was launched, and the Church Building Society of Glasgow came into being in the closest co-operation with the Assembly's committee. Before winter set in the enthusiastic group had raised twenty thousand pounds, and building operations had begun. The elaborate preparations of this western group and the speed with which they operated created problems for the committee. The public heard of money flowing in for the purposes of Church extension, and were sometimes impatient when grants were refused, not realizing that a very large proportion of the early subscriptions were locally destined.

It was natural, also, that Dr. Chalmers should regard the task laid on him as one into which he could throw all his energies. At the very first meeting he acknowledged that if he had been left to make a choice " among the countless diversities of well-doing, this was the one office he would have chosen as most congenial to his taste ; " [1] and he closed by indicating his conception of its magnitude, foreseeing a whole generation of intensive effort to make up for past neglect, before the goal could be reached, which would not be " till churches have been so multiplied and parochial charges so subdivided that there will not one poor family be found in our land who might not, if they will, have entry and accommodation in a place of worship and religious instruction, with such a share in the personal attentions of the clergyman as to claim him for an acquaintance and a friend." [2]

The financial campaign that followed—the appeal to the generosity of true friends of the Church of Scotland —may have been Chalmers' 'prentice effort, but the course of events demonstrated its soundness. Its results were immediate and continuous.

The moment it became apparent that new churches would thus be forthcoming by voluntary effort, the committee prepared its appeal to Government for aid in their upkeep. As we have seen, Dr. Chalmers con-

[1] Hanna, vol. iii, p. 451   [2] Ibid., p. 452

sidered some endowment necessary for the sixty-six admitted chapels, and for the new parochial churches, if they were to be adequate territorial agencies. For the one object of an endowment, he had insisted, was not to secure a higher stipend for the admitted ministers, nor even to provide it more easily for those who might be added to their number, but to make it possible for the seat rents to be so low that they would not deter any parishioner, however poor he might be. So, while the committee asked for an endowment for the un-endowed chapels and the churches still to be created, they made it plain to the Government that this was no proposal to increase or to stabilize the salaries of chapel ministers. To ensure this, they desired that to what-ever grant the Government was pleased to provide there be attached two definite conditions—that, immediately on its allocation the seat rents in present chapels be reduced by an equal amount, and that in those chapels and in the churches contemplated, the actual parishioners were to have their claim to sittings fully satisfied before any outsiders were admitted.

So lucidly and persuasively was the case presented that the Whig ministry gave the delegation a most favourable reception—so favourable, indeed, that they imagined their object was to be attained at once. But Lord Melbourne's government was already in deep waters, and may not unfairly be described as clutching at any straw to keep afloat a little longer. In November it was replaced by a Tory government under Sir Robert Peel. An official approach to it met with the most cordial response, and success seemed to be within grasp when the Church found this paragraph included in the king's speech, " I feel it also incumbent on me to call your attention to the condition of the Church of Scotland,

and to the means by which it may be enabled to increase the opportunities of religious worship for the poorer classes of society in that part of the United Kingdom." [1] This clearly foreshadowed a Government measure designed to implement the request of the committee and the Assembly.

But the public announcement of this intention gave rise to a veritable tornado of protest. The organized Voluntaries took the field at once. They accused the Assembly, and Chalmers in particular, of misleading the Government by this pretence of concern for the poor. Under cover of this pious aim they were seeking the annihilation of every religious body outside the Church of Scotland. " A sufficiently thick-set Establishment " was intended to squeeze them out. Was the Church of Scotland, they asked, making an adequate use of its present endowments ? They bombarded the Government with statistics about the number of unlet sittings in the existing parish churches, especially in Dr. Chalmers' own city of Edinburgh. In the light of these, they triumphantly asked, could it be contended that there was any demand for more churches, particularly in Edinburgh ?

In pamphlet after pamphlet Dr. Chalmers strove to repel the attack. He was particularly pungent on the Edinburgh situation. Here are the titles of two of his polemics : *On the evils which the Established Church in Edinburgh has already suffered, and suffers still, in virtue of the seat-letting being in the hands of the Magistrates : with remarks on the unjust and injurious tendency of a late document, published by their authority, on the subject of the Unlet Sittings* ; and *Re-assertion of the Evils of the Edinburgh system of seat-letting, with new proofs adapted to recent objections.* While it might

[1] Hanna, vol. iii, pp. 462–63

146

be interesting to recall some of the more trenchant strokes, the details of the magistrates' speculations in soaring seat-rents were only a side issue. His main aim was not to expose a scandal, but to plead with the Government not " to confound the effects of an Establishment rightly conducted, with the effects of its wretched mal-administration in the town of Edinburgh." [1] And always he returned to his great positive aim, to provide in every churchless territory a minister, whose specific business it would be, not to fill his new church from the wide bounds of the city, but to " fill that church out of that parish." [2] The storm of protest made the Government hesitate, and it was still hesitating when it was thrown out, and Lord Melbourne returned to office. Dr. Chalmers himself went to London to deepen the impression the delegation had made a year before, only to be told on arrival that, since the basic facts on which the Prime Minister's favourable consideration had been promised had been publicly challenged, the Government had decided not to take the matter up, but instead to appoint a Royal Commission of Inquiry into the Provision of Religious Instruction in Scotland. The Commission was duly set up. It had such a wide remit and such extensive powers, and it comprised so many members known to be hostile to the Church, that throughout the Church of Scotland there was a widespread feeling of alarm. Even leading Moderates regarded it as a most flagrant attack upon the Church's privileges and liberties.

Recalling Chalmers' drastic handling of an earlier Commission, many expected that he would lead the onslaught on this one. But this he refused to do. He was bitterly disappointed ; but he was not going to

[1] *On the evils, etc.*, p. 23   [2] *Ibid.*, p. 39

impede its work. Every facility, he contended, should be given to any inquiry. The more searching the investigation, the more fully justified would the Church's claim for endowment emerge from the test. It would become manifest that what was sought from Government was not calculated to promote clerical enrichment or ecclesiastical status, still less to depreciate or decrease the auxiliary forces of the Seceders, but solely for the uplift of the neglected poor, and that money spent in such a cause would assuredly decrease other demands on the national exchequer, for prisons and poor relief in particular. He placed his accumulated statistical material at the disposal of the Commission, and set others to the task of providing the like for their own localities.

The one real personal quarrel of his career arose out of evidence given before the Commission, and the various pamphlets on the moderatorship controversy are best forgotten. It was more than two years before all the estrangements which arose from it were overcome. Dr. Chalmers' sole concern had been that one who had shown himself in his public testimony needlessly unfavourable to the cause of Church Extension should, on no account, be raised to the Moderator's chair ; and while he won his point friendships were broken in the process.

The Commission duly made its various reports. They proved more favourable than was expected from its composition. The inadequacy of the provision was admitted. The Government was now bound in honour to implement its promise. It professed to do so in a Bill—in the committee's eyes a most inadequate Bill. The Church felt constrained to remonstrate. The leaders of an official deputation saw Lord Melbourne personally. They solemnly pointed out that both in content and implications the Bill was an injustice to the Church of Scotland. " That, gentlemen," said the Premier in the easiest tone of banter, " that is your inference. You may not be the better of our plan, but—hang it !—you cannot surely be worse." [1]

It became abundantly apparent that there was no real hope from Parliament. The Whigs could not afford to alienate two main groups of their supporters, the Dissenters in England and the Voluntaries in Scotland. The Tories, while at the moment full of promises, were not in the position to implement them. Later, when they did have a real chance, a new development in the situation had emerged which interfered with their benevolent intentions.

Must the great Church Extension scheme, then, be abandoned because the prospect of endowment had disappeared ? Would the ardour of Dr. Chalmers and his colleagues, lay and clerical, cool down and fade away ? Was there no possible alternative ? Was necessary Christian work in Scotland to be left undone through the inaction of careless statesmen ? In confronting this serious problem, a fresh aspect of Chalmers' genius and resource bursts forth. His long preoccupation with economic problems begins to bear ecclesiastical fruit. In 1835 Alexander Duff had returned to Scotland on his first furlough. By his report of his work in India he had roused the General Assembly to a high pitch of enthusiasm. But he had not stopped there. He had toured the country on the first Foreign Mission campaign within the Church of Scotland. He had awakened interest wherever he went. He had found financial support in the most unlikely quarters. Might not some similar action for the Home Mission produce similar

[1] Hanna, vol. iv, p. 23 (note)

results? So Dr. Chalmers persuaded the General Assembly of 1836 to give its benediction to an organized campaign of popular meetings. Their slogan was, " We want more churches, and we pledge ourselves to pay for them."

In the early stages Dr. Chalmers was adviser rather than participant. He felt that direct appeal and dealing with hecklers was not his *métier*, and that there were others to whom it would be sheer joy, a breathing of their native air. Despite many troublesome incidents, duly recorded with glee in the *Voluntary Church Magazine*, the campaign was a triumphant success. " As the ear of the Government seemed to close, the ear of the country seemed to open," [1] and Dr. Chalmers himself seemed to feel that he had found a more potent way of ensuring the co-operation of the Government than sending deputations to London. All this stir in the constituencies might be more effective than the reasoned appeal of a few Church representatives.

In the Assembly of 1838 he was able to announce that nearly two hundred churches had been erected or were in process of erection ; that the enterprise had not reached its zenith ; and that there was abundant evidence of rising fervour. Yet he was far from satisfied. To undertake this vast work the Committee had been forced to proceed by way of grants. The normal grant was proportioned to the sittings to be provided, and amounted to only about one quarter of the cost. The rest had to be raised locally. This meant that the most desperate cases had to be left untackled. An adequate local contribution was out of the question. This impasse must, somehow, be resolved. Such was the atmosphere of those days that the dilemma had only to be brought

[1] Hanna, vol. iv, p. 32

forcefully before the notice of his friends for a way out to be devised. It was the suggestion of another Glasgow layman, Mr. William Campbell, that the next hundred churches might be confined to such areas, and that he and his friends would raise a supplementary fund so to augment the normal grant that the whole cost of churches in such areas of proven destitution would be provided. Forty thousand pounds was raised for this end alone.

It was the intention of Dr. Chalmers to hand over his responsibilities at the Assembly of 1840, after six years as convener. In order to make things as easy as possible for his successor, he made a special effort in what was to have been his final year. He planned and executed a personal campaign through a great part of Scotland during the autumn of 1839 before the opening of the university session. Despite his doubts as to his fitness for such a task, he thoroughly enjoyed his arduous labours ; and his close association with the Church in many hitherto unknown regions, both north and south, increased both his knowledge of the Church and the Church's knowledge of him. In what was meant to be his final speech he brought the figures up to date, intimating that in the six years nearly £290,000 had been raised and 216 churches had been added to the strength of the Church of Scotland. The sternest critic of Voluntaryism had demonstrated its usefulness within an endowed Church, only, as he was careful to point out, it was not the futile Voluntaryism *ab intra*, but the more admirable, though still inadequate, Voluntaryism *ab extra*.

It is interesting to note that £5,000 of the total was raised in London in 1838 when he was delivering his six lectures on Establishments.

This zeal for Church Extension was not, however, the only manifestation of the new life coursing in the

Church's veins. It found outlet in many directions, new and old. Foreign Missions were prosecuted with growing ardour, and supported with a mounting enthusiasm. The call of exiled fellow-countrymen in distant colonies was heard and answered, and a committee charged with this special duty. No longer were the Seceders to have practically a monopoly of this branch of overseas work. The desire to spread the blessings of efficient education —a religious education—at home found expression in the new activities of an old committee, with Normal Schools for the training of teachers and the provision of facilities in every neglected industrial area as the main objects of its endeavour.

No project of these days had quite the excitement and the thrill of the inquiry into the distribution and state of the Jews in Europe and in Palestine. Prominent in the commission was that fervent and dedicated evangelist, Rev. R. M. MacCheyne, who owed his position on it to the fear in the hearts of his friends that he was not long for this world if he continued to spend himself in his labours in Dundee and throughout Scotland with the same prodigality of passionate affection. The report is one of the major documents in the history of Jewish Missions, and its effect was enhanced by the crusading efforts of the commissioners themselves on their return. No vessel was ever launched with greater acclamation and hope than the Church of Scotland's Jewish Mission.

If anyone should approach the history of this period with the key-phrase " Ten Years' Conflict " dominating his mind, he would be surprised to find that for five years of the period (1834–39) the Church of Scotland was a throbbing centre of uninterrupted and accelerating activities. At no period in its previous history, not even in the days it looked back to as heroic, had it displayed such energy and sacrifice for the evangelization of the nation and of the world. The minor controversies, whether with the Voluntaries outside, or between parties and individuals within, do not diminish the impression of an alert army on the march. Old possessions had been re-occupied, new territory had been won, and fresh conquests were in sight. There was only the tiny cloud of the first stages of the Auchterarder Case to indicate that a desperate Four Years' conflict was about to begin against old forces armed with new and unheard-of weapons.

This judgment which, even now, can be gathered from the records of the time, is confirmed by the testimony of one to whom these years were, when he spoke, a living memory. In the General Assembly of 1870, Dr. Norman MacLeod said : " I remember 1838, when our Church devoted itself chiefly to its practical work, leaving mere abstract ideas and ideal constitutions alone. We never saw a period in our history, I think, in which all parties were so united—in which, in fact, all party seemed so to disappear. Coming into personal contact, we began then to understand one another better, to sympathize with one another more, to unite in a great common sentiment for good." [1] It is significant, as reports to the Assembly show, that the annual revenue of the Church for all her Christian enterprise was in 1839 fourteen times greater than it had been in 1834. These figures might have remained more memorable had not Dr. Chalmers after 1843, as leader of the Free Church, gone on, to use a modern phrase, to break his own record.

What was in some respects the apex of this epoch was the admission to the Church of Scotland in 1839

[1] *Patronage, Presbyterian Union, and Home Work of the Church of Scotland,* p. 134

of the majority of the congregations of one branch of the Secession, the denomination called in popular speech the Old Light Burghers. In 1733 when the Secession first arose, the four brethren expelled had appealed from the decision of the Commission of Assembly that extruded them to " the first, free, faithful, and reforming Assembly of the Church of Scotland." The Assembly of 1834 having awakened hopes that this had now come into being, this minor branch of the Secession began to make overtures for return. The way having been prepared by careful action, not unopposed, within the Church of Scotland, the Synod of that smaller Church dissolved itself in 1839, so that a majority of its ministers and congregations might be received as within the framework of the Church of Scotland. It was not so much a union as a return, and, while at the moment it seemed as though it might be the first of many such, it has thus far remained unique and without successor. The accession of thirty-one ministers, nearly all of them with their congregations, was not a very weighty reinforcement, but Dr. Candlish at least saw in it a symbolic crown to five years of Evangelical witness and an earnest of greater things to come, and said so in one of the best of his early speeches.

These years 1834–39 were not only a strenuous time of most profitable and fruitful work for Dr. Chalmers, they saw also the high-water mark of his outside recognition. In addition to London's homage to him as a lecturer, there were two most notable academic distinctions. In 1835 the university of Oxford bestowed on him the degree of Doctor of Laws, specifying four main reasons for the award—his Bridgewater Treatise, his eloquence, his St. John's scheme, and his most acute defence of the Church of Scotland, and, inferentially, of the Church of England. On his visit to Oxford for graduation, he showed a somewhat naïve delight in the whole atmosphere of the place, lamenting only the reserve he encountered in some of the leading Tractarians with whom he would have desired more intimate talk on the deepest topics. The other distinction had come even earlier. In 1834 he received the unexpected intimation that he had been elected a corresponding member of the Royal Institute of France. In view of the fluctuation in the estimate of such Continental honours, it is important to note that Dr. Chalmers himself regarded this as the peak of his academic achievement. " I cannot imagine," he wrote, " a higher object of ambition to him who aspires after a name in philosophy than to have his labours associated with the transactions of so illustrious a body " ; [1] and even fugitive polemical tracts carefully record the distinction after his name. From the time of the receipt of this intimation it was his fixed intention to visit France and to present a contribution in person. No opportunity occurred till the summer of 1838, when he made an extended stay. He preached on two Sundays in a French Protestant chapel to the most crowded and cultured audience its walls had ever held ; he read before the Institute a long and closely reasoned paper on the *Distinction, both in principle and effect, between a Legal Charity for the Relief of Indigence and a Legal Charity for the Relief of Disease ;* he basked in the favour of distinguished savants, who hailed him as a pioneer in the inter-relations of the moral and the economic ; he was made welcome in congenial homes not only in Paris itself, but all over the North and Midlands of France.

The writer knows of no other minister of the Church of Scotland who has had this double honour, from Oxford

[1] Hanna, vol. iv, p. 2

and from Paris. The young recruit to Evangelicalism who had so resolutely turned his back on the absorbing ambition for academic distinction had attained it in a degree far beyond what had been his rosiest dreams.

These were his last glimpses of that quiet realm the guidance of a Church in jeopardy was henceforth to absorb every energy and power he possessed.

Chapter Twelve

FIRST REVERSE IN THE LAW COURTS—
AUCHTERARDER

1838–39

While Dr. Chalmers was busily and happily immersed in the manifold activities of his campaign for Church Extension, the Church as a whole was manifestly responding to the stimulus of its recovered powers, under the two new measures. The Chapel Act not only strengthened the courts of the Church by an influx of eager members, it actually brought a chapel minister with the concurrence of all parties to the Moderator's chair in 1836 in the person of Dr. Norman MacLeod of St. Columba's, Glasgow, the father of the more famous Norman. He himself did not belong to the now dominant party that had made his election possible. It was as a representative of their opponents that he had been chosen, which indicated how completely the Moderates had now acquiesced in that Act. The Act anent Calls, the Veto Act, was working, on the whole, smoothly and satisfactorily, with hardly a single case of protest. But out of one protest in its first year a situation was slowly developing which was to become, to the surprise of even the best-informed, fraught with menace. This was the Auchterarder Case which, although related in detail in scores of histories and biographies, must be reviewed once more in order to make intelligible the conflict which led to the Disruption.

The initial circumstances are plain, and can be

plainly stated. In August 1834 the parish of Auchterarder became vacant through the death of its minister. The patron was the Earl of Kinnoul. At the meeting of the Presbytery in October a presentation was laid on the table in favour of a Mr. Robert Young of Dundee, a recent licentiate of the Church. By appointment of the Presbytery, Mr. Young preached on two Sundays in the parish church. Early in December a meeting of the congregation was duly summoned to moderate in a call. In a large meeting two parishioners came forward to sign the call, and with a third signature, by mandate, for the non-resident patron, the call was completed. In accordance with the Act anent Calls an opportunity was then given to the male heads of families to give in dissents. Two hundred and eighty-seven out of the 330 on the register came forward to do so. At a meeting held a fortnight later in accordance with the regulations of the Act, one of these dissents was withdrawn. The Presbytery had therefore before it a call signed by two parishioners, and a roll of dissent of male heads of families of 286.

Since the legal agent of the presentee had taken a technical exception to certain alleged defects in preparing the roll, and had appealed to the Synod, it was decided not to proceed immediately to a final judgment, but to await the issue of this appeal. The Synod in April dismissed it. From that decision a further appeal was taken to the General Assembly. There it was again dismissed, and the Presbytery was instructed to proceed in terms of the Act anent Calls. In July the Presbytery met and rejected Mr. Young " so far as regards his present presentation " to Auchterarder. Against this rejection, Mr. Young's legal agent protested and appealed to the Synod.

Up to this point the case can be paralleled in all essentials by a host of cases in the eighteenth century. In every one of these cases patron and presentee had accepted the considered verdict of the Church courts as final. It is at this point the new element enters. Instead of following up the second appeal to the Synod, intimation was made of an appeal to the civil courts. It had become obvious that there was no hope of getting the Church to ordain a presentee with two signatures to his call and seven-eighths of the parish vigorously and openly protesting against his settlement. It has been suggested that the presentee intended to take his case to the civil courts from the very beginning, having been convinced that the Act of 1834 was a stretching of the Church's prerogative beyond its legitimate bounds. This is manifestly unfair to him, for so long as he acted in conjunction with his first legal agent, he tacitly accepted that law as operative, appealing only against alleged deficiencies in its administration.

It is with the emergence of his new legal adviser, Mr. Hope, the Dean of Faculty, that his attitude alters. How the two came together is still obscure. Despite many darker hints, it is most likely that the Earl's factor saw a hope for the future of his young relative, the presentee, in the dissent which Mr. Hope had lodged in the Assembly of 1834, and in consequence called him in for consultation. This is confirmed by the first form of the appeal to the Court of Session which simply concerned Mr. Young's right to the possession and enjoyment of the stipend of Auchterarder, as being validly presented to that parish. It would have been possible for the Church, in spite of an adverse verdict in this case, to have ordained some one acceptable to the people to the charge of Auchterarder, the Church being responsible herself for

his support, thus disjoining, for the time, the benefic
and the cure.

But it speedily became clear to Mr. Hope that there
were complications which would prejudice this simple
issue. It was deliberately, therefore, amended to on
more complex and far-reaching, a declarator that the
Presbytery had failed in its duty by allowing the Veto
Act to control its proceedings. The exact words were :

" That the Presbytery of Auchterarder, and the
individual members thereof, as the only legal and com
petent court to that effect, by law constituted, were bound
and astricted to make trial of the qualifications of the
pursuer, and are still bound so to do ; and if, in thei
judgment, after due trial and examination, the pursue
is found qualified, the said Presbytery are bound and
astricted to receive and admit the pursuer as minister o
the church and parish of Auchterarder, according to law
That the rejection of the pursuer by the said Presbytery
as presentee foresaid, without making trial of his qualifi
cations in competent and legal form, and without an
objections having been stated to his qualifications, o
against his admission as minister of the church and parish
of Auchterarder, and expressly on the ground that the
said Presbytery cannot, and ought not to, do so, in respec
of a veto of the parishioners, was illegal and injurious t
the patrimonial rights of the pursuer, and contrary to th
provisions of the statutes and laws libelled : " [1]

The Court of Session, to put it bluntly, was asked t
decern that the Presbytery had acted wrongly in obeyin
the General Assembly, and must now, despite the Veto
proceed, after formal trials, to ordain and induct Mr

[1] C. Robertson, *Report of the Auchterarder Case*, vol. i, Appendix, p. 10

Young, in order that he might have the legal title to occupy the manse and glebe, and to collect the stipend.

It was not until the November of 1837 that the case was argued for three solid weeks before a bench of thirteen judges ; and it was not until the 8th of March 1838 that the sentence of the court was pronounced in favour of the pursuer by eight votes to five.

The two stout volumes in which are gathered together the whole speeches of the First Auchterarder Case, while they seem at first sight to present a formidable barrier of antiquarian technicalities, especially to one untrained in law, make even to-day interesting, if at times painful, reading. It would be difficult to find so many rash and unfounded statements about the Church history of Scotland gathered together in like compass anywhere. Bench and bar are almost equally responsible ; and generally speaking, where the parade of erudition is most ostentatious, the percentage of errors is highest. It would be a not unprofitable line of research to examine the various utterances in detail in the light of ascertained historical fact. But this byway ought not to attract us away from the main drift of the argument.

In the consideration of the fundamental question as to the right of the Church to regulate calls, as exercised in the passing of the challenged Act, the two main opposing approaches should at least be indicated. Did the Act restoring Patronages of 1712 leave room for any weight to be attached to the call, concurrence, or effective assent of the Christian people ? The Solicitor-General (Rutherfurd) had no difficulty in showing that the Church had always so considered it, and that both patrons and presentees had uniformly acquiesced in this interpretation. The records of the Assemblies and

Commissions showed that after 1712 scarcely a single year passed without cases in which they were asked to judge as to the sufficiency of a call. It was admitted that the tendency had been downwards, towards reducing the extent of the concurrency required as indispensable, but " in not one of these cases, down to the present day, has it ever been held, even by the party most adverse to the popular interests, that a Call could be dispensed with ; or that it was an irrelevant point of consideration, whether the Call was sufficient." [1] Further, principles governing the decision of these special cases had been abundantly confirmed by Assembly legislation. The Acts of 1736 and 1782 [2] directly affirming the necessity of the Call were perhaps not so important in this respect as those of 1753 and 1759 against simoniacal practices, both of which placed bargains with, and bribes to, a patron to secure a presentation, on a complete par with those to heritors and others " in order to obtain a concurrence with the said presentation or otherwise to procure a Call to a vacant parish " [3] as being equally just cause of deposition in the case of a minister or of deprivation of licence in the case of a probationer. " It humbly appears to me, therefore," thus he concluded this part of his argument, " that no one can review the history of the Church—her statutes—her course of decisions—and attend to her immemorial use and practice, and deny that the Call is an essential part of the process of induction ; and which it is peculiarly in the province of the Church to regulate." [4]

The other line of approach is best represented in the lengthy speech by the Dean of Faculty. These con-

[1] C. Robertson, *Report of the Auchterarder Case*, vol. i, p. 366
[2] See pp. 117–118
[3] *Report of the Auchterarder Case*, vol. i, p. 363   [4] *Ibid.*, p. 378

iderations of, and decisions as to, calls could, he contended, be dismissed as totally irrelevant. They were nothing more than the Church attempting to save her credit with the people after patronage had been re-enacted. Patronage in any adequate sense was totally incompatible with giving any substance to the call, as the Church was wise enough to recognize in earlier days.[1] To find the Church's relation to a presentee it was only necessary to look at the relevant statutes ; the Church could have no power outside of them ; beyond the definite prescriptions of statutes strictly interpreted the Church had no right to trespass. Now, the call, he asserted, is never mentioned or even hinted at in any existing statutes ; there it is uniformly laid down that the Presbytery is to make trial of the qualifications of the presentee. It cannot hand over its statutory obligations to another body, the " male heads of families." It cannot accept the decision of its superior court and stretch the well-understood term " qualifications " to cover such things as " acceptability to the parishioners." If it attempts to do so, it is evading its duty. When a presentation is laid upon its table, the Presbytery is bound and astricted to take the presentee on trials for ordination. It may, and indeed ought to, pay heed to relevant objections taken to his life or doctrine ; but it may not, and must not, pay heed to any dissents *qua* dissents, even when they demonstrate a notorious universal repugnance on the part of the people of the parish. Throughout the twenty-two years (1690–1712) during which patronage was abolished, the nominee of the heritors and elders

---

[1] Individual churchmen had done so, *e.g.* Principal Hill in the 1782 debate had argued that a call is incompatible with patronage, and therefore nugatory ; but although leader of the Moderate party, he failed to carry his motion. Dr. Cook, *Life of Hill*, pp. 114–56

could be disapproved by the congregation, but even then, he contended, against all the weight of evidence, simple disapproval was insufficient. Definite reasons had to be stated, and it was on the merits of these reasons, not on the prevalence of the opposition, that the Presbytery was to proceed. Even then, however, he asserted, relying on one conceivable interpretation of the words of statute against the construction of them on which ecclesiastical and civil authorities had hitherto proceeded with absolute uniformity, even this shadow of a right to a consultation on the part of the congregation had been obliterated by the statute restoring patronages ; for the words of that Act, " as . . . before the making of this Act," whatever they may mean, cannot refer to the years immediately before the making of the Act, but must relate to some earlier period when patronage had been the law of the land. On the basis, therefore, of statute law, and of statute law alone, and interpreted only by statute law, without reference to the historical circumstances of its evolution or to the practice of the Church, the Dean contended that the Church had exceeded its statutory authority in making the Veto law, and that in consequence, if anyone, such as his client, suffered damage to his interests or reputation through its action, the Presbytery must be told how incompetent its action had been, and that it should now proceed in the matter in the terms of the legal statutes from which it had its whole legal jurisdiction in the matter of collation.

Out of the mazes of the trial and the relevant pamphlets of the time, there can be caught the outlines of three very different pictures of the Church of Scotland.

The first is that of Dr. Chalmers, founded on his analogy of the planter calling in the Moravians, in the interests of his labourers—a picture of the State in Scotland, recognizing that it must make provision for the adequate moral and religious instruction of its citizens, entrusting this duty to a Church which was from the beginning, and remains, entirely self-determining in regard to the gospel to be preached, its control of the men who are to preach it, its whole organization of its own resources and the resources entrusted to it. Such a Church may, and did, pay for State privilege and support, not only with its services, but by accepting certain agreed restrictions in the destination of funds provided for it. But essentially it is a Church free of secular control in its spiritual affairs, free to order its life and activities by the Word of God and under the headship of Christ, that has freely made this compact with the State. " She did not make over her liberties to the State at the time when she entered into fellowship with it ; she only made over her services." [1]

The second is that of the Dean of Faculty, at least in his pleadings. In the light of other utterances, it is well to remember that he spoke then as an advocate.[2] There he has given us the picture of the State in Scotland determining in 1560 to replace the proved inefficiency of the Papal Church by something new and better. " A new and vigorous—a young and untried fabric, full of energy and power, was created by the State, in the room of that which the State overturned and abolished. I say *created*—for it was devised, formed, moulded, instituted, and created wholly, and of new, by the State." [3] On this view any idea of a compact is absurd. The Church of Scotland was formed, instituted, established, created by

[1] Hanna, vol. iv, p. 108

[2] In any estimate of his real views, account must be taken of his private letter to Dr. Chalmers on the Church's independence and privileges being threatened by the Royal Commission of Enquiry. *Vide* Hanna, vol. iii, pp. 485–86   [3] *Report of the Auchterarder Case*, vol. i, p. 183

the State ; it is " wholly of statutory creation, of statutory authority, and statutory jurisdiction. Its powers are the result of special statutory grant." [1] And any power it ventures to claim beyond the verge of those specifically conveyed is a hallucination of grandeur on the part of ecclesiastics. The talk of a power " to legislate and regulate bestowed on the Church by its great spiritual Head . . . is the most pernicious error by which the blessed truths of Christianity can be perverted." [2] This is essentially the Nazi theory of the Church as an organ of the State, controlled and directed at all points and in all details by the supreme executive authority for its own ends.

The third picture may here be connected with the name of the advocate who immediately followed the Dean—Rutherfurd, the Solicitor-General. It is that of a Church which, despite the State, and in face of its continued and determined hostility, had been, long before 1560, manifesting a vigorous life, and shaping its own confession, worship, and institutions. This living Church received a certain recognition in 1560, and its formal establishment in 1567. But long before that establishment it had been functioning freely in Scotland. Its supreme court, the General Assembly, had been meeting much more frequently than at any later date, and transacting business even more varied, as was natural in those days of transition. The statutes do not " create, but recognize an established order of things." [3] All the statutes refer to an existing discipline, and are to be read in the light of it. Even that portion of the Acts of 1592, which gave the first statutory recognition of the court of the Presbytery, was setting its seal on an organ

[1] *Report of the Auchterarder Case*, vol. i, p. 222   [2] *Ibid.*, p. 184
[3] *Ibid.*, p. 352

of the Church which had been functioning for a dozen years, and expressly declares that in regard to collation and ecclesiastical matters within their bounds these Presbyteries are to "put order . . . according to the discipline of the Kirk." [1] Therefore—and this is the gist of his major contention—"to see what it is that the Parliament approved and ratified, your Lordships must look to the practice of the Church herself, and to her records, and must find in her statute books and in her practice the more exact definition and explanation of that constitution which the Parliament generally, and by reference, sanctioned and ratified." [2]

Dr. Chalmers' picture, though attractive, and though anticipating in a remarkable way the post-1929 constitution of the Church, is not free from the suspicion of being an idealistic construction, loosely attached to the facts of history. The Dean of Faculty's is a perverse novelty which has been homologated by no churchman of any note within the Church, before or since, though, perforce, acquiesced in, at least in its implications, by some for a time, and hailed with delight by some of the Voluntaries outside who found in it a confirmation of their own worst suspicions. The Solicitor-General's, as a description of the actual position of the Church as established in 1838, has substantially stood the test of a century of controversy and research.

Why, then, was it that the Dean of Faculty's plea commended itself to a majority of Scottish judges ? There were many contributory factors, such as the previous commitments of their Lordships, but on reading the pleadings and the verdicts in their totality, the main one seems to have been the adroit handling by the Dean of one specific aspect of the whole problem. The Procurator

[1] *Report of the Auchterarder Case*, vol. i, p. 350   [2] *Ibid.*, p. 352

of the Church had contended that the form of the action really asked the Court of Session to pronounce a judgment which it could not enforce. " In one word," said he, " I ask your Lordships, could the court charge us—an ecclesiastical court—to find the presentee qualified for the office, and consequently to induct him into it ? Or failing of our doing so, could you do it yourselves ? " [1] Matters were heading straight for a conflict between the civil and ecclesiastical judicatories.

In dealing with this issue the Dean showed consummate address and marked psychological skill. He treated this as a blustering declaration of defiance against the supremacy of the law. Triumphantly he built up before the court a most glowing picture of its own dignities and prerogatives. The hard facts of Scottish history not affording a broad enough canvas, he skilfully enlarged it by imported patches from other lands. In particular, he made one significant addition by bringing in the United States of America to exhibit the scope of the authority of judicial determination.

" When the federal union of the United States of America was formed, with a common legislature for general purposes, but each state retaining its separate rights and laws and customs, and individual executives and legislatures, the problem at once arose, how the probable encroachments by the general legislature on the rights of individual states might be prevented or checked. The wisdom of Washington and Hamilton solved the problem. They proposed that the Supreme Court of the whole states, as the ultimate resort of all conflicting interests—the Court of Law of the Union—should decide the question, even as to the competence and legality of

[1] *Report of the Auchterarder Case*, vol. i, p. 101

the acts of the supreme legislature. The result has proved the wisdom of the recommendation. In the wildest outbreaks of American democracy, in the fiercest conflict of parties and the most violent collision of passions, fostered by provincial jealousies and embittered by provincial interests, when the acts of Congress have been challenged as unconstitutional, as incompetent, because inconsistent with the fundamental law of the Union, the stern and unbending decisions of the court of law have silenced the contentions of that great republic, and awed by the majesty of the law, their mighty parties have retired in submission from the political objects which the Court told them could not be legally carried through." [1]

As a digression, which is not really a digression since it has much light to shed on this whole conflict from start to finish, it may be said that had the Dean been able to foresee later happenings, he might not have been so unqualified in his panegyric. From 1935 to 1937 President Roosevelt's main difficulties were with this Supreme Court. It threw out one constituent part after another of the New Deal, generally on the ground that factories, stores, and farms belonged to the department of *intra*-state commerce, and it was only with *inter*-state matters the Federal Government could deal. The National Industry Recovery Act and the Agricultural Adjustment Administration were the two main measures which it disallowed. Any federal economic law seemed banned. But when it had achieved this result, the majority of the court, having tasted blood, proceeded to throw out a State minimum-wage law. " The result was staggering ; nobody could legislate on wages and

[1] *Report of the Auchterarder Case,* vol. i, pp. 263-64

hours." People began to talk of the " nine old men " of the Court, to hint openly at " arterial hardening," to demand a drastic reconstitution. Its defenders could hardly continue to assert " that the processes of the Court were impersonal and unpolitical, an Olympian matching of the text of an Act with the text of the constitution." The President's intimation of a " clarifying amendment " evoked general approval. This and the consequent change of mind in some, and the resignation and replacement of others, gradually eased the tension, and the New Deal went through, if not without amendment, yet on the whole unimpaired. But the Supreme Court itself had not passed through the ordeal so unscathed. One " mighty party " had not " retired in submission from the political objects which the Court told them could not be legally carried through." [1]

Returning to the point at which this digression started, by means of the American pseudo-parallel the Dean had built up in the minds of the bench a picture of themselves as of right adjudicating on matters that had never before come within their jurisdiction, matters with which their predecessors had more than once expressly refused to meddle—as set up in fact to vindicate sound conservative law against the incipient radicalism and unconcealed contempt of authority manifested by a Church captured for the moment by the high-fliers, who must be disciplined in time lest worse should follow. Hence we find his own father, the Lord President, following his lead, and forsaking the dubious ground of Court of Session precedents, equating the Court to quite dissimilar courts in France and in England, and preening himself in the con-

---

[1] For an accessible account of the whole episode, v. F. L. Allen, *Since Yesterday*, pp. 163–64, 220–21, 250–51.

templation of an unlimited jurisdiction. If these Courts can deal with courts-martial, is not the Court of Session empowered to deal with courts ecclesiastical? Here and there, throughout the other deliverances of the majority, there are distinct traces of the same feeling. It was in this psychological climate that the Court delivered its verdict of declarator, and was led to hint not obscurely that if the Church refused to acquiesce, the Court would find means to make its decision effective. Relying largely on false analogies, the Court of Session had definitely overstepped its hitherto recognized bounds.

It was on the 8th of March, 1838, that the verdict was given. At its first meeting thereafter Mr. Young presented himself before the Presbytery of Auchterarder, and in accordance with the declarator, demanded to be taken on trials for ordination forthwith. The Presbytery decided to refer the whole matter to the synod, where- upon Mr. Young handed in a notarial protest, " by which he held the members of the Presbytery, conjointly and severally, liable to him in damages " [1] for refusing to act on the decision.

The way of appeal to the House of Lords was still open, and when the General Assembly met it resolved unanimously to take that way, but lest the step should be interpreted as an acknowledgment of jurisdiction in these matters, it first of all passed a resolution on the subject of spiritual independence. Dr. Chalmers was not a member of Assembly, and the motion was moved by Mr. Buchanan, who afterwards became the historian of the Ten Years' Conflict from the Free Church side. In the language of the second part of the motion there are traces of the fact that the Church, in its celebration of the bicentenary of the National Covenant, had been

[1] Buchanan, *Ten Years' Conflict*, vol. i, p. 401

vividly recalling the Covenanters ; and this language had come to stay. It was worded thus :

" That the General Assembly of this Church, while they unqualifiedly acknowledge the exclusive jurisdiction of the Civil Courts, in regard to the civil rights and emoluments secured by law to the Church, and the ministers thereof, and will ever give and inculcate obedience to their decisions thereanent ; do resolve that, as it is declared in the Confession of Faith of this national Established Church that ' the Lord Jesus Christ as King and Head of the Church, hath therein appointed a government in the hands of Church officers distinct from the civil magistrate,' and that in all matters touching the doctrine, government, and discipline of the Church, her judicatories possess an exclusive jurisdiction founded on the Word of God, which ' power Ecclesiastical (in the words of the Second Book of Discipline) flows from God and the Mediator, Jesus Christ, and is spiritual, not having a temporal head on earth but only Christ, the only spiritual King and Governor of his Kirk.' And they do farther resolve that this spiritual jurisdiction and the supremacy and sole Headship of the Lord Jesus Christ, on which it depends—they will assert, and at all hazards defend, by the help and blessing of that great God who, in the days of old, enabled their fathers, amid manifold persecutions, to maintain a testimony, even to the death, for Christ's kingdom and crown. And, finally, that they will firmly enforce submission to the same upon the office-bearers and ministers of this Church, by the execution of her laws, in the exercise of the ecclesiastical authority wherewith they are invested." [1]

The resolution was carried by 183 to 142, against a

[1] *Acts of the General Assembly, 1638–1843*, p. 1085

motion which incorporated a similar doctrine but was prepared to grant wider bounds to the civil courts in matters which they considered bore on civil and temporal rights.

It is worth while recalling that it was after the verdict of the Court of Session and before the meeting of Assembly that Dr. Chalmers delivered to electrified audiences in London those lectures on Establishment that were dealt with in a previous chapter. Some sentences acquire a new ring in this context : " We own no head of the Church but the Lord Jesus Christ." Establishment had been entered into " without the slightest infringement of the spiritual prerogatives of the Church, or the ecclesiastical independence of her clergymen." " External force might make an obnoxious individual the holder of a benefice ; but there is no external force in these realms that can make him a minister of the Church of Scotland." The note sounded by Chalmers in London is at least as uncompromising as that which rang from the Assembly in Edinburgh.

It was more than a year after the Scottish decision before the appeal in the Auchterarder case was heard in the House of Lords before Lord Brougham, a past Lord Chancellor, and Lord Cottenham, who then held that office. The speeches before their lordships are not given in Mr. Robertson's report, which merely states that " as the arguments maintained from both sides of the Bar were almost identical with those maintained in the Court of Session, it is unnecessary to repeat them here." [1] But fortunately the judgments, both highly unfavourable to the Church, are given in extenso. That of Lord Brougham is almost incredible. It is at once superficial, jaunty, and pontifical. He could not see what all the fuss was about.

[1] *Report of the Auchterarder Case*, vol. ii, Supplement, p. 1

How the Scottish bench found difficulties and was so nearly equally divided he could not fathom. The case was simple in the extreme. The Church was interfering with the plain rights of patrons. He could not refrain from picturing what his venerable relative, Dr. Robertson, would have thought of the case, " the contempt, the scorn, the indignation " [1] with which he would have met such pretensions. " Male heads of families," forsooth. " Shall nothing be said of women in the matter of salvation, and in the administration of the Church to which they belong? We are living under the Christian and not the Mahomedan law." [2] And why not lodgers? Why not a respectable scholar, more learned than all the parish together? The Call? May not a mere presentation be a Call? " Why may not the patron's connection with the parish in respect of that advowson be held to be sufficient for the purposes of giving a Call?" [3] Take an analogous instance. Take the coronation. " It is a decent and convenient solemnity to present the Sovereign to the people, and the people are supposed to take part in the choice—a part, however, so immaterial that, if they were all with one voice to reject, the coronation would be just as good, would go on exactly in the same way, and the rejection or recalcitration of the assembled people would have no more weight than the recalcitration of the champion's horse in Westminster Hall during the festival attending the great solemnity. It is an obsolete right, which has not within the time of known history been exercised by any people." [4]

Lord Brougham's verdict may have its defenders, but the reasons for it are a mixture of irritating irrelevancies, fancied analogies, non-existent cases, wrapped up in a

[1] *Report of the Auchterarder Case*, vol. ii, Supplement, p. 26
[2] *Ibid.*, p. 30   [3] *Ibid.*, p. 35   [4] *Ibid.*, p. 36

ush of sentiment and threats. There were times when
ne might have supposed that the judgment, since it was
ot written, must have been mangled by an imperfect
nd indiscreet reporter, but no ! There was at the end
n inset page with a Notice to Publishers : " The
peeches contained in these volumes, which have been
evised by the judges and counsel for this work, are copy-
ight." And this was the same Lord Brougham who
ad congratulated the General Assembly five years
arlier on its wisdom in passing the Act anent Calls.
f this verdict were a main element in assessing Lord
rougham's legal attainments, it certainly would give
oint to Daniel O'Connell's gibe that " if he had known
little of law, he would have known a little of every-
hing." [1] A contemporary sketch of Lord Brougham
ncludes this : " Marvellous things are related concerning
ord Brougham's quickness in doing any thing, as well
s his rare faculty in being able to do all things at the
ame time. We have heard that he can read, so as to
naster perfectly, the contents of two quarto volumes in
ne hour—' that he can despatch three letters, three
ewspapers, three bottles of wine, and three applicants for
vings, in a quarter of an hour.' " [2] It is only charitable
o suppose that it was one fragment of such an over-
rowded quarter of an hour that he devoted to the
onsideration of the Auchterarder case.

Lord Cottenham's verdict, which was just as un-
esitating and unfavourable, was quite on another plane.
Though, inevitably, his thoughts of the rights of patrons
vere moulded by English conditions, he had certainly
lone his best to master the Scottish statutes. But he
onfined himself to these ; and having found what he

[1] J. B. S., *Random Recollections and Impressions*, p. 91
[2] W. Jones, *Biographical Sketches of the Reform Ministers*, p. 71

imagined to be an authoritative contemporary interpretation of the earliest movement towards the first
statute of 1567, which unfortunately had no connection
with it save that of date—an interpretation which seemed
to confine the Church's whole demand and the State's
whole concession to an ecclesiastical examination of the
literature, life, and good morals of the presentee—he was
able to produce, in the light of this, a highly plausible
and consistent résumé and analysis of subsequent statutes
which, if sound, would have proved that the Church had
been exceeding its power at practically every period of its
history. In form and substance, however, it was certainly
much more dignified and more worthy of the occasion.
But its effect was not only to destroy the Act anent Calls,
but to preclude the Church of Scotland from taking into
account in any shape or form the reaction of a parish to
its presentee—from taking into account anything but
general professional qualifications.

These verdicts were pronounced on the 4th of May
and the Assembly was to meet on the 16th. During the
winter, while the Court of Session verdict was all that
was before the Church, Dr. Chalmers more than once
expressed himself in favour of a repeal of the Act anent
Calls, to which he had never been thirled as the only
expression of the principle of Non-intrusion. He was
willing to fall back on his early plan of the Assembly,
through a series of decisions in individual cases, on what
constituted an adequate concurrence to justify the
formation of the pastoral relation, gradually reinstating
and strengthening the Call. But now, in May, he found
the ground cut away from his feet. He seems to have
tried to make himself believe that only the confirmation
of the verdict of the Court of Session mattered, but he
could not ignore the *dicta* of the judges, the grounds behind

their verdict. If these grounds acquired any legal validity, as well they might, no such possibility was left to the Assembly. A novel interpretation of the old statutes now existed in which the Church simply could not acquiesce. So, in some haste and heat, he drafted a motion to meet the new situation. Here are his words, as recorded in a contemporary report of the debate, and though they are not to be found in the revised version published as *The Substance of a Speech*, they bear the marks of a genuine utterance.

" The motion which I have the honour to submit was concocted by myself. It was never out of my hands except for a day or two. How many saw it, or who they are, with two or three exceptions, I am entirely ignorant. My object in giving it out of my own hand was my anxiousness to have my views put in the practical shape of a motion by those better acquainted with such forms than I am. It was returned in a right shape and with no change of substance. If there was any change it was in this, that it came back with a more mild and conciliatory complexion than, with my most strenuous endeavours, I had been enabled to give it." [1]

This disposes of Dr. Bryce's suggestion that the motion had been put into the hands of Dr. Chalmers by the extreme anti-patronage group, and that he was arguing a case that was not his own in what Dr. Bryce calls " the most strange and heterogeneous harangue that ever, perhaps, fell on the ears of a Church court." [2]

The motion is so important that it must be given in full.

[1] *Auchterarder Case : Report of the Debate, etc.* (Dundee, Frederic Shaw), p. 19

[2] J. Bryce, *Ten Years of the Church of Scotland*, vol. i, p. 94

" The General Assembly having heard the report of the procurator on the Auchterarder case, and considered the judgment of the House of Lords affirming the decision of the Court of Session, and being satisfied that, by the said judgment, all questions of civil right, so far as the Presbytery of Auchterarder is concerned, are substantially decided, do now, in accordance with the uniform practice of this Church, and the resolution of last General Assembly ever to give and inculcate implicit obedience to the decisions of civil courts in regard to the civil rights and emoluments secured by law to the Church, instruct the said Presbytery to offer no farther resistance to the claims of Mr. Young or the patron to the emoluments of the benefice of Auchterarder, and to refrain from claiming the *jus devolutum*, or any other civil right or privilege connected with the said benefice.

" And whereas the principle of Non-intrusion is one coeval with the Reformed Kirk of Scotland, and forms an integral part of its constitution, embodied in its standards, and declared in various Acts of Assembly, the General Assembly resolves that this principle cannot be abandoned, and that no presentee shall be forced on any parish contrary to the will of the congregation.

" And whereas, by the decision above referred to, it appears that when this principle is carried into effect, in any parish, the legal provision for the sustentation of the ministry in that parish may be thereby suspended, the General Assembly, being deeply impressed with the unhappy consequences that must arise from any collision between the civil and ecclesiastical authorities, and holding it to be their duty to use every means in their power, not involving any dereliction of the principles and fundamental laws of their constitution, to prevent such unfortunate results, do therefore appoint a committee for the purpose of considering in what way the privileges of a National Establishment, and the harmony between Church and State, may remain unimpaired, with instructions to confer with the government of the country, if they shall see cause." [1]

The presupposition of his motion was therefore that since there has arisen through this verdict and its foundations an intrusion by a civil court into the sphere of a co-ordinate ecclesiastical court through unexpected interpretations of former statutes, the only remedy is for the legislature to intervene, the Church meanwhile placing no barrier in the way of the civil consequences of the decisions of the civil courts.

The official motion of the party opposing was tabled by Dr. Cook. The gist of it was that the Church must now acknowledge the Veto Act illegal, and revert to her practice before 1834 as though the Act had never been, the Presbytery making trial of the qualifications of presentees and considering all relevant objections made to them as in the past. Further, he was willing to append to his motion, that all ministers presented to kirks be tried as to whether they are qualified for the places to which they are appointed, in addition to their ordinary trials. Now, this was not unlike the course of action which Dr. Chalmers had favoured up to the 4th of May, but which, he then discovered, was, if the legal pronouncements of Lords Brougham and Cottenham were to regulate future decisions, to return to a course quite as illegal as procedure under the Veto Act. There was a third motion before the Assembly. All that need be said of it is that it was irenical in intention, striving to steer a course midway, but actually nearer to Dr. Cook than to Dr. Chalmers.

[1] *Auchterarder Case: Report of the Debate, etc.*, pp. 5, 6

Though Dr. Chalmers' speech in support of his motion seems brief in comparison with any of the speeches by advocates in the Court of Session, it occupied three hours in delivery. And alike in its frank and full statement of the gravity of the issues, its unsparing exposure of the fallacies of the recent judgments, its clear exposition of the essential differences between the practices of ordination and induction in Scotland and England, and its undismayed reassertion of the essential liberties and spiritual independence of the Church, it is a masterpiece.

A few extracts may serve to indicate its quality and its line of argument.

" We refrain from aught that touches their department ; and all we ask is that they shall refrain from what touches upon ours. After the sentence they have given forth, we are not asking at their hand the temporalities of the benefice of Auchterarder : but they are requiring at ours that we shall ordain for that benefice a man on whom by the laws of the Church and on our views of what is best for the good of Christianity we must refuse to confer that privilege. After this, which of the two parties, we ask, is it that makes encroachment on the domain of the other ; or which of them is chargeable with taking hold of a heterogeneous ingredient, and dragging it into their own category ? " [1]

" I hold it to be quite an axiom—a first and elementary truth—that we are never in any instance, to depart from the obligations which lie upon us as a Christian church, for the sake either of obtaining or perpetuating the privileges which belong to us as an Established church." [2]

[1] *Substance of a Speech . . . on the Case of Auchterarder*, 1839, pp. 12, 13
[2] *Ibid.*, p. 16

" We should be degraded far below the level of the sister Church [of England], if we remain in connection with the State, and submit to their new ordinance, or, if you will, to this new interpretation of their old ordinances." [1]

" If we succeed in demonstrating of this sentence that altogether it is grounded upon error, is it too much to hope of an enlightened legislature, that it will grant a new law which might correct the interpretation, or rather misinterpretation, that has been made of their old ones." [2]

" I would take the verdict of a congregation, just as I take the verdict of a jury, without reasons." [3]

It was, says Dr. Hanna, " a great and exhausting effort "—so exhausting, indeed, that it was nearly his final speech, as this entry in the diary of a friend serves to indicate. " Heard Dr. Chalmers speak nearly three hours with great power. At the conclusion of his speech, he went to the vestry and lay down—his physical energies greatly prostrated. Was with him, and felt much alarmed for the result. . . . His friends were, in the evening, very anxious about him. The great exertion and fatigue he had encountered, and his intense earnestness in delivering his powerful and impressive speech, had been, in fact, too much for his physical strength." [4] Was it of this speech, or of some other, that Francis Jeffrey is recorded to have said, " He buried his adversaries under the fragments of burning mountains " ? [5]

Dr. Chalmers was not present at two in the morning to vote for his own motion, but it was carried by a

[1] *Substance of a Speech . . . on the Case of Auchterarder*, 1839, p. 22
[2] *Ibid.*, p. 27   [3] *Ibid.*, p. 33
[4] J. Anderson, *Reminiscences of Thomas Chalmers, etc.*, p. 274
[5] Rainy and MacKenzie, *Life of Cunningham*, p. 64

majority of 49 (204–155). In terms of this decision, a strong committee was appointed to negotiate with the government, and though two of the nominees, Dr. Cook and the young Earl of Dalhousie, refused nomination, one quietly, and the other dramatically, it immediately set to work with what seemed a bright prospect of a successful issue.

CHAPTER THIRTEEN

COMPLICATIONS FROM LETHENDY

1838–39

BEFORE the formal appeal to government came to be fully pressed by the committee appointed for that purpose, the situation was to be further complicated by the final stages of another case. This was the disputed succession to the united parishes of Lethendy and Kinloch, commonly known as the Lethendy Case, one much more involved in its elements than that of Auchterarder.

The minister of Lethendy finding himself, by reason of age and infirmity, no longer able in any sense to perform his duties, suggested an assistant and successor. The patron was the Crown. The Rev. Thomas Clark, a probationer who had preached for a short period in the church, had proved so welcome a relief to the ministrations of the enfeebled incumbent, that in 1835 a petition to the Crown in his favour was forwarded with the large signature, for this sparse district, of 108 parishioners. There being no actual vacancy, a regular deed of presentation could not be issued. But, following the normal procedure, a letter of presentation or sign-manual conveyed the royal assent to the settlement asked for, with the further provision that upon the death of the senior minister Mr. Clark was to be entitled to the united stipend " in the same manner as if he had been presented upon the vacancy of the said united parishes." [1]

The Presbytery of Dunkeld, with all the documents

[1] C. G. Robertson, *Report, etc., in the Lethendy Case*, p. 2

before it, decided to proceed. After Mr. Clark had preached in both places by its appointment (this being after a further four months' experience of his ministry), a meeting was held for moderation in a call. It was signed by 22 parishioners. On dissents being called for 53 male heads of families, being a considerable majority of the 89 on the register, recorded their dissents. At a later meeting, none being withdrawn, the Presbytery rejected the presentee. It throws a somewhat revealing light on the impression made by Mr. Clark, that of the 53 who now recorded their dissent, 40 had signed the original petition in his favour. Appeal was taken to the synod and thence to the General Assembly; but in vain. By the decision of June 1, 1836, it seemed as though Lethendy had heard the last of Mr. Clark as minister.

But in January 1837 the old minister died. There was now a regular vacancy. Two steps were taken. Mr. Clark, on the one hand, raised an action in the Court of Session, claiming that the Presbytery, despite his rejection under the Veto Law, was now bound and astricted to take him on trials for ordination. The Crown, on the other hand, while this action was pending, issued a formal presentation in favour of the Rev. Andrew Kessen. On receipt of this the Presbytery sustained the presentation, appointed Mr. Kessen to preach in both churches, and fixed a day for moderation in a call. There being an adequate call, and no Veto, the Presbytery was prepared to proceed to his trials and settlement, when Mr. Clark obtained an interim interdict from the Court of Session against their giving effect " to the alleged presentation in favour of Mr. Kessen." [1]

After various transactions in the Presbytery, in the course of which Mr. Kessen's trials for ordination were

[1] C. G. Robertson, *Report, etc., in the Lethendy Case*, p. 7

pointed, heard, and sustained, and after appeals to the
[S]nod, the whole situation was referred to the General
[As]sembly of 1838, which, through its Commission, after
[aff]irming that " admission to the pastoral charge of a
[pa]rish and congregation is entirely an ecclesiastical act," [1]
[or]dered the Presbytery to proceed to his ordination
[u]pon the call in his favour, according to the rules of
[th]e Church." [2] This motion was carried with only two
[dis]senting voices. Not one party alone but the great bulk
[of] the other denied, at this time, the authority of the
[Co]urt of Session to intervene by interdict in a Presbytery's
[ex]ercise of its function as a spiritual court. Just a year
[be]fore, the Moderates had been united, in a somewhat
[sim]ilar case, that of the parish of Cadder in the Presbytery
[of] Glasgow, where there were two ministers claiming the
[pr]esentation, and the one rejected by the Presbytery had
[ob]tained what he averred to be an interdict from the
[Co]urt of Session against the Presbytery's proceeding to
[th]e ordination of his rival until a civil action as to the
[va]lidity of the presentation had been tried. In the
[Pr]esbytery, Principal MacFarlane of Glasgow had said,
[" H]ad it been an interdict, as it was said to be, it could
[no]t prevent the Presbytery from carrying their previous
[re]solution into effect. No man had a greater respect for
[th]e judges of the land than he had ; but he could not
[for]get that he was a minister of the Church of Scotland,
[wh]ich acknowledged no other head than the Lord Jesus
[Ch]rist, and which disallowed all interference with their
[ec]clesiastical proceedings." [3] And it had been on the
[mo]tion of Dr. Cook himself that the Presbytery was
[in]structed to proceed. This, of course, was before the
[de]cision in the Auchterarder case, but this Commission

[1] C. G. Robertson, *Report, etc.*, in the *Lethendy Case*, p. 12
[2] *Ibid.*, p. 12   [3] *Scottish Guardian*, May 1837

of Assembly, shortly after that decision, was almost unanimous in the case of Lethendy as the Assembly its« had been earlier in the case of Cadder.

Not for one moment, however, did the Commissior decision deter or baffle Mr. Clark and his astute advise the Dean of Faculty. The old interdict was no long adequate. It had inhibited the Presbytery from pr ceeding on an alleged presentation. A fresh one w devised and secured. This interdicted Mr. Kessen fro presenting himself for induction, and the Presbytery, a body and as individuals, " from inducting the sa Rev. Andrew Kessen upon the pretence of the alleg« call in his favour, or on any other ground whatever.' Faced with this formidable document the Presbyte referred the case to the August Commission. At th meeting, by 52 votes to 6, it was decided that this bei a purely spiritual act in regard to which the civil cour had no authority, the Presbytery of Dunkeld ought proceed to the ordination and induction without dela Two of the notable speeches in favour of this course we made by leaders of the Moderate party. It was furth resolved that, should Mr. Clark persist in his action, libel should be prepared charging him with offenc against the doctrine of the spiritual independence of tl Church, and in violation of the vows of obedience take on his licence as a preacher of the gospel.

When the Presbytery met in August a new obstac was thrown in its path. This was a letter from the De; of Faculty, who, it should be noted, had been one of tl minority of six. It was not only its threats that ma« it menacing ; it was its further development of the id« of the Church of Scotland as a creature of statute. Di consequences would fall on the Presbytery if it obey«

[1] Robertson, *Lethendy Case*, p. 13

the Commission of Assembly, and disobeyed the Court of Session. To fancy themselves immune was to live in a fool's paradise : " the members of Presbytery will most infallibly be committed to prison, and most justly, for an offence of the most grave nature, and the more aggravated in proportion to the status of the parties by whom it is committed." [1] The two new points which emerge in his notion of the Church are that the Commission of Assembly has no authority whatsoever, not being mentioned in any statute, and that the Church of Scotland had no control over its own admission to membership, " every man in this country who adheres to its doctrines is entitled to be a member of the established church." [2] This letter was not without effect. It shook the confidence and constancy of some of the members. So much so, that it was only by the casting-vote of the Moderator that the Presbytery proceeded to set a day for Mr. Kessen's admission.

On the appointed day, 13th September, the Presbytery met at Lethendy for the ordination and induction, which was duly carried through. Its significance was enhanced by the solemn and weighty address of the senior member of the Presbytery, which dealt with the threats and intimidations of the letter in a spirit of high resolve, referring to it as an insult " never offered to any lawfully constituted court since the worst days of the Charleses and the Jameses." [3]

Two months later Mr. Clark initiated an action against Mr. Kessen and the Presbytery for breach of

[1] Buchanan, *Ten Years' Conflict*, vol. ii, p. 8   [2] *Ibid.*, p. 9
[5] *Ibid.*, p. 11. Did the speaker know how closely he was reproducing Mr. Hope's own language about the Royal Commission—" an attempt not paralleled, I think, by anything in the reigns of James or Charles I "? Hanna, vol. iii, p. 485

interdict. The issue was confined to this point. There was no plea, as there might have been a little later, that the ordination should be annulled. And, with the Auchterarder decision now fully confirmed, there could be little dubiety as to the technical breach of an interdict. Lord Moncrieff, indeed, contended with vigour and point against the conclusion, but even Lord Cockburn was forced to join the majority in finding it proven. "But though," he concluded, "I cannot avoid this result, I must add that, considering the circumstances, and without prejudging or anticipating any repetition of the offence, and believing, as I do, that a conscientious, though erroneous, feeling of right and of duty entered largely into their motive, I can recollect no breach of interdict which had a stronger claim to be leniently dealt with." [1]

The Court of Session having decided that both Mr. Kessen and the Presbytery had to be punished, and having, by a narrow majority, decided that this must take the form of a solemn public censure, the final scenes of this strange case took place on the 12th and 14th of June, 1839. On the first day both Mr. Kessen and the Presbytery of Dunkeld appeared, accompanied by a few of the leading ministers of Edinburgh, who desired to lend support to their brethren by their presence. In answer to a request from the Lord President for an explanation of their conduct, the briefest of answers were read and handed in. That of the Presbytery, read by its senior minister, is worthy of record.

"My Lords, we appear in obedience to the citation of your Lordships, inasmuch as we hold it to be the duty of all subjects to render their personal compearance when

[1] Robertson, *Lethendy Case*, p. 84

cited by the civil courts : and being deeply impressed with the obligation of giving all honour and reverence to the judges of the land, we disclaim any intention of disrespect to the Court in what we have done. But, in ordaining to the office of the holy ministry, and in admitting to the pastoral charge, to which, in our proceedings complained of, we strictly limited ourselves, we acted in obedience to the superior Church judicatories, to which in matters spiritual we are subordinate, and to which at ordination we vowed obedience." [1]

On the second day of their citation the formal judgment was read, and then the Lord President continued :

" In obedience to the orders which I have received from the Court, I have, in the most solemn and emphatic terms, to pronounce upon you the solemn censure of the Court : and, in doing so, I am also directed by the Court to signify that it was not without considerable difficulty their Lordships brought themselves to adopt this lenient measure : but they desired me to state that if you, or any other Presbytery of the Church, were ever brought before them again under similar circumstances, you and they will be dealt with in a very different manner. The ordinary punishment for disobedience to the law by a breach of interdict is imprisonment ; and I am directed to say, that if a case like this present should occur again, that punishment will be resorted to ; and the length of the imprisonment will depend entirely on the heinousness of the offence committed. But I hope and trust that such a case never will occur again ; and therefore you are to consider yourselves as solemnly censured and rebuked accordingly." [2]

[1] Buchanan, *Ten Years' Conflict*, vol. ii, p. 15
[2] Robertson, *Lethendy Case*, pp. 210–11

It would have been wiser and more dignified to have stopped at this point, but the learned judge could not resist the temptation to continue, and to lecture the Church through the Presbytery before him. After a sound elementary legal exposition of the nature of interdict, he, unfortunately, went on to a much less trustworthy exposition of the constitution and history of the Church of Scotland. One paragraph deserves citation.

" As for those ministers of the Church whose conscience cannot submit to the law so long as it remains the law, I am afraid nothing remains for those ministers but to retire from the Established Church. It is impossible that they should remain ministers of the Established Church, and yet reject the law by which they have become an Established Church. That great and good man,[1] Ebenezer Erskine, a hundred years ago, did not so think. He did not resist the law—he did not think that he could remain a member of the Established Church if he did not submit to the law ; and as he did not think that he could conscientiously submit to the law, he withdrew from the Church and founded the Secession. No man, I am sure, will regret more than I shall do, if that shall be the fate of some distinguished members of the Church ; but, alas ! I see no remedy. Either they must submit to the law, or they must retire from the Church."[2]

It would hardly be possible to compress more glaring mistakes about Ebenezer Erskine into a similar compass. What law did he protest against ? There was no clash with civil law in the whole process.

[1] This judgment of his lordship is on a par with Lord Brougham's concern for women's suffrage.   [2] Robertson, *Lethendy Case*, p. 217

It was against a new law of the Church, passed by the prevailing party, and the general legislation of that prevailing party, that he raised his protest. Nor did he secede until he and the others had been expelled. And they did not withdraw from their churches and manses. They kept them for seven years, until they were deposed by formal process. To press home the parallel of Ebenezer Erskine should have meant that it was incumbent on Dr. Cook and his party to withdraw from a Church in which they could not conscientiously fall in with one definite Act and the whole trend of the legislation of the prevailing party. Than the action of that " great and good man, Ebenezer Erskine," nothing could have been more irrelevant to his lordship's purpose.

The broad result, however, of the Lethendy case was this : that where the issues were imperfectly understood, particularly in England, it was possible to represent the Church of Scotland as in rebellion against the law of the land, refusing to respect legal decisions regularly arrived at. It certainly did not predispose the ears of the Government to listen to the plea of the Church of Scotland. It was with this additional deadweight of prejudice that the Committee set out on its task to persuade the party in power to legislate in relief of the Church.

CHAPTER FOURTEEN

THE CHURCH AND THE POLITICIANS

1839-40

THE Non-intrusion Committee, with Dr. Chalmers as convener, proceeded at once to prosecute with all diligence its remit from the Assembly. Its activities were twofold. In a series of short popular pamphlets dealing with specific aspects of the problem, it sought to educate the membership of the Church in the principles at stake. These appeared at weekly intervals, beginning immediately after the Assembly. With a huge circulation, they played no mean part in influencing popular opinion ; and since governments come at times under suspicion of being less attentive to sheer reason and justice than to the prospects of the next election, it was considered that they might not be without effect on the Committee's main aim. This was the endeavour to obtain governmental intervention, either in the way of giving statutory effect to the Church's Veto Act, or, at least, of protecting the Church from the civil courts by making room, in some other way, for the principle of Non-intrusion.

It was with high hopes that the Committee entered on its task. For one thing, they had not a shadow of a doubt about the soundness of their case. The more fully the matter was looked into the more clearly it would appear that the law courts were making claims never asserted before. For another, the Whig party was in power, and a party which had fought long, and finally victoriously, for an extended franchise, might well be

:pected to be in sympathy with the parallel ecclesiastical
anifestation of regard for the will of the people. Indeed
e law officers of this party had quite definitely declared
eir view in 1834 that the Veto Act was within the
hurch's competence. Since that date, there had been
a expression of opinion, at least among the Scottish
embers of the party, that the Church was due some
paration for the earlier refusal to help her in her great
heme of Church extension. There was also a general
>pe that the Church would be able to go forward to the
:gotiation undistracted by new hostile manœuvres, that,
aving suspended till next Assembly all cases arising out
' the operation of the Veto, its opponents would likewise
ow some restraint in response to the appeal of Dr.
halmers, " Let me only hope that the forbearance will
: mutual—that a season of repose and opportunity will
: allowed for the settlement of this question—some
>mmon ground laid open on which piety and patriotism
ight meet together." [1]

There were, however, certain less favourable omens.
>rd Melbourne had a notorious and unconcealed dislike
Dr. Chalmers. His aggressive Christianity, his per-
:tence in the interests of Church Extension, and his
>parent affiliations with the Tory party combined to
ace him so manifestly in the bad graces of the Prime
Iinister that his word would carry no weight. Further,
e continued action of the plaintiff in the Lethendy case,
ith the appearance of the Presbytery of Dunkeld at the
ar of the Court of Session declining its jurisdiction in a
atter it impenitently regarded as purely spiritual, had
ven plausibility to the slogan that the Church was in
bellion. And still further, as Marnoch and other cases
owed, there was no decrease in the hostility and in the

[1] *Substance of a Speech . . . on the Case of Auchterarder,* 1839, p. 28

ingenuity displayed in the fresh disturbances with whic the Church was assailed. To this Dr. Chalmers thu referred in a pamphlet of the following year : " In th absence of all formal evidence, however effective, it wer obviously improper to mention names ; but it is th resistless conviction of all wakeful and intelligent on lookers that there is secretly at work against us a busy active, and hitherto irrepressible spirit of mischief, ber on defeating the objects of the Church, and for thi purpose of thickening in every direction the embarrass ments by which she is surrounded." [1] In this charge he was careful to explain, he was making no referenc to the Court of Session, but to those unseen originator who devise and instigate the processes, " the actions fo damages, the motions for interdicts, and the othe countless forms of molestation which have been con trived and set on foot pending the attempt of the Genera Assembly to have the question of co-ordinate jurisdictio settled in the alone competent and constitutional quarter which is the British Parliament." [2]

In the high summer of 1839, the Scottish Churc deputation held in London a multitude of interview not only with the Government, to which, naturally, thei attention was mainly directed, but with leading statesme of the Tory party, their case being, they felt, one tha should never be degraded into a mere party issue There were moments when they felt themselves on th very threshold of success, and that some satisfactor legislative measure was not only possible but certai within the next few weeks or months. But no govern mental measure was introduced, or even authoritativel prepared, within the limits of their stay. At the meetin

[1] *What ought the Church and the People of Scotland to do now ?* p. 12
[2] *Ibid.*, p. 12

of the August Commission, however, Dr. Chalmers gave in a highly favourable report of the progress of negotiations—a report which contained these paragraphs :

" First, we can state our having received the assurance of the Government that they were fully impressed with the importance of the subject, and would give it their most serious consideration, and that they would give instructions to the Lord Advocate to prepare, along with the Procurator, a measure to be submitted to the Cabinet. And for those who might desiderate something more definite, and as they perhaps feel, more substantial than this, we have the satisfaction of announcing, if not yet a specific measure by the Legislature, at least a specific and most important concession to the views of the Church on the part of the Government. They have authorized us to state that, in the disposal of these livings which are at the nomination of the Crown, its patronage will most certainly be exercised in accordance with the existing law of the Church, a resolution which applies to nearly one-third of the parishes of Scotland."[1]

Other patrons, he hoped, would speedily follow that good example.

It is no wonder that there was considerable elation in the evangelical phalanx at this announcement, though it failed to give what would have rejoiced them more, some definite governmental assurance of immediate legislative action. This rejoicing was hardly damped by the statement of Dr. Cook that what he had just listened to amounted to no less than a proposed violation of the law of the land on the part of the Crown. Nor was it

[1] Hanna, vol. iv, p. 122

much damped by the appearance a little later of an enormous pamphlet by the Dean of Faculty in the form of *A Letter to the Lord Chancellor*,[1] a pamphlet designed primarily for circulation among Members of Parliament. Few pamphlets have ever received such immediate and crushing replies. One of the many was by Dr. Chalmers himself : *Remarks on the Present Position of the Church of Scotland, occasioned by the publication of a Letter from the Dean of Faculty to the Lord Chancellor.*

The Dean's pamphlet and this particular reply demand at this point a brief consideration. Reading the pamphlet carefully, just one hundred years after its publication, when attention is not focused on the misstatements of facts and of positions which instantly drew forth indignant corrections and denials, one is forced to agree with the first impression of all the contemporary readers that it totally lacks coherence and unity and merits Chalmers' comment, " a mighty maze, and quite without a plan." It has all the marks of a composite structure, with some materials much more weathered and ancient than others. It suggests notes made at various times by a clever debater, turning to account now an apparently inconsistent utterance of Chalmers, now a violent outburst of Cunningham, now an unwary admission of Candlish. All these unused notes are loosely patched together and pitchforked on the public, and supplemented hurriedly by a reference to the August Commission, which proved to be the storm-centre of the

[1] There was a suspicion, current even among his colleagues, that Sir Robert Peel had himself commissioned this pamphlet and laid down its lines. But when it came to his ears he wrote to Sir James Graham : " I have as much to do with John Hope's pamphlet as with the last speech of O'Connell. Whenever I employ John Hope to speak my opinions, I will ask him to convey them more briefly and more methodically than he conveys his own." S. Parker, *Life of Sir James Graham*, vol. i, p. 378

whole. Although a scheme is not apparent, the purpose is plain. It is to create in the minds of English Members of Parliament a terrifying bogey of a Church given over to fanatics, with Popish dreams of clerical power, but pandering at the same time to the passions of the people. A smoke-screen—a Scotch mist, one might say—is thrown over the last seven years in Scotland, through which may be dimly seen gigantic shapeless monsters menacing the Church of England and the whole order of society. It is all very skilfully done ; the very confusion of the arrangement enhances the effect. It is calculated to make the flesh of the legislators creep at the bare thought of giving more power to these insatiable clerical usurpers. " The agitations of the present time have not raised a question of more serious import to the liberties of the country, and to the interests of religion, than that which the Church of Scotland has forced upon the country. . . . There is a plain, practical course to be followed—Let the law be obeyed and enforced." [1] Firmness will succeed, as it has succeeded before.

Dr. Chalmers' reply is also composite, in that it is divided into two distinct parts. The first part is a detailed explanation to one whom he is comforted to think of as " a gentleman and man of honour " of the apparent inconsistencies in his personal action. There have ever been two guiding principles of his action, Non-intrusion by restoring the place of the call, and the independence of the Church within its own spiritual sphere. As to the former, whatever particular policies were devised for its exercise, he had always stood for effect to be given to a *bona fide* dissent : to substitute a *bona ratione* dissent was a delusion and a snare. As to the latter he had never wavered in his assertion. " The

[1] *A Letter to the Lord Chancellor*, p. 286

State can take from us what they gave—the mainten-ance of our clergymen : but they may not take from us what they never gave—the right of determining our own methods, and prescribing our own requisites for the ordination of clergymen. They may withhold from our minister all that they ever gave civilly. But they may not control us in what we require of him ecclesiasti-cally." [1]

In the second part, the tone changes. He had just come across the last section of the Dean's *Letter*—the supplement—in which he deals with the August Com-mission and the report to it of the negotiating committee.[2] He had missed it, he explained, because he had been looking for places where charges were brought against him by name, and his name was absent from these pages. Nevertheless it was against himself that their charges of bad faith were levelled. The deputation, it was averred, could have no authority for the use that they made of Lord Melbourne's name in their report. " I suspect," wrote the Dean, " that Lord Melbourne has been very ill-used in the whole of this affair." [3] Now, Mr. Alexander Dunlop at the same time was dealing with this charge. He printed in his reply side by side the deputation's statement and a statement by Lord Melbourne in the House of Lords, showing that, in all essentials and even details, they said the same thing. Dr. Chalmers took the line of consulting the deputation and the notes of the deputation, printing in a footnote a letter from Dr. Gordon ; and then, after his investigation, he asserted firmly, " we will uphold the perfect integrity and good faith of that document, against the alleged testimony

[1] *Remarks on the Present Position of the Church of Scotland*, p. 46   [2] *v.* p. 196
[3] *A letter to the Lord Chancellor*, p. 277.   The words are given a separate paragraph and printed in italics.

of all the Peerage in the Empire." [1] " Let us hope," he concluded, " for his own sake, that the Dean of Faculty will yet make avowal of his regret for those unguarded and most unseemly paragraphs." [2]

It is evident that Dr. Chalmers was grievously wounded by this insinuation of duplicity. The rest of the pamphlet has a sterner ring. Nothing that he ever wrote is marked with such crispness and decision. " We do not expect ever to find access to his mind for the *truth* of our proposition : but, more helpless still, we cannot even find access for the *meaning* of it." [3] " The Dean of Faculty wonders that I should have changed my resolution in the short space of eighteen days. I should have wondered at myself if, after the perusal of the speeches of Lords Brougham and Cottenham, I had taken eighteen minutes to make up my mind anew upon the subject." [4]

Whether due or not to the influence of the Dean's *Letter*, later deputations were unable to procure any definite assurance of a government Bill. Interest began to concentrate on the friendliness of Lord Aberdeen, when it became known that this prominent Tory peer was not disinclined to test the possibility of a non-party measure, to be introduced first in the House of Lords, and by himself. This project appealed specially to Dr. Chalmers who, after his twofold experience of the delusive promises and dilatory tactics of a Whig government, was inclined to pin his faith rather to the superior Tory integrity. Negotiations began. Meetings of consultation were held. Letters were interchanged. It was definitely known that Lord Aberdeen was unwilling to go the whole length of a Bill legalizing the Veto Act

---

[1] *Remarks on the Present Position, etc.*, p. 80   [2] *Ibid.*, p. 81
[3] *Ibid.*, p. 82   [4] *Ibid.*, p. 89

as to its civil consequences, but all the early interchanges seemed to indicate that he was quite in favour of a plan which would allow the Presbytery, in its judicial capacity, at the trials of a presentee, to take into account his " acceptableness to the parishioners " as one element in the decision, *i.e.* that while he was unwilling that a veto without reasons should in all cases and automatically mean the rejection of a presentee, yet it might, by any particular Presbytery in any particular case be given effect to by a judicial decision that it was not for the good of the Church that this particular presentee should be inducted to this particular parish. He was understood to be in favour of what was called the *liberum arbitrium* of the Presbytery, its freedom to reject judicially, apart from its verdict on qualifications as narrowly interpreted by the House of Lords. Outlines of such a Bill were supplied to him, and Dr. Chalmers undertook to convince his colleagues that such a Bill, while not giving all that had been sought, came within their remit as a measure preserving both the principle of Non-intrusion and that of the independence of the Church.

Thus the matter was left, and Lord Aberdeen without any consultation with the committee set himself to draft a Bill with the help of parliamentary lawyers. It was understood that the terms of it would be available in time to be considered at the General Assembly of 1840, since the approval of the Assembly was a requisite step to its parliamentary success.

On the 5th of May a copy was dispatched by Lord Aberdeen to Dr. Chalmers with a covering letter : " I believe that the peace of the Church is at this moment in your hands ; for although, from the accident of birth and social position, I have had the means of proposing this measure to the legislature, it will depend on you whether it is to receive life and efficacy." [1] When he read the accompanying measure, Dr. Chalmers was stunned. It did not seem in the least to represent the conclusions arrived at in discussion. He read it again and again in growing disillusionment, and finally, he wrote to Lord Aberdeen a letter which began, " I have now examined the Bill, and it is with inexpressible grief and concern that I am forced to confess myself dissatisfied. . . I little thought, my Lord, after my incessant labours all last year to bring others down to the point at which I conceived your Lordship willing for a settlement, I should have met with a fresh obstacle in finding that your Lordship had taken up a position so much lower than I was counting on." [2] He followed this up by a last-moment appeal for a revision of the terms before the measure came before the General Assembly, for its benediction or the reverse. When this proved vain, Dr. Chalmers had to adjust his mind to the ordeal of the approaching Assembly where, for the second year in succession, he would have to make a motion totally different from the one he had hoped for a fort-night before.

It meant for him another three hours' speech. It was not such an exhausting effort as the year before, much of it being occupied with the reading of the corres-pondence which had passed, but in the closeness of its reasoning and in its searching analysis of policies that per-mitted and precluded the exercise of essential principles, it must take no mean rank among his public utterances. His motion was to the effect that the Bill was totally inacceptable, not only as failing to provide what the Church was looking for, but as in itself, inconsistent with

[1] *The Correspondence between Dr. Chalmers and the Earl of Aberdeen, etc.*
1893 edition), pp. 90–91   [2] *Ibid.*, pp. 91–92

the principles of the Church, and that " it is the duty of this Church to use every effort to prevent its obtaining the sanction of the Legislature." [1]

An amendment was moved by the Rev. James Robertson of Ellon, who was evidently loth that the high motives of Lord Aberdeen should appear to be slighted, and who put a much more liberal construction on the terms of the Bill. He thought that it did give increased power and security to every Presbytery in its judicial task. He quite agreed with Dr. Chalmers that if it did not give a Presbytery power to consider even the inarticulate but genuine revulsions of the lowly saints, it was a bad bill. " If a congregation of such honest and conscientious people—if even a small number of such persons, much more if a majority of heads of families, were to come forward and tender the objection to the presentee that he did not preach the gospel of Christ to their hearts, there must be a singular want of analysis in that Presbytery if they were not able to lay their hands upon the discourses preached to these illiterate people, and to say fearlessly in the face of the country that these discourses were not conceived in the spirit of the Gospel." [2] If Mr. Robertson's interpretation of the Bill had been sound, the distinction between a *bona fide* and a *bona ratione* dissent had been narrowed to a very fine point.

Mr. Robertson's qualified welcome was not, however, to be the basis of the official amendment, which was moved by Dr. Cook. This approved of the general tenor and spirit of the Bill, and incorporated the appointment of a committee " to watch over its progress, and give to the noble mover such suggestions as may, in their opinion, tend to promote the important objects contemplated by

[1] *Proceedings of the General Assembly of 1840*, p. 130   [2] *Ibid*, p. 156

it." [1] After a prolonged and somewhat confused debate Dr. Chalmers' motion was carried by a large majority, larger than at one time seemed likely.

It remains to ask : Can the cause of the genuine misunderstanding be laid bare, that misunderstanding which led Lord Aberdeen to expect from Dr. Chalmers a favourable reception for his Bill as framed, and led Dr. Chalmers to declare in the report to the Assembly :

" The noble framer of the Bill had ceased to honour them with his correspondence for some weeks previous to its introduction into parliament ; and coming greatly short even of that measure in favour of which they had been led to contemplate the full consent of all the influential members of both Houses with whom he is associated, the appearance of the Bill in question could not fail to be met by them with feelings both of disappointment and surprise." [2]

The correspondence has long been before the public in printed form, first in 1840, and again, more completely, in 1893, but it is still hard from it to fathom how a genuine misunderstanding arose. It may be that Lord Aberdeen was misled by the phrase " judicial powers " of the Presbytery, though it was made explicit that " acceptableness " in the mind of Dr. Chalmers was one essential ingredient in their judicial consideration. It may be that Dr. Chalmers and the committee laid greater stress than was warranted on Lord Aberdeen's instancing of even " red hair " as one of the things that might be taken exception to in a presentee. It may have been that Lord Aberdeen's attitude had been unconsciously altered by situations which had arisen

[1] *Proceedings of the General Assembly of 1840*, p. 166   [2] *Ibid.*, pp. 113–14

during the year in his own corner of Scotland.[1] Whateve
happened, there is no ground for doubting either th
genuineness of Lord Aberdeen's good intentions or th
astonishingly meagre, and indeed disastrous, nature o
their fruition.

Unfortunately, Lord Aberdeen, despite the ver
adverse vote, persisted with the Bill, and allowed himsel
in moving the second reading to insinuate that he hac
been unfairly dealt with, and that the Assembly's com
mittee had been " unscrupulous in their statements.'
When through lack of support it had finally to b
dropped, it came to Dr. Chalmers' knowledge that ir
the bitterness of his disappointment he had told th
House of Peers that Dr. Chalmers, after having led th
Church into her present difficulties, had now desertec
her, to find as best she might her own way out of them
In this he referred to the fact that Dr. Chalmers had, a
the Assembly, laid down his convenerships both of th
Church Extension and of the Non-intrusion Committees

By way of reply, Dr. Chalmers simply reiterated th
words he had spoken in the Assembly at his resignation
" The truth is, that in this harassing warfare I am abl
to hold out no longer. Irrespective of this, I should
have tendered my resignation of every office I hold
from the Assembly. . . . For more than a twelvemonth
I had made up my mind to do this in the Assembly o
1840, and during that twelvemonth the resolution ha

[1] Sir Arthur Gordon, in the *Earl of Aberdeen*, while laying the mai
blame on the younger hotheads of the Non-intrusion Committee, speak
also of an " unfortunate " visit of the Dean of Faculty to Lord Aberdee
at a critical stage of the negotiations. " Thoroughly self-confident, an
possessing that influence which a strong, narrow mind of a positive, over
bearing type often exerts on a mind of much higher quality, in whic
humility and self-distrust are leading characteristics, the Dean succeede
in persuading Lord Aberdeen to defer to his advice " (p. 134).

been strengthened every day by the infinity of calls
and conflicts and tracasseries innumerable to which my
twofold situation of Convener of Church Extension and
Convener for Non-intrusion has exposed me ; and to
crown and consummate all, there have not only been the
fatigues, but within these few weeks, or rather, few
days, the sore, bitter, crushing disappointment—*the
blasting of all my fondest hopes for the good and peace of our
Church, in my correspondence with public and parliamentary
men.*" [1]

The first appeal to the legislature, undertaken with
apparently soundly based hopes, had ended in unrelieved
and crushing defeat.

[1] *What ought the Church and the People of Scotland to do now ?* p. 61.
The central part of Lord Aberdeen's Bill—not the amended form
which became an Act in 1843 after the Disruption—was " That if the
Presbytery or other Church court shall be of opinion that, in respect of
any of the said objections or reasons, the individual presented ought not to
be settled in the said Parish, the Presbytery or other Church court shall set
forth and specify in their Deliverance the special Ground or Grounds on
which it is founded." *The Correspondence between Dr. Chalmers and the Earl of
Aberdeen* (1893 edition), p. 130.

CHAPTER FIFTEEN

THE STRATHBOGIE TANGLE

1838-41

IF any episode at all like the Marnoch case had appeared in the pages of Scottish fiction in the days of Sir Walter Scott and John Galt it would have damned for ever the reputation of its author. Every reader would have protested against the insult to his intelligence. "How can the author take us for such gullible creatures as to imagine this credible?" "How can he expect us to swallow such a hotch-potch of impossibilities?" And indeed at no other moment of time in Scottish history than just on the heels of the Auchterarder and Lethendy decisions could it conceivably have happened. Only amid the confusions created by these verdicts and the Church's reactions to them could this case have taken the tortuous course it did. At all other times it would have come to an end at the first General Assembly, if it had not been finally quashed in the lower courts. But, coming when it did, this case was to raise the most crucial issues, and practically to make the Disruption inevitable.

Marnoch was and is in the Presbytery of Strathbogie, in the county of Banff, just over the Aberdeenshire border. It was quite a populous parish, and by no means a poor living. The patronage was vested at the moment in a firm of lawyers, representing the trustees of the Earl of Fife. The former minister had been unfit for full duty for some years. Since there was within the parish a licentiate of the Church acting as a parish schoolmaster, a Mr. John Edwards, his services had been utilised by the minister as occasion demanded for the filling of the pulpit and other necessary duties. However acceptable he may have been as an unofficial assistant to begin with, various causes had contributed to the decline of his popularity. Relying on some biased reports from outside sources as to his continued acceptability, the acting patrons, on the intimation of the vacancy in 1837, presented him to the parish. At the meeting for moderation in a call, only one member came forward to sign. Perhaps too much was made of the fact that he was the local innkeeper, Peter Taylor. Of the 300 male heads of families on the roll, 261 came forward to register their dissent. The peculiarity of the situation arose from the fact that the Presbytery was divided on the legality of the Veto Act, at that time *sub judice* in the Auchterarder case. Seven ministerial members belonged to the party that opposed it, four to the party which upheld it. Its regulations, therefore, were not immediately applied.

The case was taken to the General Assembly of 1838, which ordered the Presbytery to proceed in terms of the Veto. The Presbytery obeyed.[1] Mr Edwards was rejected, whereupon the patron made a second presentation, a Mr. Henry. Shortly after Mr. Edwards applied to the Court of Session, following the precedent of the Lethendy case, for an interdict against the Presbytery's proceeding on the second presentation, and raised an action to have it declared that since he was the genuine presentee, the Presbytery of Strathbogie was bound and astricted to receive and admit him to the Parish of Marnoch, if found qualified after the customary trials. When the interim interdict had been granted, and the other case was pending, the Presbytery of Strathbogie by a majority

[1] June 6, 1838. *Vide* Bryce, *Ten Years of the Church of Scotland*, vol. i, p. 104

resolved to sist procedure, *i.e.* to desist from taking the necessary steps towards the settlement of Mr. Henry, until a legal decision had been reached. Their ground was—and this was the first ominous feature of the case—that the Court of Session had authority in matters relating to the inducting of ministers, and that its interdict consequently must be obeyed. The minority, who had advocated a reference to the August Commission, on losing that motion intimated an appeal and complaint to the Synod of Moray. The Synod came to the finding that, since admission to a pastoral charge is an ecclesiastical act, subject to the exclusive jurisdiction of the spiritual courts, the Presbytery had been at fault in the sisting of procedure at the bidding of a civil court ; but it refrained from declaring that the Presbytery should forthwith proceed, and referred the whole case to the General Assembly of 1839.

This General Assembly, with so many other urgent matters before it, and having no foresight of the proportions this particular case was likely to assume, referred it to the Commission due to meet at its close for any necessary action, and the Presbytery was enjoined, in the event of any change of circumstances, to report the matter to a future meeting of the Commission, which was given authority to determine thereon. The June Commission, in harmony with the general policy of a standstill pending the issue of the appeal to the legislature, while expressing its sympathy with the parishioners of Marnoch in their prolonged vacancy, simply instructed the Presbytery to suspend all proceedings unless it should so happen that Mr. Edwards withdrew his opposition, in which case they ought to take steps for the settlement of the second presentee.

Within a month the Court of Session issued its decision

in Mr. Edwards' case, finding that the Presbytery was still bound and astricted to take him on trials for ordination.

All eyes were now on the Presbytery, concerning the future action of which there were now contradictory injunctions, the earlier from the ecclesiastical court suspending all proceedings, the later from the civil court, not, indeed, ordering them to proceed, but declaring them obliged to do so. There is no doubt that both sides sought and procured expert advice from Edinburgh. Had the matter been delayed till the next ordinary meeting of the Presbytery, both injunctions would have been on the table. Since this would have put the majority in a dilemma a way out was sought. Could there not be summoned a *pro re nata* meeting to consider Mr. Edwards' claim to be taken on trials in the light of the Court of Session decision ? This would mean that they could deal with the later civil decision, while they were still in judicial ignorance as to the earlier ecclesiastical one. The minority, however, had one tactical advantage. The Moderator, who alone could summon a *pro re nata* meeting, belonged to their number. So, when the requisition signed by the seven reached him he summoned the meeting as in duty bound, but he put both injunctions on the billet of business, and he fixed the date so near to the meeting of Commission that no irreparable step could be taken by the majority before the case came before it.

The day fixed for the special meeting of Presbytery saw a most confused and disorderly scene, or series of scenes. The majority objected that this was not the *pro re nata* meeting which had been requisitioned by them, that the Moderator had no authority to enlarge the terms of the requisition, that it was incompetent to receive the Commission's injunction, and decided to

adjourn all further consideration of the case to the next
regular meeting on 4th December.

The minority, in obedience to the instruction to
report to the Commission any change of circumstance,
referred the matter to that body. At its November
meeting the Commission decided unanimously to enjoin
the Presbytery to appear "either personally or by procurator" at a special meeting on 11th December.

On the 4th, at its regular meeting, the Presbytery
decided by a majority that the injunction of the civil
court, being the later and more authoritative of the two
before it, was to be obeyed, and resolved to take Mr.
Edwards on trials. At the same time they refused to
hear an agent commissioned by the protesting parishioners of Marnoch. Further, they simply ignored the
fact that the last mention of Mr. Edwards in their own
records was that of his definite rejection as presentee
eighteen months before.

The Commission had therefore before it a most
thorny problem. They had been authorized, in any
change of circumstance, to determine the case. But
how were they to deal with a Presbytery which had
come to such a resolution? After various preliminary
skirmishes on relevance and an able debate on the
merits, it was decided, in order that the position of the
Church be not more deeply compromised by any further
action of the Presbytery in disobedience to the ecclesiastical courts through obedience to the civil, that the seven
ministers of the majority be suspended from their office
until the next General Assembly. It was insisted that
the sentence was not so much a punishment for past mis-
deeds as a preventive of future mischief. Further, since
this sentence deprived a part of the country for the time
being of regular pastoral services, it was remitted to the

minority with the help of a central Church committee to make provision for the means of grace being available in these parishes. The majority behind this decision was 121 to 14. During the discussion a suggestion was made that an influential committee might be appointed to hold conference with the Presbytery and with Mr. Edwards. This being approved, a committee was named, with Dr. Gordon, the honoured minister of the High Church of Edinburgh, as convener.

With this sentence solemnly pronounced, but not yet locally intimated, the " seven " of Strathbogie seem to have put themselves into the hands of the Dean of Faculty. He advised an interdict from the Court of Session against any of the Presbytery or any minister deputed by the Commission intruding into their parishes to intimate the suspension. This, for once, was too much for the court, which, however, granted an amended interdict forbidding them to enter the " churches, churchyards, or schoolhouses " for the purpose of such an intimation. The Church did not hesitate to accept this decree. The civil tribunal had the right, it allowed, to decide what was to be done, or not to be done, with the property of the Church. The sentences were, therefore, intimated in the parishes in the open air.

The religious services of the parishes were under the same handicap. But so effective were the preachers that in places the gatherings were beyond expectation. This led to the application for the more notorious " extended " interdict, which, after refusal in the Outer House, was granted by the First Division of the Court of Session. This interdicted any minister of the Church of Scotland from entering the parishes of any of the " seven," and holding services without their consent. Despite the interdict, none of the ministers appointed failed to fulfil

their engagements ; [1] on the contrary, such engagement
were sought after, and not a few of the leading Evangelica
churchmen counted it as one of their greatest honours t
have been permitted to serve the Church in such a cause
Dr. Bryce commends the moderation of the " seven,"
who refrained from prosecuting for breach of interdict
not wishing to subject " any of their brethren to fine o
imprisonment." [2] Nothing, however, would have pleased
the Evangelicals better than an appearance at the ba
of the Court of Session to answer such a charge. I
would have demonstrated to Scotland and to the world
the full extent of the intrusions of the civil court int
spiritual things.

Meanwhile the special Committee which went north
to hold conference with the " seven " had been compelled
to return in vain. A written document declining th
interview, presented by a lawyer, was the sole fruit c
their journey. The main grounds of their declinatur
were that the Committee had no power to undo th
sentence of the Commission, and that any conferenc
should have come before, not after, that sentence.

The case came before the General Assembly of 1840
There were three separate and distinct phases.

First, on the dissents recorded to the findings of th
Commission there was necessarily a review of its actions
It was moved by Dr. Cook that the Commission had
exceeded its powers in the pronouncement and execution
of the sentence, and a long and learned debate followed
on the existence, nature, and extent of these powers i
general, and on the alleged over-stepping of the specifi

[1] One of these was the Moderator of the General Assembly, Dr. Henr
Duncan of Ruthwell, to whom the messenger-at-arms handed the interdic
" with downcast looks and stammered apologies, as by one ashamed of h
office." G. J. C. Duncan, *Memoir of the Rev. Henry Duncan, D.D.*, p. 274
[2] Bryce, *Ten Years of the Church of Scotland*, vol i. p. 136

remit. The Commission's action having been vindicated by a considerable majority and the complaints dismissed, the way was opened for the second phase.

Mr. Alexander Dunlop moved the first motion, finding the " seven " censurable, but that before pronouncing any sentence " a Committee of this House shall be appointed to deal with those men, and to report to a subsequent diet of this Assembly." [1] He supported this in a long and lucid speech which, while condemning their actions, was not unsympathetic with their perplexities. Dr. Cook's motion was essentially to find that they were not censurable for what they had done. There was a small party in the Assembly which felt drawn to neither proposal. They wanted a conference, without any preliminary condemnation. No definite motion, however, was submitted. The final vote showed a large majority for Mr. Dunlop's motion.

The third phase followed on the report of the conferring committee. It had received certain explanations in regard to minor offences, but no profession of penitence or promise of amendment. The motion it submitted through its convener, Dr. Patrick MacFarlane, was " that the sentences of suspension should be continued ; that they should be cited personally to appear before the Commission in August, and if they then continued contumacious, and refused submission to the Church courts, that they should then be served with a libel for that contumacy, and that the Commission should proceed until the case was ripe for the next General Assembly." [2] Dr. Cook's counter-motion was to remove the suspension. An intermediate motion, to suspend them from their judicial and administrative functions, while permitting them to minister within their parishes, was made and

[1] *Proceedings of the General Assembly of 1840*, p. 182   [2] *Ibid.* p. 240

seconded. In the final vote Dr. MacFarlane's motion became the finding of the Assembly by a majority of 64 over Dr. Cook's, the figures being 166 to 102.

The " seven " now suspended by a judicial act of the Assembly lost no time in appealing to the Court of Session, which found that the sentence was invalid, and interdicted the Assembly from executing it or acting further upon it. Being thus civilly " de-suspended," they returned to their churches and manses to exercise their functions as parish ministers.

Early in July the first steps were taken by a group of their friends towards the formation of a Moderate League to stand by the " seven " in their struggle, the intention being to convert a local mutiny into a widespread insurrection. It was countered at once by a rival combination, whose " engagement " was to " maintain in all our actings, and at all hazards to defend, those fundamental principles relative to the government of Christ's house, His Church on earth, for which the Church of Scotland is now called to contend." The Strathbogie case was thus the occasion of the first appearance of definite opposing parties, and July 1840 is the date.

This open array of forces and principles lent an almost painful interest to the proceedings of the August Commission. The " seven " did not compear. Instead they gave notice through an agent that they could not " without acting inconsistently recognize or sanction any part of the proceedings which have been suspended as illegal." By this they openly affirmed that they renounced allegiance to the courts of the Church, and stood by the courts of law. The question now to be decided was, " Proceed to serve them with a libel, or not ? " The principal speech was made by Dr. Chalmers. Three months before, at the Assembly, he had intimated his resignation of his official Church responsibilities. Wearied and worried by his fruitless efforts to move the legislature to devise some *modus vivendi*, he had contemplated leaving the arena altogether. But at this point he felt that there was involved something even deeper than the Veto Act and alternative expressions of Non-intrusion. On 7th August there is this entry in his journal : " The Church matters seem fast hastening to a crisis, and a disruption seems inevitable. I pray for counsel and fortitude, and all the proper virtues of such an emergency from on high." [1] He girded himself afresh for the fray. And in this speech he said :

" We must stand out against this series of aggressions thus rising in magnitude one above the other, else the most sacred, the most sacramental of our institutions, the very innermost recesses of the sanctuary, will be opened to the invader and trampled under foot. . . . The Headship of Christ—the authority of the Bible as our great spiritual statute book, not to be lorded over by any power upon earth—a deference to our standards in matters ecclesiastical—and a submission unqualified and entire to the civil power in all matters civil. These are our principles, and these principles we are asked to give up by men who have put forth unhallowed hands upon them." [2]

By 180 votes to 66 it was decided to frame and to proceed with the libel. At the continued discussion in the November Commission the libel was sustained as relevant.

Meanwhile Mr. Edwards had been persistently demanding of the " seven " that, having sustained his

[1] Hanna, vol. iv, p. 262   [2] Buchanan, *Ten Years' Conflict*, vol. ii, pp. 177–78

trials, they should proceed to his ordination and induction. This step they refused to take. So a new action was devised by Mr. Edwards and his counsellors. In it he craved that the Presbytery of Strathbogie, including both its unsuspended and its de-suspended ministers, should be ordained " forthwith to admit and receive the pursuer as minister of the church and parish of Marnoch," and to decern further that, if they failed to do so, they must pay to him, Mr. Edwards, " the sum of £8,000 in name of damages," and a " further sum of £2,000 in reparation of the injury done to the pursuer's character and usefulness, and to his status in the Church of Scotland, and as a *solatium* for the injury done to his feelings." [1] While the minority put in defences, the " seven " indicated that they, on their part, were not unwilling to submit. A decree was given, not touching the question of damages, ordaining the " seven " to receive and admit the presentee.

On January 21, 1841, Mr. Edwards was ordained at Marnoch. No scene in Scottish church history has been more frequently described. It is not necessary here to add another to the number. It is enough to quote the brief and pointed summary of its significance given by Dr. Hanna. " It was an ordination altogether unparalleled in the history of the Church, performed by a Presbytery of suspended clergymen, on a Call by a single communicant, against the desire of the Patron, in face of the strenuous opposition of a united Christian congregation, in opposition to the express injunction of the General Assembly, at the sole bidding, and under the sole authority, of the Court of Session." [2] One element only is missing in this description : " in a church, empty

[1] Buchanan, *Ten Years' Conflict*, vol. ii, p. 185
[2] Hanna, vol. iv, pp. 218–19

of parishioners, but filled with a jeering crowd from a distance."

It may be asked, why did not the parishioners use their opportunity of bringing specific objections against Mr. Edwards if he was so obnoxious to them ? The answer is, that to have done so would have been to acknowledge the suspended " seven " as at least in some sense a Presbytery. In the protest, read before the parishioners left in a body, this was clearly stated. " We, the subscribers, elders and others who have signed for ourselves, and as representing the other parishioners of Marnoch opposed to the settlement of Mr. Edwards as minister of that parish, do represent to you that it is with extreme pain and disappointment that your personal position, as suspended ministers of the Church of Scotland, precludes us from appearing before you to lodge and prove the objections which have been prepared, and are ready to be substantiated, before any competent Church court." [1]

At the March Commission the libels against the " seven " and against Mr. Edwards were, after various evasive activities, found proven.

At this point all the contemporary summaries of the case lose sight of the conditions in Marnoch itself. Only in the newspapers can there be found any adequate account of the next steps taken by and for the parishioners. The Aberdeen *Banner* has this notice in an early February issue. " The parishioners of Marnoch, who withdrew in a body from the Church, on the 21st ult., after entering their solemn protest against the pretended ordination of Mr. Edwards, wish to avow that, while their conduct on that trying occasion declared their adherence to the divine principles for the exercise of which the Church is

[1] Hanna, vol. iv, p. 217

contending, and that their opinions of Mr. Edwards were unchanged and unchangeable, it [their conduct] also emphatically expressed their most cordial attachment to the ministry of the Rev. D. Henry, the second presentee, who has so zealously discharged the duties of an affectionate pastor among them for nearly two years, and who has stood by them so faithfully in all their trials." And the *Witness* of 6th February in a leading article made a financial appeal for a new church and school for the parish of Marnoch, asking local committees to be formed all over Scotland with a view to raising £8,800 for this purpose—a sum which would, it was calculated, provide not only the buildings, but also adequate endowments for both minister and schoolmaster, who could labour under the Presbytery of unsuspended ministers.

The Assembly of 1841 had to face this case at the very outset, for there were rival nominations to its membership from the " seven " and those who adhered to them, and from the four and those elders who acted with them. The nominees of the " seven " were rejected.

In this Assembly there were again three separate parts, or rather two parts and an unforeseen appendix.

The decisive step in the first part was taken by Dr. Chalmers in moving that the Assembly find the libel drawn up by the Commission to be relevant and proven. In a speech which shirked no issue he declared that he could find no conceivable excuse for the " seven " ; even the irrelevant plea of conscience which might be advanced by the worst of heretics was not to be credited to them. He did not mince words in pillorying the details of their contumacy, and when he came to describe its crown and consummation—their putting " forth their unlicensed hands on the dread work of ordination," [1] the Assembly, though already familiar with the facts, could not repress a fresh shudder of horror.

Dr. Cook, with what can only be described as conspicuous courage in view of the mood of the Assembly, moved a counter-motion. This proposed to condemn the whole proceedings, past or present, against the " seven " as incompetent. He argued that the determination of these men to be guided " by the injunctions of the supreme tribunals of the country was in perfect conformity with their duty, and ought not to have subjected them to censure," [2] far less should it have resulted in this trial for contumacy and dereliction of duty.

There can be few more grave or penetrating debates in the records of the General Assembly than this one of 1841. Irrelevant considerations may at times have been introduced, but no light or unworthy argument marred its high seriousness. In the end Dr. Chalmers' motion was carried by a majority of 97 (222 to 125).

The second stage saw this decision carried to its logical consequences. Dr. Chalmers moved the sentence of deposition. No counter-motion was made, but a protest was laid on the table by Dr. Cook. After prayer the solemn sentence of deposition from the office of the holy ministry was pronounced by the Moderator on the "seven" by name. The case of Mr. Edwards followed, and was speedily disposed of. It was felt to be ruled by the greater case, and not equally capable of de-

---

[1] *Report of the Proceedings of the General Assembly of 1841*, p. 199
By placing the deposition before the Ordination, Professor Carnegie Simpson missed an essential feature of this case (*Life of Rainy*, p. 55). Mr. Stuart Parker, by placing the suspension after the Ordination, gave it a strange twist (*Life and Letters of Sir James Graham*, vol. i, p. 373).
[2] *Report of the Proceedings of the General Assembly of 1841*, p. 215

fence. His irregular ordination being of course ignored, the Assembly deprived him of his status as a licentiate of the Church.

Two days later came the third scene. A letter was delivered to the Moderator, intimating that a messenger-at-arms was at the door of the Assembly Hall with a communication from the Court of Session. This was a fresh interdict to prevent the Moderator or any other from carrying into effect the sentence of deposition. The final upshot was a series of resolutions submitted by Mr. Candlish, embodying a protest against this further intrusion of the secular arm into the ecclesiastical province, and drawing the attention of the Government to this climax of the continued assaults on their freedom as a Church. The resolutions were adopted by an overwhelming majority, though Dr. Cook did not let them pass without protest.

One closely related matter came before this same Assembly. This was a petition by 399 male communicants of Marnoch, asking for the settlement of a minister among them. Without a vote, it was agreed that since Mr. Edwards was not, and never had been, the minister of Marnoch, the Assembly found " that Mr. Henry is the only presentee, and that authority be given to the Presbytery of Strathbogie to proceed to his settlement." [1]

Thus ended the Marnoch case, with two ministers, churches, and congregations within the parish both claiming to be the genuine Church of Scotland ; with a similar rivalry within the parishes of each of the " seven " ; with two separate bodies claiming to be the Presbytery of Strathbogie ; and with certain ministers of the Moderate party appearing to court a similar deposition through open association with the " seven,"

[1] *Report of the Proceedings of the General Assembly of 1841*, p. 265

even at sacramental occasions. The case was ended, but its repercussions were to continue throughout the Church, and to hasten the Disruption.

The presentation of this case as a continuous story has led beyond the point reached, the Assembly of 1840. In the next chapter it will be necessary to turn back to consider other happenings contemporary with its later stages.

Chapter Sixteen

IN RETIREMENT FROM LEADERSHIP

1840–41

When Dr. Chalmers retired from his two main offices at the Assembly of 1840 he was succeeded in the Non-intrusion Committee by Dr. Robert Gordon, of the High Church, Edinburgh, and in the Church Extension Committee by Dr. Robert Buchanan of Glasgow.

He had made it abundantly clear that it was not because his faith in the Church's cause was weakening, nor his hope for a fortunate issue extinct, that he had withdrawn into the background ; it was that his experience of political negotiations had convinced him that he was not the man to continue these. He could make nothing of either party, and they perhaps as little of him. He felt himself totally nonplussed by the astonishing result of past conferences and correspondence. That Lord Aberdeen or any other to whom he had opened his mind should have expected him to be a party to a solution which entailed the Presbytery being free to consider reasons of dissent, but legally limited to reasons capable of substantiation, seemed to him incredible. This was manifestly not the arena for which he was equipped. Other younger men must now step into the breach. They might be able to acquit themselves better in the political field in which he had so signally failed.

But would he be able to keep out of it ? He could not, at least during the session, betake himself into retirement at Burntisland or elsewhere. If he still remained

at headquarters in Edinburgh, would he not be danger-
ously accessible in every emergency? It is this desire
to get out of range that seems to explain the first step
of his retirement. The chair of Divinity in Glasgow
was vacant. Names were being discussed. Various
prominent Evangelicals were in the field. The main
Moderate candidate was Dr. Hill of Dailly, a son of
Principal Hill, Dr. Robertson's successor as the leader
of the party. In view of the constitution of the board
of nomination, it looked a certainty for him. But then
it became known that, though he would not apply, Dr.
Chalmers was willing that his name should be brought
forward. The excitement grew. It appeared that there
were Moderates on the board who were willing to
abandon their party affiliations to secure Dr. Chalmers
for their university. A great deal turned on the Lord
Rector's vote. He was Sir James Graham, who in his
rectorial address had spoken almost fulsomely of the
scholarly fame of Dr. Chalmers, but who had since been
closely associated with Lord Aberdeen in his bill. He
travelled from London to vote—against Dr. Chalmers.
Dr. Hill was appointed. Dr. Hanna says, " The same
university which had refused the chair of Logic to
Edmund Burke, refused that of Theology to Dr.
Chalmers." [1] On this judgment there is an interesting
comment by a later occupant of the chair : [2] " In our
chastened view of to-day it may seem not improbable
that the Glasgow Senate were wise in preferring efficiency
to eloquence, in both cases." But neither quality entered
deeply into the determination of the electing body ; the
dominant factor was ecclesiastical politics.

[1] Hanna, vol. iv, p. 213
[2] Professor H. M. B. Reid in *The Divinity Professors of the University of
Glasgow*, p. 310

It is significant that, a little later, Candlish was actually nominated to the new Chair of Biblical Criticism in Edinburgh, but on questions being asked in the House of Lords about the appointment of one who had notoriously and openly flouted Strathbogie interdicts, the Government withdrew its nomination. So while Lord Melbourne's Government adhered to its policy of administering Crown patronage according to the law of the Church—*i.e.* the Veto Act—its whole weight in professorial appointments was thrown against the party which was responsible for the Act.

Released from the burden of leadership, Dr. Chalmers returned to an earlier love. Early in 1840 there had appeared a pamphlet by Dr. Alison on the administration of the poor laws in Scotland. Though an able and persuasive statement, it ran counter to all Dr. Chalmers' convictions. He was at one with its delineation of the deplorable conditions, as to the prevalence both of destitution and of the diseases produced or intensified by the kind of housing that accompanied extreme poverty ; but he totally disagreed with the remedy proposed. This was that Scotland should come into line with England, and that there should be in every part of the land assessments for the poor ; that these poor rates should be so levied as to bring in an annual revenue of £800,000 immediately ; and that the indigence which arose from unemployment should be a charge upon the fund. As we have seen, Chalmers had always been convinced that the English system was wasteful, ineffective, and totally lacking in remedial value ; and his experience in Glasgow had, he felt, demonstrated a better way.

His first and public answer to Dr. Alison was at a meeting of the British Association in Glasgow. Though his paper drew an unprecedentedly large meeting of the section, and though it was well received, he felt that its effect on listeners would be so evanescent, and its impact on readers of the reports so limited in range that something more was incumbent on him. So during the winter session he delivered to his students and the general public that course of lectures from which we have already quoted,[1] and which was almost immediately published as the twenty-first volume of his *Collected Works*. This volume he sent out widely to men of influence in thought and politics. It was in acknowledging his copy that Thomas Carlyle wrote : " It seems to me a great truth this fundamental principle of yours, which I trace as the origin of all these hopes, endeavours, and convictions in regard to Pauperism, that human beings cannot stand on selfishness, mechanical utilities, economics, and law courts ; that if there be not a religious element in the relations of men, such relations are miserable and doomed to ruin. . . . With a Chalmers in every British parish much might be possible ! But, alas ! what assurance is there that in any one British parish there will ever be another ? "[2]

Another phase of Dr. Chalmers' withdrawal from the limelight of leadership was the zest with which he threw himself into the movements for adult education. While some of these were political in origin, and tinged with an anti-Church bias, he accepted many invitations to lecture to them even on subjects like chemistry and the laws and phenomena of heat, so long as it was understood that he was free to utter his views on the necessity of religion for the well-being of men. Nor did he despise invitations to areas remote from the great centres of population. In stimulating scientific curiosity, he felt

[1] Pp. 60 and 61.   [2] Hanna, vol. iv, pp. 199–200, 201

that he was doing a service for the nation and for the Church.

During the early part of this short period of detachment from Church courts and committees he prepared an ecclesiastical pamphlet, of which singularly little notice was taken by friend or foe. There is this reference to it in his journal : " July 9, 1840. Going on leisurely, I think feebly, with, I hope, my last controversial pamphlet on the Church question." [1] Its title was, *What Ought the Church and the People of Scotland to do now ? Being a pamphlet on the principles of the Church Question. With an Appendix on the Politics and Personalities of the Church Question.*

After a glowing description of the possibilities of a reinvigorated Church of Scotland and a powerful analysis of the meaning of the impasse which now faced it, he goes on to lay down definitely in four points the immediate tasks of Church and people. It seems highly probable that these points were carefully prepared for the speech that he had intended to make in the Assembly of 1839, before the deliverances of Lords Brougham and Cottenham wrought a vast change in his programme. They are as follows. (1) The Veto Law ought to be repealed by the Church. He had never been tied to that particular law as the sole machinery for preserving the principle of Non-intrusion. And this was not, as has been suggested, a capitulation to the Moderate Party ; for their policy was not to repeal that law, but simply to treat it as non-existent from the moment the civil courts had finally declared its enactment *ultra vires*. (2) Having relinquished the Veto, the Church, unshaken in her historic witness for Non-intrusion, must fall back upon the call, and restore to it, in the exercise of her judicial

[1] Hanna, vol. iv, p. 251

power, all the significance and effect which it had in other days. (3) The Christian people must play their part. They ought at once to petition the Government importunately for a larger measure of influence, a definite improvement of their standing, in the election of their ministers. (4) There must not be forgotten a matter which to some might seem trifling and local, and yet was fundamental—the position of the ministers of Strathbogie. " It is impossible for the Church to give in, without the abandonment of her most sacred prerogatives as a Christian Church." [1] No Church which sets any store on its independent jurisdiction can, at the bidding of a civil court, regard ministers whom it has solemnly suspended as unsuspended or even as reponed. This firm statement helps to explain why Dr. Chalmers was called in at every crucial moment in the Marnoch case.

In the Appendix the most notable point is that after having detailed all his political hopes and their shattering, one after the other, he concludes thus, " The proofs are multiplying upon us, that what Charles Fox said of the African slave-trade is true of Scottish patronage —it is a system not to be regulated, but destroyed." [2] These were strong words for one whose policy at the outset had been, " Do not destroy patronage, but regulate it."

Now, if this was Dr. Chalmers' considered programme in the autumn of 1840, and if his word was still as powerful with the Evangelical party out of office as in, why did not the Assembly of 1841 initiate procedure for rescinding the Veto Act ? Was this course of action deemed too humiliating by the younger and fiercer spirits now in control ? No, there was another very different reason.

[1] *What ought the Church and the People of Scotland to do now ?*, p. 50
[2] *Ibid.*, p. 62

There had already been introduced into Parliament a new legislative measure which seemed a veritable beacon of hope. This was the Duke of Argyll's Bill. Prepared in consultation with the Non-intrusion Committee, it went far to legalize the Veto Law. Its main differences were two : substituting " male communicants " for " male heads of families," and strengthening the provisions for a Presbytery's disregarding the Veto, where there was proof of factious motives or causeless prejudices.

Though the Bill was bitterly opposed at its introduction in the House of Lords, the Duke of Argyll was confident that he could carry it if only it were backed by a united General Assembly. Two separate tasks, in consequence, devolved on Mr. Candlish. He had to secure the approval of his own committee to it as a final settlement, and he had to persuade the other party to give it their blessing. In the former task he was successful. He made a bold bid for the second in one of the most powerful speeches he ever delivered. But it was not destined to meet its full reward. An amendment was proposed dividing the Assembly, although not supported by anything like the full strength of the Moderate party, many of them having responded to his appeal. By the largest majority on any general issue up to that time the General Assembly expressed its approval of the Bill. To many the prospect still seemed rosy, but before the second reading the Whig Government fell, and Sir Robert Peel became Prime Minister. From him there was little to be expected. He had already declared his mind, when in opposition, that the terms of Lord Aberdeen's Bill were the utmost the Church could hope for, and that even these terms were available only for a Church which had given up disobedience to the law.

During the summer of 1841 there was another approach made to Parliament by a very different group in the Church. This was a section of the Moderate party, that section which had been upholding the "seven" of Strathbogie, and were in consequence of their association in danger themselves of coming under definite Church censures. In their memorial to Parliament they protest against any change in the law of the land. The present law must be enforced. Those who break it must be strictly dealt with ; and those who suffer at present for their obedience to it must have the full protection of the State.

When the Commission met in August 1841 it had to take account of the ominous situation created both by the action of certain prominent ministers in countenancing, recognizing, and associating with the deposed "seven," and by this memorial of theirs to the Government. It was the former with which it mainly concerned itself. It decided that the deliberate insubordination displayed in treating the Assembly's sentence of deposition as null and void should be reported to the Presbyteries of the offenders for necessary action, and that a " solemn remonstrance and warning " should be drawn up and addressed to them. When this had been carried Dr. Cook lodged reasons of dissent which were still more ominous, containing as they did a declaration that he and those who agreed with him must now " take such steps as may appear most effectual for ascertaining from competent authority whether we who now dissent, and they who concur with us, or they who continue to set at nought the law of the land and the decisions of the Civil Courts in what we esteem a matter of civil right, are to be held by the Legislature of the country as constituting the Established Church, and as entitled to the privileges and endowments conferred by Statute upon the ministers of that Church." [1] Despite the assurance of Dr. Cook "that they had no desire to take steps at present to follow out their opinions," [2] the dissent could mean nothing less than the expression of a resolution on the part of the Moderate party to drive their opponents out of the Church. Should it come to this complete separation, Dr. Cook further said, "we would not proceed to depositions; we would declare them to be no longer members of the *Established* Church." [3]

It is not hard to appreciate the general apprehension that the final crisis was just on the threshold. Energetic measures were deemed necessary. An extraordinary meeting of Commission was summoned for 25th August, a fortnight later. Although no special appeal was issued, the popular interest in Scotland was so intense that the meeting overflowed its customary place in the High Church, and was compelled to adjourn to St. Luke's. Dr. MacFarlane of Greenock was entrusted by the Evangelical majority with the motion to be submitted. It was long and detailed, occupying nearly a column in the newspapers. After affirming anew the principles at issue, and protesting against the kind of governmental interference sought by one section of the minority, it continued :

"In accordance with these resolutions, the Commission agree to propose a conference with the parties above referred to, with the view of leading them to reconsider their present position, and persuading them to pause in their dangerous and disastrous career. And farther, in reference to the purpose openly avowed by these said parties, the Commission resolve to oppose, by

[1] Hanna, vol. iv, pp. 232-33   [2] *Witness*, August 14, 1841   [3] *Ibid.*

all constitutional means, any attempt that may be made to interfere with the rights of the Church, and to take measures for bringing the principles and privileges of this Church, as well as the dangers that may threaten her, before the Government, the legislature, and the country at large, by deputations, public statements, meetings, and such other methods as may appear expedient." [1]

It concluded by nominating a huge panel of prominent ministers and elders to be ready to render such services. In support of the resolutions Dr. Chalmers made a brief but notable speech, not in order, he affirmed, " to stir up the wrath of our enemies, just as little to propitiate their favour, but simply and altogether to open their eyes." [2] He hoped that the language of determination would not be construed as the language of defiance. He felt it as of the utmost practical importance that the state of matters should be plainly understood ; for nothing could " exceed the misconceptions, and especially of the higher classes, both in this country and in London." " Be it known unto all men, then, that we have no wish for a disruption, but neither stand we in the overwhelming dread of it. We have no ambition, as has been pleasantly said of us, for martyrdoms of any sort, but neither will we shrink from the hour or day of trial." [3] Since a counter-motion that was made failed to find a seconder, the resolution was adopted unanimously. A second member asked his dissent to be recorded, and after discussion this was allowed.

No time was lost in putting the resolutions into operation. The first of the public meetings was held that very night, of which an experienced journalist wrote that it was " the most crowded and enthusiastic meeting

[1] *Witness* (Special Supplement), August 28, 1841   [2] *Ibid.*   [3] *Ibid.*

we ever witnessed." [1]   Organized meetings followed all over the country ; current newspapers are filled with their reports.   Local committees were instituted ; and before the end of 1841 there were to be found in every corner of the land many who had publicly taken some such pledge as this : " The Ministers and elders present declare their resolution to stand by each other, and by the Church, in the maintenance of the principles hitherto professed by them, and to which they again avow their determined adherence, praying Almighty God that He will give them strength to maintain them to the end." [2]   This was the wording of the first Edinburgh pledge, and reports show that it supplied the pattern for many others elsewhere.

Brilliantly successful though the popular appeal was, the approach to a Government headed by Sir Robert Peel seemed entirely a forlorn hope.   Yet there followed another promising negotiation, which, in the end, proved a mere will-o'-the-wisp.   One of the leading Scottish Members of Parliament, Sir George Sinclair, was an elder in Dr. Candlish's congregation.   Brooding over the approaching crisis, he lit upon what seemed to him a heaven-sent inspiration to avert it.   Would it not be possible to so amend Lord Aberdeen's Bill as to make it acceptable ?   Would not one additional clause serve the purpose ?   That Bill, it may be recalled, gave the Presbytery authority to decide upon any reasons submitted.   Could not that power be extended thus ?   " Or in respect that the reasons or objections, though not in the judgment of the Presbytery in themselves conclusive, are entertained by such a proportion of the parishioners, as in the opinion of the Presbytery to preclude the prospect of the presentee's usefulness in that particular

---

[1] *Witness*, August 28, 1841   [2] *Ibid.*

parish." [1] Lord Aberdeen, on being consulted, thought that this conceded too much ; indeed " it would make the repeal of the Veto Act illusory." Therefore he was disinclined to accept the clause, as carrying with it a condoning of past offences.

Sir George, however, arranged more than one meeting between Dr. Candlish and the Dean of Faculty. And although Mr. Hope said that he feared that this would enable the Church courts " to enforce the Veto, in every particular instance, if they chose," a tentative agreement was reached. Dr. Candlish accepted the assurances that the form of words did provide for the discretionary liberty of the Presbytery to give effect, in any case, to the dissent of the people. But he was careful to add that he was not to be regarded as personally committed, until a selected legal expert confirmed this interpretation. To the consternation of the Moderate party Lord Aberdeen, on an approach by the Dean of Faculty, gave his approval to the clause ; and to the disgust of extreme Moderates like Dr. Bryce, both Sir George Sinclair and the Dean began in different ways to bring pressure on the Strath-bogie " seven." For a brief period during the October of 1841 matters looked hopeful indeed ; the essence of the Non-intrusion principle seemed on the point of being conceded. But again it proved illusory. The amended clause which seemed so satisfactory in itself, when introduced into the text of the Bill, and read in that context, apparently meant no more than a judicial finding on the reasons for any dissent, however widespread. Practically the same misunderstandings that had marked Dr. Chalmers' correspondence with Lord Aberdeen were seen to have been at work in the conferences between Dr. Candlish, Sir George Sinclair, and the Dean of

[1] Bryce, *Ten Years of the Church of Scotland*, vol. ii, p. 179

Faculty. The Non-intrusion Committee were compelled to reject the amended Bill as unsatisfactory.

It was not through any lack of industry or goodwill that Sir George Sinclair failed. His attempt to secure the benediction of Dr. Chalmers was totally unavailing. He had had enough of ambiguous parliamentary phrases. He saw no ray of hope in any measure emanating from what had been his own favoured Tory party—a party which he now declared supported the National Church not " for the sake of its religious and moral benefits to the population," but only as " a mere congeries of offices, by which to uphold the influence of patrons and subserve the politics or the views of a worthless partisanship." [1]

As though this failure were not enough in the way of heartbreak, a fourth major case had emerged which was still further to cripple the Church and undermine its remaining powers.

[1] Hanna, vol. iv, pp. 242–43

CHAPTER SEVENTEEN

CULSALMOND AND AFTER

1841–42

THOUGH much less has been made of the case of Culsalmond than of the four—one yet to be considered—which are normally regarded as the critical cases, its historical importance is little inferior to theirs.

Culsalmond is in the Presbytery of Garioch, and thus within the Synod of Aberdeen. The conditions which led to the peculiar embroilment there had their roots in the fact that while the Presbytery's leanings were distinctly towards the Moderate side, there was a very wide-awake and active Evangelical minority. The minister of Culsalmond intimated in the autumn of 1841 that he desired an assistant and successor. The patron presented the Rev. William Middleton, who had acted for some time as interim assistant. On the Presbytery's receiving the presentation it resolved, somewhat surprisingly, to follow, at least so far, the procedure of the Veto Law. It doubtless expected an almost unanimous Call when it took steps to prepare a roll of the " male heads of families."

The meeting for moderation took place on 28th October. On the Call being submitted it was signed by all the elders and by 41 communicants. But immediately thereafter dissents were tendered by 70 " male heads of families," a majority of those on the roll. The Presbytery's duty, if it were to obey the General Assembly, was plain. That supreme court had ordered that no further steps, either of rejection or admission, were to be taken in any case arising out of the operation of the Veto Law, but that all disputed settlements were to be referred to the Assembly. Yet the Presbytery proceeded to deliberate on the call. A motion was made to the effect that the Presbytery sustain the call, in respect that the Veto had been declared illegal by the civil courts. This was met by a counter-motion, not that the Presbytery forthwith reject Mr. Middleton, in terms of the Veto, but that, in obedience to the Assembly, it should sist procedure. The former motion was carried by 7 votes to 5. The minority intimated an appeal to the Synod of Aberdeen. An agent for the dissenting parishioners protested and appealed on their behalf. Yet the Presbytery went on, by the same majority, to fix 11th November as the day of Mr. Middleton's induction.

At this point, seeing that the mere majority of dissents was ineffective, the agent for the parishioners tendered "special objections." There was nothing of the nature of a libel about them, but some were matters that deserved investigation, *e.g.* "cold, unspiritual preaching" and "attending to secular pursuits on the Lord's Day." [1] The Presbytery refused to receive them on the ground that the dissentients were the same who were taking their stand on the Veto—on the mere fact of their being a majority. There is no reason to believe that the Presbytery planned from the beginning to use the Veto Law to thwart the majority of the parishioners. But when, as a matter of fact, they began on the Veto Law procedure, then discarded it altogether, and finally brought it in again to bar the regular procedure of the days before the Veto Law, it did look like a pre-arranged

---

[1] Buchanan, *Ten Years' Conflict*, vol. ii, pp. 314–15

plot, and many of the dissentients interpreted it as such.

On the day fixed for the induction, the Presbytery, quite naturally, anticipated opposition. They called in the sheriff and a posse of constables to see them through. But the uproar in the church was such that the whole party had at length to beat a retreat to the manse. There, behind closed doors, they inducted Mr. Middleton.

The first ecclesiastical body to meet thereafter was the commission of Assembly on 17th November. To it there was presented a petition from the dissentient male heads of families, now 89 in number, asking redress, and craving supply of religious ordinances on the ground that they could not recognize Mr. Middleton as their minister. By 54 votes to 3 the commission decided that Mr. Middleton, while left in undisturbed possession of his manse and stipend, be prohibited " from officiating and administering ordinances in said parish." [1] until a final deliverance was given at the General Assembly, and that the minority of the Presbytery of Garioch be empowered to make arrangements for the supply of ordinances.

Meanwhile, the alleged ringleaders in the riot were being brought to trial before the High Court of Justiciary and, on their acquittal, the doctor in Culsalmond, regarded by the Moderates as the prime instigator, was entertained at a public breakfast in Edinburgh. This was in no sense an official action of the Non-intrusion Committee, though one prominent member did take the leading part. It might well have been dispensed with, for it did appear to some as giving the benediction of the Church on what was, despite all provocations, a somewhat discreditable scene. Yet Dr. Robertson himself seems to

[1] *Culsalmond Case : Report of the Opinions of the Judges,* etc., p. 8

have been a worthy and stalwart citizen, dragged to the bar through local jealousies. There was no stint in the heartiness of the felicitations extended to him.

Before the General Assembly of 1842 met, two further steps had been taken in this case.

The Synod of Aberdeen heard the appeal in April when, after a very long and somewhat confused discussion, it was decided by a small majority " that any interference with Mr. Middleton's settlement can neither consist with justice nor tend to edification ; " [1] against which decision an appeal was taken by the minority to the General Assembly.

The other step was an appeal by Mr. Middleton to the Court of Session to have the prohibition laid upon him by the Commission arrested and set aside. This crave was at first refused. Lord Ivory, who heard the case, declared : " The only question here is, shall the court interfere with the proceedings of a proper Church court, where that court, acting within its own province, is dealing with a proper ecclesiastical cause, and this, too, while the cause is actually depending before them ? " [2] " No civil interest, either of the patron or presentee, is thereby affected." [3]

But Mr. Middleton persisted and appealed to the Inner House, which proved more compliant. A majority of judges found in his favour on March 10, 1842. The Lord President insisted that the petitioner had a right to the protection of the civil court, for civil interests were affected. By his suspension " a gross stigma had been fixed on Mr. Middleton and his sacred character as a minister of the gospel." [4] Nothing was more manifest than that Mr. Middleton's civil rights were affected by

[1] *Record for Respondents*, etc., in *Assembly Papers, 1842*, p. 2
[2] *Witness*, January 15, 1842   [3] *Ibid.*   [4] *Culsalmond Case*, p. 12

his suspension from his official duties and administration of ordinances in the same parish where he had acted as ordained assistant. The verdict itself was disconcerting, but the *dicta* of the Lord President were still more alarming. For if depression of personal status in the eyes of a local community were to be regarded as a civil wrong, there was no ecclesiastical sentence which might not have this element alleged in it, and consequently be brought under the review of the civil courts. It was little wonder that the Church appealed this case to the House of Lords, and when it came up in the General Assembly through appeal against the Synod's verdict, the Court of Session's declaration was rightly almost totally ignored, the matter still being *sub judice*.

There were other contemporary cases, like those of Glass and Daviot and Stewarton, which introduced new points, but these may be passed over, the third to be dealt with later, in view of the importance of two other happenings or series of happenings which demand consideration before the highly complicated General Assembly of 1842 can be adequately reviewed.

Attention has been drawn to the fact that not infrequently during the years 1839–41 there had been proposed at Assemblies and Commissions, in addition to the motions emanating from the Non-intrusion Committee and the Moderate party, intermediate motions, the intention of which was, almost uniformly, to mitigate the severity of sentences without compromising the spiritual independence of the Church. These motions did not emanate from a definite group. There had been intermediate motions, but there was no Middle Party.

It was in March 1842, in the manse of Govan, that a distinct third party was formed, under the leadership of the minister of the parish, Dr. Matthew Leishman. It was composed of men who claimed to be loyal to the non-intrusion principles they had hitherto professed, but who felt that, in order to prevent a schism, the Church ought to accept the best terms within the range of practical politics which were embodied in Sir George Sinclair's amendment of Lord Aberdeen's Bill, which might be still further amended by continued negotiations. One month later, at the meeting of the Synod of Glasgow and Ayr, the new policy had its first airing. Dr. Leishman made a considerable sensation in the Synod and in the country by his speech in introducing it, of which it will be well to quote the central part.

" An end, if possible, should be put to our unhappy conflicts with one another, and to our conflicts with the courts of law. For myself, I have no hesitation in saying that I would prefer the Duke of Argyll's Bill. That Bill, I am persuaded, would work more pleasantly than any other. But still, rather than that the Church should remain a single day longer in her present position, assailed as we are, both from within and from without, I would most thankfully receive Sir George Sinclair's measure—indeed, any measure which would not offend my principles, and at the same time would warrant any hope of being instrumental in saving the Church from destruction. I have in my hands at this moment, the written adhesion of more than forty ministers, at present attending this meeting of Synod, and all professing Non-intrusion principles, to the following *Declaration* : Whereas the difficulties and dangers with which the Church of Scotland is now surrounded, and which are every day increasing in number and magnitude, are of a most serious and alarming character, not only obstructing her operations and paralyzing her exertions in every department of practical usefulness, and tending to sunder the bonds of Peace and Unity among her members, but threatening her safety. and even her existence, as a National Establishment ; and whereas it appears from the published minutes of the Non-intrusion Committee, a measure of settlement has been proposed, as we understand with the concurrence of the Government, by which the Church courts, acting in their judicial capacity, are left at full liberty to reject a Presentee in every case in which they may think it proper to do so, either in respect that the objections or reasons stated by the Parishioners are judged by the Presbytery to be in themselves valid and conclusive ; or in respect that the said reasons or objections, though not, in the judgment of the Presbytery, in themselves conclusive, are entertained by such a proportion of the Parishioners as, in the opinion of the Presbytery, to preclude the prospect of the Presentee's usefulness in that particular Parish, our understanding of the said proposed measure being the interpretation which has been put upon it by Sir George Sinclair in his published correspondence : We, whose names are undersigned (without expressing positive approbation of this particular mode of settlement, and whilst other modes, were such in our option, might be preferred by us severally) would feel ourselves conscientiously at liberty to submit to it if passed into law." [1]

Although, in his remarks introducing the document, Dr. Leishman claimed that all professed Non-intrusion principles, there were not a few among the " forty " who had not been generally suspected of upholding these, but had been fairly consistent Moderates. Of Dr. Leishman himself there could be no doubt. He had

[1] J. F. Leishman, *Matthew Leishman of Govan*, pp. 130–32

been one of the " gallant forty-two " who voted against patronage in 1833,[1] before he became one of the " forty " who thought it sufficiently curbed by a provision of dubious import and an interpretation thereof already officially disowned. Although his modern biographer calls him the " Head and Front of the Forty," it was Dr. Simpson of Kirknewton who seems to have been generally accepted by contemporaries as the framer of its policy and the main director of its activities in Scotland and in England. Unquestionably, however, Dr. Leishman made a bigger impression in his Western Synod than Dr. Simpson in his Eastern.

The other movement was a parliamentary one. Among the Scottish representatives in the House of Commons, there were many who longed for legislative action. One of the most zealous was Mr. Campbell of Monzie, the member for Argyllshire. His first definite action was to move for a Select Committee to inquire into the Scottish Church difficulties " with powers to send for persons, papers, and records." [2] With Sir Robert Peel openly, though mildly, hostile, it was inevitable that the motion should be defeated. His next step was, with the Duke's concurrence, to introduce the Duke of Argyll's Bill in the House of Commons. It met, at the first reading, a more favourable reception than the most optimistic looked for. The second reading was fixed for 4th May, not long before the Assembly. On the morning of that day, Mr. Campbell was informed that the Government had decided to introduce a satisfactory measure. He was

[1] In one of the New College copies of *The Wheat and the Chaff*, an interleaved one with many MS. notes, which belonged to the Rev. Robert Boog Watson of Cardross, there is this note opposite p. 53 : " I remember (as a small nephew) his boasting that he belonged to the ' gallant forty-two ' in the Anti-patronage vote of 1833.—R. B. W."

[2] *Witness*, March 19, 1842

242

prepared to withdraw his on this assurance. But when it appeared from the speeches delivered from the Government bench that the proposed Bill went no further than Lord Aberdeen's, he resisted the effort to postpone the second reading of his. Naturally, he failed. The Bill was postponed. Another ray of hope had been extinguished. There can be no doubt that, through the formation of the Middle Party, the terms of its declaration, and exaggerated reports from Scotland that it was making phenomenal progress both among the ministers and among the people, the Government was led to think the revival of Lord Aberdeen's Bill a satisfactory solution.

Meanwhile, in preparation for the Assembly, the Evangelical party, amid all the gathering clouds, had been drafting and subscribing a lengthy overture on the position of the Church. The actual draughtsman was Mr. Alexander Dunlop, but it passed through many hands. Dr. Chalmers was concerned that it should not be too much occupied with the incidental and local features of the trouble, but should concentrate on the great issue of spiritual independence. For this issue, he wrote, " is that great Erastian controversy, in which all states and all churches have a common interest. The other question has more, certainly, of a local character. It is a Scottish peculiarity which not even our near friends and neighbours, the Methodists of England, can altogether go along with ; and I do confess that I have often felt when Non-intrusion was spoken of out of Scotland, that it was the inopportune presentation of such a topic as gave a certain cast of provincial littleness to a cause which might be so stated as to create a responsive and deep-felt interest in every land where national establishments of Christianity were known." [1]

[1] Hanna, vol. iv, p. 285

As printed in the Assembly papers, the overture is named as " for a declaration against the unconstitutional encroachments of the civil court," [1] and is signed by a hundred and sixty-one members of the Assembly. This resolute assertion of principle was to become the Claim of Rights of 1842 which, although it lost in 1929 the place which it had held in the Free and United Free Churches in every ordination and induction, either in the questions then addressed to the entrant upon office, or in the preamble prefixed to these, and while it is not even mentioned in the Basis of Union of that year as one of the historic documents of permanent validity and value, has been, as it were, sublimated in the Articles of the Church of Scotland (1921 and 1926) and in the United Free Church Act anent the spiritual independence of the Church (1906), wherein is to be found the constitution of the re-united Church in this matter.

All these varied cross-currents combined to make the General Assembly of 1842 one of the most crowded, tense, and significant in the whole history of the Supreme Court from its institution in 1560 down to the present day.

[1] *Assembly Papers*, 1842

CHAPTER EIGHTEEN

THE LAST UNDIVIDED ASSEMBLY AND THE CLAIM OF RIGHT

1842

AT this decisive Assembly, on which all eyes were turned with painfully keen expectation, the queen's representative was the Marquis of Bute. He was commissioned specially, it was felt, with the view of strengthening the Middle Party, and securing a more general welcome or at least assent for the government Bill already outlined and promised. The moderator was Professor David Welsh, the colleague whom Dr. Chalmers had so warmly welcomed to the Chair of Ecclesiastical History in Edinburgh eleven years before. While he had never been prominent in any of the phases of the conflict, he had contributed no small part to the renaissance of the Church of Scotland through his enlightened and persistent devotion to the cause of a national Christian education.

The first trouble arose at the very outset, when the roll of the Assembly was under consideration. Two sets of Commissioners had been sent up by the Presbytery of Strathbogie, one set claiming to sit in the name of the " seven " deposed, and the other in the name of the undeposed. This seemed a very simple matter. There were those, indeed, who were prepared to censure the Assembly officials for allowing the names of the nominees of the " seven " to appear, even tentatively, on the roll as rival claimants. Their nomination, they held, should have been totally disregarded. We have seen that

Dr. Chalmers had been recalled from his partial retirement at the two earlier phases of the case. He now intervened in one of the briefest and most incisive speeches of his career. It forms so clear a window into the deepest feelings of many in the Assembly that it deserves quotation in its fullest reported form. Dr. Cook had argued that the deposition of the " seven " had been invalid in two respects : its grounds had been matters which called for no such action, and there was a considerable party in the House which had not acquiesced in it.

" Moderator," said Dr. Chalmers, " this is the first time in my life that I ever heard it asserted that the dissent of a minority superseded the sentence of a court passed by an overwhelming majority. The proposition is, in substance, that those deposed by the General Assembly of 1841 shall, nevertheless, be allowed to sit as members of the General Assembly of 1842. Why, Sir, the proposition is so very monstrous, and so fully comes in conflict —so palpably and immediately comes in conflict—with a first principle, that I cannot hold it to be a case for argument at all. But that such a proposition should be made, that such a proposition should be ever thought of, is a very instructive fact. It discovers to what a fearful extent of anarchy and disorder the enemy within— whether by the instigation and encouragement of the enemy without, I cannot say—are resolved to plunge the Church of Scotland ; how they are resolved to strip her of the last vestige of that authority which belongs to every distinct body governed by distinct office-bearers. Never, Sir, I would say, has the character of the outrage inflicted upon the Church come out in such bold relief as at the present moment, when we have just met under the countenance of her Majesty ; when we have been ushered to our places with the form and circumstance of a great national institute ; and when we are now holding our deliberations in the presence and hearing of royalty, represented by one of the most respected of our noblemen. We are now congregated in this our first meeting of the present Assembly, by the authority and appointment of the last meeting of the last General Assembly ; and, Sir, in these circumstances, what is the first thing we are called upon to do ? Why, to pluck from our archives the most solemn deed of that most solemn convocation, and to trample it down under our feet as a thing of insignificance or a thing of nought. It is under the authority of the last General Assembly that we now hold our places, and are now met as a deliberative body ; and I must say that if there is anything more than another which could unsettle all men's notions of order and authority it would be the success of the present proposition. It would truly be an egregious travesty—it would make a farce of the proceedings of our General Assembly—a complete laughing-stock of our Church—were there left her no authority to enforce obedience from her own sons. It would present a strange contrast between the impotence of our doings and the pageantry of our forms—between the absolute nothingness of the Assembly and the mighty notes of preparation—the imposing cavalcade which accompanied us—the pealing of the clarionets with which we were accompanied into the House on the present occasion. I must say that there is not a heart which beats with more gratification, or feels more elevation, than my own, at the countenance given to our venerable Church at present by the high and honourable of the land ; but ours will be the fault, if untrue to ourselves—if, untrue to our privileges, we shall allow our

Church to become a sounding brass or a tinkling cymbal. And, to use the language of an old proverb, if men deposed in the most regular manner, by a sentence of the supreme court of the Church, shall be admitted or suffered to sit as members of the General Assembly, we shall become a hissing and an astonishment to all passers by." [1]

After this speech and its reception there was no disposition on the part of the Moderate party to insist on the sustaining of these commissions ; they contented themselves with the motion that both sets be rejected. After a short and sharp debate, in the course of which developments were hinted at, the motion was defeated by 215 votes to 85, and a motion by Mr. Dunlop sustaining the commissions of the undeposed minority adopted.

Two days later, the further developments came to light. It appeared that the rejected nominees had provided themselves with an interdict from the Court of Session prohibiting the nominated representatives of the Presbytery of Strathbogie from taking their seats in the General Assembly, or attempting to take part in its deliberations. The day between had been largely given over to devotional exercises, and to a stocktaking of the major schemes of the Church, all of which gave token of great vitality and a wealth of Christian liberality in their support. It is well to note that, despite the Church's manifold difficulties at home, she was reaching new levels in her support of her work abroad. No breath of controversy had marred that day of rejoicing. But on the Saturday morning the scene was changed. Most dramatically, even melodramatically, the matter of the interdict was brought to the notice of the Assembly. A

[1] *Proceedings of the General Assembly, 1842*, pp. 7, 8

representative elder from Strathbogie, a retired Indian officer, rose up in the Assembly with his interdict in one hand and a Bible in the other. " I am not," he declared, " one of those who treat lightly an interdict of a civil court, for I have long been accustomed to strict discipline ; but I hold that there are circumstances in which an individual may be placed, when it would be criminal to obey the interdict of any earthly court. I hold in my hand an authority in this holy Book, which does not prohibit me from standing forth in support of the principles of the Church of Scotland, in which I have been brought up ; and so long as I am permitted, I will serve God as faithfully as I have served my country." [1]

A motion on the subject was submitted by Mr. Candlish. After giving words of encouragement to the interdicted brethren, and a promise of support, it continued : " And the General Assembly do further hereby protest against the attempt now for the first time made, on the part of any civil tribunal, to interfere with the constitution of the supreme courts of this Church, and to prevent the attendance of commissioners duly elected to be members thereof, or otherwise to determine questions affecting the validity and competency of the election of commissioners thereto—the determination of all such questions, regarding its own constitution, being the undoubted right of the General Assembly alone, and being essential to its integrity as a supreme and independent court, recognized as such by the constitution of the Church and the law of the land. And the General Assembly declare, that such interference is wholly unconstitutional, and that this court cannot recognize any sentence of such civil tribunal, pronounced in a matter wholly ecclesiastical, and placed under the exclusive

[1] *Proceedings of the General Assembly, 1842*, p. 22

jurisdiction of this supreme ecclesiastical judicatory." [1] Dr. Cook, asserting that Dr. Candlish's motion " places the house in direct hostility to the law of the land," [2] moved a direct negative. A large majority voted for Dr. Candlish, and Strathbogie, for the moment, melted away into the background.

After some less thorny, but in other respects more important, matters had been disposed of, notably the rescinding of the Act of 1799, passed during a spasm of exasperation, which had so effectively fenced the pulpits of the Church of Scotland from intruders from England and elsewhere, and including improvements in the supervision of divinity students and in the election of elders and definition of their duties, the first major debate of the Assembly was that on the patronage question. In view of Dr. Chalmers' declaration of his change of mind, and of a very close vote in the preceding Assembly, the reforming group had taken fresh heart, and had greatly increased their activities. There was a notable increase in the number of overtures praying for the abolition of patronage. No fewer than twelve Synods and twenty-four Presbyteries had taken action.

Mr. Cunningham, after delivering a most massive and telling plea on behalf of the overtures, concluded by moving : " That the General Assembly, having considered the overtures anent Patronage, resolve and declare, that Patronage is a grievance, has been attended with much injury to the cause of religion in this Church and kingdom, is the main cause of the difficulties in which the Church is at present involved, and that it ought to be abolished." A counter-motion round which both the older Moderates and the new Middle Party could rally was submitted by the Procurator : " That the Assembly

[1] *Proceedings of the General Assembly, 1842*, p. 24   [2] *Ibid.*, p. 25

having considered the overtures and petitions, find it inexpedient, in present circumstances, to adopt the overtures." It is not doing any injustice to a historic debate, nor to the elaborate addresses of the accustomed leaders on both sides, to say that the two speeches awaited with the most breathless interest were those of Dr. Chalmers and Dr. Leishman. Had Dr. Chalmers overcome his reluctance to declare himself publicly against patronage, and if so, on what grounds? Had Dr. Leishman repented of his earlier vote, and if so, on what grounds?

Dr. Chalmers' speech was brief. He recounted the steps taken to mitigate the grievances of patronage. " And the ultimate issue has been, that Patronage will not allow of any deference being given to the element of the popular will. In the utter impossibility of amalgamating them, we have therefore been shut up to this, that there is no conclusive and comfortable settlement, but in the utter extinction of Patronage." [1] In his earlier speeches he had evinced a real shrinking from allowing the initiative to be in the hands of the parishioners. This evidently still remained, and found expression. " If by the people, you mean the inhabitants of the parish in general, I consider it as bad as the present system of Patronage. The Church would be in as bad circumstances . . . if over-ridden by an ungodly democracy, as if over-ridden by an ungodly aristocracy." [2] But if we continued to raise, as we had been doing, the qualifications both of the electors and of the eligible by showing increased care both in the admission of members and in the training and licensing of our students, there was bright hope for the future in a well-regulated system of popular election. He indicated quite clearly that he

[1] *Proceedings of the General Assembly, 1842,* p. 81   [2] *Ibid.,* p. 81

had always, and still, preferred a limited patronage, but events had shown that "there is no such thing as a limited patronage in this country." [1] The Church was shut up, therefore, to the demand for its entire abolition. While the whole tone of Dr. Chalmers' speech is markedly different from that of those who held that patronage was contrary to the Word of God and the will of Christ, his support of the motion was no less decided.

If Dr. Chalmers felt that the whole circumstances of the time had impelled him to this stand, Dr. Leishman was persuaded, and tried to persuade the Assembly, that the motion was singularly inopportune. These, he contended, were very critical days : the overthrow, or at least dismemberment of the Church of Scotland might be imminent, but the Government was well-disposed ; it was ready with a Bill which he felt assured would meet the situation. "Let us beware of disgusting the Government, and alienating them from us," [2] which the adoption of this motion would inevitably do. Sir Robert Peel had declared that his Bill would satisfy "the truly moderate men of all parties." Why fling this insult in his face ? He closed with these sombre words of warning : "Should the Government abandon in despair the task they have undertaken, the consequences may be disastrous in the extreme, and some, when in after life they look back upon the dispersion of their flocks, upon the extinction of the light of the gospel in many a secluded village, on the silencing of the Sabbath bell in the glens and remote districts of our native land ; when they have experienced a sad proof of the impotency of the voluntary system, and when they see their disestablished church lovely only in its ruins, some who are now present may shed over the remembrance of this evening tears of

[1] *Proceedings of the General Assembly, 1842*, p. 82   [2] *Ibid.*, p. 88

bitter sorrow and self-reproach, vainly regretting that they did not avail themselves of the last opportunity which God in His providence afforded them of restoring peace to this distracted Church and country." [1] Despite the appalling prospect so vividly placarded before their eyes, the members proceeded to vote for Dr. Cunningham's motion in such numbers that it was carried by a majority of 69 (216 to 147), in the largest vote on any issue in these eventful years.

The second major debate was on the overture from members of the Assembly against the encroachments of the civil court. It was Dr. Chalmers who moved that the Assembly adopt the overture that it might go out to the Government and to the Christian world in the name of the Church of Scotland. He had liked, he said, the proposal from the time he first heard of it. The Church was now shut up to some such measure. The Court of Session was "multiplying her encroachments." [2] The legislature thus far had failed to listen to the Church's plea for protection. This Claim of Right would demonstrate that the Church was now contending for her inherent liberties ; and what was more, as the statutes proved, for her constitutional liberties. With the Dean of Faculty's plea for firmness in his mind and its adoption by a section of the minority within the Church, he directed the main part of his speech against the futility of naked coercion, against the unthinking exercise of force. This was not the revolt of an inferior court against a superior, which, in the interests of order, must be suppressed ; it was the protest of a co-ordinate jurisdiction against an illegal invasion of its province : "There is one old Latin aphorism which shall henceforth become my adopted favourite—*Ne sutor ultra crepidam*—

[1] *Proceedings of the General Assembly, 1842*, p. 91   [2] *Ibid.*, p. 118

which might be thus translated for the benefit of those who are concerned—Let all men, whether lairds or lawyers, mind their own business, and leave us to mind ours." [1] They had no intention by this document, he continued, to operate on the fears, but on the convictions, of others. " We are not dealing in threats, but in remonstrances. . . . We are not making an experiment on English courage ; that we know would be in vain. We are making an appeal to English justice ; and that we hope will not be in vain. We are letting the capital of the Empire know a case of gross and grievous and multiplied oppression, which is now going on in one of the provinces—an oppression which if not remedied will have the effect of trampling down the Church of Scotland into utter insignificance or . . . will dissever her from the state altogether at a time when her services are most needed to reclaim a sadly degenerated commonalty," [2]—and that at the very moment when the prospects of so doing were at their brightest.

The countermotion of Dr. Cook was couched in a series of resolutions, proposing the rescinding of the Veto Act and of all the disciplinary sentences of the Church which had their origin from it ; claiming that various applications of the doctrine of the headship of Christ were possible within the one Church ; and asserting that, by falling back on the procedure before the Veto Act, the Church had sufficient security against the settlement of unqualified and unsuitable ministers.

Since the two motions were not directly opposed, the ensuing debate lacked the excitement of some others. Yet very weighty speeches were delivered on both sides. At the close, Dr. Chalmers' motion was carried by a

[1] *Proceedings of the General Assembly, 1842*, p. 124   [2] *Ibid.*, pp. 124-25

majority of 131 (241–110). The somewhat surprising extent of the majority is partly accounted for by the fact, as a scrutiny of the voting reveals, that not a few of the Middle Party followed Dr. Leishman in recording their votes for the Claim of Right.

Of what nature, then, was this document so solemnly adopted and named at its final approval by the Assembly in a revised form,[1] the Claim, Declaration, and Protest against the Encroachments of the Court of Session. Dr. Chalmers, it may be recalled, had hoped that it would be based on general principles intelligible to the whole of Christendom : and he was thoroughly satisfied with the result. And yet on a first reading there is no document ever officially adopted by any Church more closely packed with local and provincial particulars, powerful and plain enough to those who had been in the heart of the conflict, but perplexing and confusing in the extreme to those of another tradition or another age. It may be acknowledged that it was necessary, by way of preliminary, to establish not only the fact of encroachment and its nature, but also to list, item by item, the individual acts of encroachment and to assess their meaning, but it is only in the concluding paragraphs that the more universal note is struck which Dr. Chalmers so fervently desired. The four concluding paragraphs run as follows :

" THEREFORE, the General Assembly, while, as above set forth, they fully recognize the absolute jurisdiction of the Civil Courts in relation to all matters whatsoever of a civil nature, and especially in relation to all the temporalities conferred by the State upon the Church, and the civil consequences attached by law to the decisions, in matters spiritual, of the Church Courts,—DO,

---

[1] The revisions are not numerous, as a comparison of texts shows.

in name and on behalf of this Church, and of the nation and people of Scotland, and under the sanction of the several statutes, and the Treaty of Union herein before recited, CLAIM, as of RIGHT, That she shall freely possess and enjoy her liberties, government, discipline, rights, and privileges, according to law, especially for the defence of the spiritual liberties of her people, and that she shall be protected therein from the foresaid unconstitutional and illegal encroachments of the said Court of Session, and her people secured in their Christian and constitutional rights and liberties.

" AND they DECLARE, that they cannot, in accordance with the Word of God, the authorized and ratified standards of this Church, and the dictates of their consciences, intrude ministers on reclaiming congregations, or carry on the government of Christ's Church, subject to the coercion attempted by the Court of Session as above set forth ; and that, at the risk and hazard of suffering the loss of the secular benefits conferred by the State, and the public advantages of an Establishment, they must, as by God's grace they will, refuse so to do ; for highly as they estimate these, they cannot put them in competition with the inalienable liberties of a Church of Christ, which, alike by their duty and allegiance to their Head and King, and by their ordination vows, they are bound to maintain, ' notwithstanding of whatsoever trouble or persecution may arise.'

" AND they PROTEST, that all and whatsoever Acts of the Parliament of Great Britain, passed without the consent of this Church and nation, in alteration of, or derogation to the aforesaid government, discipline, right, and privileges of this Church (which were not allowed to be treated of by the Commissioners for settling the terms of the union between the two kingdoms, but were secured by antecedent stipulation, provided to be inserted, and inserted in the Treaty of Union, as an unalterable and fundamental condition thereof, and so reserved from the cognizance and power of the federal legislature created by the said treaty)—as also all and whatsoever sentences of courts in contravention of the same government, discipline, right, and privileges, are, and shall be, in themselves, void and null, and of no legal force or effect ; and that, while they will accord full submission to all such acts and sentences, in so far—though in so far only —as these may regard civil rights and privileges, whatever may be their opinion of the justice or legality of the same, their said submission shall not be deemed an acquiescence therein, but that it shall be free to the members of this Church, or their successors, at any time hereafter, when there shall be a prospect of obtaining justice, to claim the restitution of all such civil rights and privileges, and temporal benefits and endowments, as for the present they may be compelled to yield up, in order to preserve to their office-bearers the free exercise of their spiritual government and discipline, and to their people the liberties, of which respectively it has been attempted, so contrary to law and justice, to deprive them.

" And, finally, the General Assembly call the Christian people of this kingdom, and all the Churches of the Reformation throughout the world, who hold the great doctrine of the sole Headship of the Lord Jesus over his Church, to witness, that it is for their adherence to that doctrine, as set forth in their Confession of Faith, and ratified by the laws of this kingdom, and for the maintenance by them of the jurisdiction of the office-bearers, and the freedom and privileges of the members of the Church from that doctrine flowing, that this Church is subjected to hardship, and that the rights so sacredly pledged

and secured to her are put in peril ; and they especially invite all the office-bearers and members of this Church, who
are willing to suffer for their allegiance to their adorable
King and Head, to stand by the Church, and by each
other, in defence of the doctrine aforesaid, and of the
liberties and privileges, whether of office-bearers or people,
which rest upon it ; and to unite in supplication to
Almighty God, that he would be pleased to turn the
hearts of the rulers of this kingdom, to keep unbroken
the faith pledged to this Church, in former days, by
statutes and solemn treaty, and the obligations, come
under to God himself, to preserve and maintain the
government and discipline of this Church in accordance
with His Word ; or otherwise, that He would give
strength to this Church—office-bearers and people—to
endure resignedly the loss of the temporal benefits of an
Establishment, and the personal sufferings and sacrifices
to which they may be called, and would also inspire
them with zeal and energy to promote the advancement
of his Son's kingdom, in whatever condition it may be
His will to place them ; and that in His own good time,
He would restore to them these benefits, the fruits of the
struggles and sufferings of their fathers in times past in
the same cause ; and, thereafter, give them grace to
employ them more effectually than hitherto they have
done, for the manifestation of His glory."

Now what about the very long preamble, the seem-
ingly interminable procession of "And whereases"? First
of all, the doctrine of spiritual independence is stated
and elaborated from the confessional documents of the
Church; then the various statutes which recognize, ratify,
and confirm this jurisdiction are enumerated and quoted ;
then the various Acts and episodes which led to the

repudiation of any royal jurisdiction in the Church of Scotland ; then various Acts which directed the civil authority to follow ecclesiastical sentences with their proper civil effects ; then the Act restoring Patronages against which the Church had so long protested as contrary to the constitution confirmed and assured in the said Act of Security ; then the Church's adherence to the Call even in the days when Patronage was most powerful, and her giving fresh value to it in 1834 ; and finally, a review of the eighteenth-century actions in the Court of Session, citing seven cases in which that court refused to be drawn beyond civil matters, like the destination of the stipend, *i.e.* the regulation and disposal of the temporalities which were derived from the State.[1] The more distant past having been thus epitomized, there follows the more detailed review of the recent past, a survey of the various judgments from the Auchterarder Case onwards, sixteen being named in the notes, in which the Court of Session, " have exercised powers not conferred upon them by the Constitution, but by *it* excluded from the province of any secular tribunal— have invaded the jurisdiction of the Courts of the Church— have subverted its government—have illegally attempted to coerce Church Courts in the exercise of their purely spiritual functions." These and the further encroach- ments threatened being such as no true Church of Christ could permit, they CLAIM, DECLARE, PROTEST, and CALL as above.

The rest of the actions of the General Assembly may be briefly summarized. The report of the Non-intrusion Committee was approved, despite a second appeal by Dr. Leishman for a favourable verdict on the government

---

[1] It was against the accuracy of this part that the detailed criticisms of *Veritas* (A. K. MacGeorge) were mainly directed.

measure ; it was resolved to uphold the ecclesiastical rights of Chapel ministers, no matter what the civil court's decision might prove to be ; [1] it frustrated the attempts of libelled ministers to evade deposition by challenging the composition of the libelling Presbyteries ; it took an initial step for the final extinction of pluralities.

Of the many cases that came before it three call for notice. In regard to Culsalmond, it was moved that the settlement be rescinded, and that Mr. Middleton be found to have disqualified himself by his conduct. It was moved also that the settlement be not disturbed. There was a middle motion " to reduce the settlement, because of the irregularities of the procedure, and to send the case back to the Presbytery to consider the special objections." [2] The first motion was carried with very few voting against it.

The case of those ministers who had recognized as brethren in full standing and associated with the " seven " of Strathbogie in ecclesiastical acts created greater trouble. Some, for the most part, it would seem, elders, clamoured for their immediate deposition. Others thought that, after a conference, an admonition not to repeat the offence would be adequate. The sentence actually proposed by Dr. Makellar was of a quite peculiar character, and was agreed to without a vote. It was that the eleven ministers concerned " be suspended from the exercise of their judicial functions, as members of Presbyteries and all other judicatories of the Church, until after the first Wednesday of March next." [3] This would debar them from the Commission of Assembly, but would not preclude their nomination to next General Assembly.

---

[1] *Vide* pp. 28off., " The Stewarton Case "

[2] *Proceedings of the General Assembly of 1842*, p. 227   [3] *Ibid.*, p. 254

It was a peculiar sentence, and some of the Moderates naturally asked why, if this partial suspension were permissible, it had not been adopted in the original case of the " seven." The answer given was that that original sentence was not penal, but preventive ; it was to prevent them from proceeding on their declared intention of ordaining the presentee to Marnoch, and that this was a " ministerial " act, from which suspension from judicial functions would not have debarred them.

The third case raised a new issue, which was prophetic of things to come. In the parish of Rhynie a great proportion of the parishioners had left the ministry of one of the " seven," and enjoyed the services of a missionary supplied by the General Assembly. They wanted a building of their own. The whole land of the parish was controlled by one landowner. He would on no account grant a site. One which they had actually purchased they were interdicted from utilizing. Through the sympathy of a neighbouring proprietor a site was obtained, accessible to the population but outside the bounds of the parish. The consent of the Assembly was necessary if the parishioners were to avail themselves of this generous offer. It was granted by a large majority. The parishioners took action as soon as they heard the news. Fearing an interdict at the instance of other heritors, they mustered in force, carted prepared materials to the site, and before night fell the frame of the structure was practically complete. Newspapers and pamphlets of the time celebrated or ridiculed " the church built in a day." It was a fore-gleam of one of the practical difficulties the Free Church was to face.

All men felt that this Assembly had definitely cleared the issues. There could be no longer any dubiety where the Church stood. Opposition was to be expected from two powerful interests : from the aristocracy through the declaration against patronage, and from the Court of Session through the Claim of Right. But surely the legislature would be moved by that powerful appeal ; surely it would give up tinkering with half measures ; surely it would come to the rescue of a distressed and fettered Church !

CHAPTER NINETEEN

THE CONVOCATION AND ITS SIGNIFICANCE

1842

AT the close of the General Assembly of 1842 the focus of interest shifted to London. How was the Claim of Right to fare at the hands of the government? At long last the extremely critical nature of the situation must now be apparent to the British Parliament. Its members must surely be convinced that it was a first duty to devote their minds and energies to finding a way out.

The first faint glimmering of hope was speedily extinguished. Shortly after the Assembly the date fixed for the second reading of Mr. Campbell of Monzie's Bill was due. The parliamentary champions of the Scottish Church mustered for the fray. Their case, they felt, was much stronger now. Even opponents in close touch with the Government had their orations ready in expectation of a regular field-day. But no debate took place. The Bill was thrown out on a technicality. It was bound to affect the many Crown patronages in Scotland, and no such Bill could be considered without the express consent of the Crown. There is no doubt that the Bill would have failed to survive the second reading, but the method by which an open discussion on the grievances of the Scottish Church had been shelved rankled. A few days later the hopes of the Middle Party that the Government would make its own the revised version of Lord Aberdeen's Bill were just as ruthlessly quenched. The Government, declared the Prime Minister, had abandoned all hopes of effecting any good by introducing any measure relating to the Scottish Church question. So, while the formal response to the Claim of Right was long delayed, there could be little dubiety as to its contents when it did appear.

Within two months a fresh decision in the law courts worsened the Church's plight. On the 9th of August the House of Lords gave its decision in the Second Auchterarder Case. This had taken the form of an action for damages lodged by both patron and presentee against the Presbytery of Auchterarder, and in particular those members who had voted with the majority, for their refusal to take the presentee on trials for ordination, after the judgment in the first case which had declared that it was not legal for them to sist procedure in the settlement. The Presbytery's general plea was that it had respected the decision so far as the province of the civil courts extended—that is to say, it was putting no obstruction between the presentee and patron and the temporalities of the benefice, but that in the matter of ordination it was its duty as a court of the Church, and it was their individual duties as office-bearers of the Church, to obey the regulations and the instructions of the General Assembly.

Four of the leading law lords concurred in upholding the decision of the Court of Session, viz. that the Presbytery and its offending members had clearly laid themselves open to a civil action for damages. In their pronouncements there was hardly a reference to the constitution of the Scottish Church and its statutory privileges. These were taken as disposed of in the first case. The situation as it is envisaged in all the judgments is this. The Presbytery of Auchterarder has been, to all intents and purposes, instructed by the supreme tribunal of the country to take this presentee on trial. It has refused to do so. Is an action for damages, therefore, competent? Of the many precedents adduced all were English save one. Lord Brougham, evidently conscious of the weakness and incoherence of his judgment in the first case, was the most learned and the most prolific in English legal precedents. After piling up cases of the liability of corporations and the "individual liability of corporators," he castigated the Scottish Church with the whole weight of his unquestioned eloquence. " It has been said, that to suppose the Legislature, which acknowledged the Divine origin of the Church's powers, could ever intend to enforce their exercise by the sanction of temporal penalties, is to charge that Legislature with conduct as profane as it is absurd. Yet the compelling men and bodies of men to exercise faculties which they have received from Heaven is one of the most ordinary acts of legislative, of executive, and of judicial power—not to mention that it is the act of ordination itself, and not the preparatory process of trial, which the Church claims to have received from above." [1] " It is fit that these men learn at length the lesson of obedience to the tribunals that have been appointed over them, a lesson which all others have long acquired, and which they, as learning it, should also practise. It is just that they should make reparation to those whom their breach of a plain duty has injured. The duty is not doubtful. The Courts have laid it down. Their failure is not a mistaken opinion ; their fault is not an error of judgment. They knew what they ought to have done, and they refused to do it. The penalty of their transgression is to make compensation to those whom they have injured by their pertinacious refusal to perform their duty and yield obedience to the law." [2]

Auchterarder Case : Speeches by the Lord Chancellor, etc., p. 16   [2] *Ibid.*, p. 17

The actual verdict was not unanticipated, but the accompanying dicta on the Church's subjection to the civil power seemed to strip her of the last shreds of independent jurisdiction. What made the situation more alarming was that, not only were the judgments published *in extenso* in the Press, but they were immediately issued in pamphlet form, finally at the cost of one penny, by a group acting " under the full conviction that they will produce the most salutary effect upon the public mind." [1] The immediate reaction of Dr. Candlish and the Edinburgh stalwarts of Non-intrusion forms the main theme of all the histories and diaries and biographies of the period. What is more significant for the future course of events is the effect the full reports had on Dr. Chalmers.

At the time of the promulgation of the decision he was enjoying a welcome vacation in the north of Ireland. It was no time of idleness, for he had preached to crowded congregations in Belfast. One of the most pleasing features of his visit was an address of welcome and appreciation from ministers of the Irish Presbyterian Church who had been his pupils in Edinburgh. Within his reply to this address we find his spontaneous reaction to the verdict.

" They would strip us of that spiritual independence which has long been the undisturbed birthright of the Church of Scotland, and the only bulwark behind which the cause of religious Establishments can permanently stand. . . . Meanwhile the Church of Scotland, in the midst of these conflicting influences, between the last governing party which refused to extend her, and the present governing party which is attempting to enslave her, will steer her own rectilinear way. She will never

---

[1] *Auchterarder Case : Speeches by the Lord Chancellor, etc.* Preface

relinquish the principle of a National Establishment, yet will rather be driven from all its privileges and endowments than receive a mandate or pay respect to an interdict from the civil power in things ecclesiastical. In other words, she will consent to be a Voluntary rather than an Erastian Church ; and if our rulers will persevere in their present blind and ruinous policy, acting the part of Destructives under the name of Conservatives, she will, if abandoned by the State and erased from the institutions of the country, commit her righteous cause to that God who will not forsake her in the day of adversity, and to the sympathy and support of the people of Scotland." [1]

The Voluntaryism which he had fought with all his might seemed now a lesser evil than the State control, which was assuming gigantic proportions. It was clear to him that the parting of the ways had drawn appreciably nearer. Still, there was as yet no adequate justification for the renunciation of the State endowments. Though the highest judicial tribunal had spoken, there still remained the feeble hope of parliamentary intervention. What then could be done to impress Parliament, and at the same time to prevent a premature " going out in driblets " ? [2] Would it not be well to have a frank, free, and private consultation of all the ministers known to be sympathetic ? It is in a letter shortly after his return to Edinburgh that we find the first mention of any practical steps towards that end.

" Mr. Hanna suggested to me a general convocation of all the right-minded clergy on the subject ; a suggestion which I am pushing among the brethren here, and with greater acceptance than I at first anti-

[1] *Witness*, September 3, 1842   [2] Hanna, vol. iv, p. 305

cipated. I wish it to come in the shape at first of a requisition from some twelve or twenty of the most venerable of the senior clergy in all parts of Scotland, so as to divest it altogether of the aspect of Edinburgh leadership, and give it the appearance, as well as the reality, of a great, and general, and withal spontaneous remonstrance from the collective mind and conscience of the Church, against the Erastian invasion made by the recent decision of the House of Peers on the rights and liberties of the Church of Scotland." [1]

It was frequently suggested in the newspapers of the day, alike in the leaders and in the correspondence columns, that the convocation of November 1842 was an adroit exploitation of the soreness left by the Auchterarder judgment ; that it was a clever device of the younger hotheads of the Non-intrusion party to increase the nominal roll of their supporters by pledges from the waverers. Writing seven years later, Dr. Bryce persisted in the charge. " The snare that was laid proved as successful as it was cunningly devised ; and it was believed that many were entrapped into pledges of which they never dreamt when they left their homes to attend this celebrated convention." [2]

It is clear, however, that the scheme did not emanate from these " young and fiery spirits," [3] but from Dr. Chalmers, and the letter through which he sought concurrence from the other signatories is perfectly clear and explicit.

[1] Hanna, vol. iv, pp. 306–7, from a letter to Chalmers' other son-in-law, Mr. MacKenzie

[2] Bryce, *Ten Years of the Church of Scotland*, vol. ii, p. 311

[3] Dr. Candlish, presumably one of the " young and fiery spirits," writes to Mr. Alexander Dunlop, presumably another, on 13th September : " The more I think of it, the more I like Chalmers' proposal." W. Wilson, *Memorials of R. S. Candlish*, p. 213

" The truth is, that every effort has been made to foster the delusion in the minds of our rulers that the late proceedings of the Assembly are due to the factitious influence of a few leaders which, when once broken up, will leave the Church in a condition to be moulded into a willing conformity with the reigning and Erastian policy of the times. There is nothing more fitted to dissipate this imagination than a spontaneous and free expression, the result of a conference, held for days together, by clergymen assembled in a great and general body from all parts of Scotland ; and giving forth such a solemn and deliberate representation of their sentiments and views, as might convince all men that the determination *to stand or fall* with the spiritual independence of our Church, is both so strong and so general as not to be overcome but by a violent oppression of conscience, which, if attempted on the part of our civil authorities, will lead to the degradation and eventual overthrow of the best and greatest of our national institutes." [1]

Further, while it is true that the circular issued spoke of the value of united prayer and Christian fellowship at such a time of crisis, and laid stress on the wholesome effect on the Government of a united front, it must have been obvious to all who read the invitation through, that some expression of the determination to abide, at whatever cost, by essential principles would be made by the gathering. Any member who looked forward to a devotional conference without any practical resolutions must have been singularly blind both to the realities of the situation and the terms of the summons.

The convocation began with a great meeting for public worship in St. George's on the 17th of November,

---

[1] Hanna, vol. iv, p. 308 (*italics supplied*)

and it closed with another open meeting in Lady Glen-orchy's on the 24th, both fully reported in the Press. The week between was spent in private conferences in the Roxburgh Church, which was chosen for its size, which was suitable, and for its acoustics, which did not prove quite up to expectation. No account of these conferences was given to the newspapers, which were, however, full of rumours, generally wide of the mark. Dr. Bryce and Mr. Turner, in their descriptions, were dependent on the memories of some who had been present during some at least of the sessions ; Dr. Buchanan, who was present, so stringently observed the seal of confidence that his record is the most meagre of the three. But twenty years after the latest of these histories Dr. Wilson, in his life of Dr. Candlish, published [1] a summary of the proceedings made night by night from notes taken during each day by one whom he calls a " thoroughly competent reporter," Dr. James Henderson of Glasgow. It is a notable document, frank to a fault, revealing the many cross-currents of opinion which finally blended into one strong stream.

It has always been known what a wise and sure lead was given to the proceedings by Dr. Chalmers' sermon in St. George's on the text, " Unto the upright there ariseth light in darkness " ; but this narrative discloses that his was the guiding hand throughout. During the private sessions he manifested himself as a real master of assemblies. When extremists were inclined to persist in the incorporation of their principles in the resolutions, when old feuds seemed to be on the point of breaking out afresh, when the prospect of the unendowed future seemed to dismay the timorous, he uniformly intervened with the very word for the emergency. About one such

[1] W. Wilson, *Memorials of R. S. Candlish,* pp. 219–59

occasion Dr. Henderson confessed himself unable to give more than an impression. Chalmers was dealing at the moment, with the hesitant who dreaded not their own plight in the future, but the restricted activity of an un-endowed Church. " If free," Chalmers contended, " the Church of Scotland might be the rallying point for evangelical truth throughout the world." At this point, continues the report, " he burst forth into a description of enthusiasm as peculiar to times of trouble and excite-ment, etc." And then in brackets there follows : " He was himself the most striking impersonation of the passion which he so eloquently and vividly depicted. I cannot recall it—it burst like electricity upon us—not less brilliant and effective than the most brilliant and striking of all the productions of his mind. The effect was astonishing." [1]

This lofty flight which defeated his reporter was not, however, his most breath-taking contribution. This found utterance on the Monday evening. It was a com-plete plan for financing a Church bereft of her patrimony —" not a voluntary Church, but a voluntarily endowed and supported Church " [2]—with the congregations de-pendent not on fluctuating local conditions, but on a stable central fund, out of which an equal dividend would be paid to all ministers, " leaving to the private kindness of people to show any additional kindness to their own " [3] ministers. The proposals he outlined were to provide the complete blueprint for the Free Church finance of days to come.

It is quite apparent that the fact that Dr. Chalmers with his genius for finance had already been gathering in gifts and promises, and had thought out the whole problem of support down to the last detail, came as an

[1] W. Wilson, *Memorials of R. S. Candlish*, p. 252   [2] *Ibid.*, p. 233
[3] *Ibid.*, p. 233

astonishment to the majority of the convocation. The one memory of these days that those who were present seem to have taken most pleasure in recounting is thus reported by Dr. Henderson : " Dr. Paterson moved thanks to Dr. Chalmers the philanthropist, who had brought a lifeboat to the rescue when the ship was sinking. The only objection he had was that the lifeboat was made to look better than the ship "—(great laughter).[1]

But practical proposals absorbed only a small portion of the time of the convocation. The members seemed quite content to leave these to Dr. Chalmers. And almost the only unworthy note came when a prominent Edinburgh minister, realizing that in the event of a separation the civil courts would claim even the Church Extension buildings for the Establishment, said that " it was a custom with a distressed army when they could not carry away their guns to spike them. If we cannot get the Extension Churches, lay a heavy burden of debt on them, which will make them of little use." [2] Despite his great popularity and eloquence, this advocate of a " scorched earth " policy seems to have made no impression.

The mind of the convocation was gathered up in two series of resolutions. The former series was a brief restatement of the Church's grievances, concentrating on that involved in the recent Auchterarder judgment, " the supremacy of the Civil Courts over those of the Established Church in the exercise of their spiritual functions," [3] and declaring that they felt it indispensable that this type of encroachment should be fully prevented in time to come. Four hundred and twenty-three [4] ministers signed this first set of resolutions. The second series contains a

---

[1] W. Wilson, *Memorials of R. S. Candlish*, p. 234   [2] *Ibid.*, p. 253
[3] Hanna, vol. iv, p. 314   [4] This is the number given by Buchanan, vol. ii, p. 395, and Turner, p. 322. Hanna says (vol. iv, p. 314n.) 427

declaration that they conceived it to be their duty, should the State refuse to grant the indispensable minimum to abandon the Establishment, " to tender the resignation of their civil advantages which they can no longer hold in consistency with the full and free exercise of their spiritual functions, and to cast themselves on such provision as God, in His providence, may afford." [1] This second set of resolutions was signed by 354 ministers.[2]

At the close of the convocation various practical steps were taken. Two of these were more official. The resolutions, embodied in a memorial, were transmitted to the Government, submitting the question to the decision of Parliament ; and in an address to the people of Scotland, the significance of the resolutions and the urgency of the crisis were expounded with a view to the utmost possible publicity.

These, however, were supplemented by local activities. Public meetings were held, not only in the cities and towns, but in many of the rural parishes, which seldom dispersed without a resolution to stand by the principles enunciated and their defenders, whatever betide.

Not long after the convocation separated the tardy official answer of the Government to the Claim of Right was transmitted through Sir James Graham.[3] It was quite unmistakably a refusal to entertain the Claim at

[1] Hanna, vol. iv, p. 317

[2] On this figure Buchanan (vol. ii, p. 397) and Turner (p. 322) agree, but Hanna (vol. iv, p. 317n.) gives 333. The *Witness* for February 11, 1843, gives as the numbers adhering to the first set 517, to the second 469. But as the names given in this and previous issues show, it includes ordained missionaries as well as ministers, together with many who signed after the convocation had separated.

[3] Lord Cockburn says : " It is certainly not written by Sir James Graham, the Home Secretary, who signs it. Some give it to Duncan McNeill, the Lord Advocate ; who, however, I don't believe wrote it. . . . It is all much liker Lord Aberdeen." *Memorials*, vol. i, p. 341

all. By dint of deliberately confusing that document's statement of the indispensable minimum of relief required from the legislature and the General Assembly's resolution against patronage transmitted at the same time, it contrived to represent the Church as a body insatiable in its demands, advancing by leaps and bounds to swollen pretensions which were unprecedented and intolerable in any ordered State. One main part of the letter was devoted to a justification of patronage as an ancient institution, and as a safeguard against clericalism. To yield to the demands of the Church would simply promote its strong inclination towards "despotic power." There was no patient examination of the Church's statement of her historic rights. Instead, there was a stern rebuke to the Church for her assault on vested interests, and a not obscure insinuation that the leaders of the Church of Scotland were emulating the arrogant pretensions of the See of Rome.

An official answer to this was speedily prepared, and adopted at a meeting of the Special Commission within a week of its receipt. It fills five columns of the *Witness* ; yet there is not a trace of haste in its weighty paragraphs. Intended to serve a temporary need, and sponsored by a commission which was no normal court of the Church, it does not seem ever to have been reprinted. It certainly deserved to be ; for in no document are the whole issues more fully set forth, or more vigorously and lucidly expounded. No minister of the Crown who read it through could any longer credibly profess ignorance of the Church's position. In particular, the effects of the two alternatives, granting the Claim of Right or refusing it, were most strikingly exhibited.

" If the *Legislature* shall adopt the same views [*i.e.* as the civil courts] the Church will have only this alternative, viz. to fulfil conditions, and to submit to a state of subjection to secular power, in matters spiritual, which she deems inconsistent with the Word of God, and at variance with her own laws and standards *or* to relinquish the temporal benefits of an Establishment clogged with such conditions, and implying such subjection. The LEGISLATURE also will have an alternative submitted to them, viz. Whether to force on a Disruption of the Established Church of Scotland, with all its attendant evils, *or* to restore the Church to the state in which she was between 1834 and 1838, when the Veto Act had not been declared illegal . . . and the jurisdiction of the civil courts, which has since been so largely exercised, had not been claimed. That the state of the Church during this period was one of usefulness and comparative harmony and peace none will deny. The practical operation of the Veto Act had removed much of the dread with which it had been viewed, and many of the objections which had been made to it. Those who had opposed its adoption in the Church courts had come to acquiesce in it, and even to talk of it as likely to prove a ' blessing ' to the country. The Government had exercised the Crown patronage in accordance with it, with a happy experience of its beneficial and peaceful working. None of the *extensive* private patrons opposed it, or complained of it ; and the resistance to it proceeded from one individual alone. A general and cordial co-operation in the great cause of advancing religion, promoting education, and improving the morals of the people prevailed among all parties in the Church. Those bodies who had in the preceding century seceded from her communion were returning within her pale. She was extending herself with a rapidity unknown at any former period of her history, and new life and vigour were apparent in every department of her labours. That the total disruption of the Establishment should be *preferred* to the restoration of the Church to the state in which she was during this period the Special Commission would be unwilling to believe." [1]

This elaborate and powerful document drew forth an equally speedy reply from Sir James Graham. But there was nothing elaborate about it. A few lines sufficed. " Sir James Graham loses not a moment in acknowledging receipt of Dr. Gordon's reply to his letter ; and as the Church have appealed the matter to Parliament, he feels it unnecessary to correspond farther with the Commission on the subject." [2]

The policy behind this curt and laconic reply is plain. You appeal over our heads to the Legislature. Well, then, do it. We shall not hinder you making the attempt, but once it is made we shall oppose you to the utmost of our power. You will speedily find out how little that appeal will profit you.

Such official interchanges, however, do not fully convey the atmosphere of this winter of 1842–43. The days were full of ferment and stir among the people. Hardly had the educative mission of the convocation begun with its serious meetings ending in solemn pledges when a new campaign opened, with no official sponsors, in which the atmosphere was less religious and more political. Sir James Graham's reply was torn to pieces on many a Scottish platform. No picture of the period would be complete without some account of these other meetings. One may be instanced as a sample. On Thursday, 19th January, there was held in the Roxburgh Church (where the convocation had met) a crowded meeting of the Edinburgh Tradesmen's Church

---

[1] *Witness*, January 14, 1843 [2] *Ibid.*, January 25, 1843

Association, at which Mr. Begg of Liberton scintillated for two hours. He dealt largely in apologues. Here is one of them—as reported.

" The grounds of two proprietors, one much more powerful than the other, are contiguous. It occurs to them that they might unite and live in one house. But the less powerful one says, ' I have a very precious flock of sheep, and I shall not unite with you unless you swear upon the open Bible that you will guard these sheep with the utmost care.' A bargain is struck, but lo ! the first dark night the other brings a furious wild beast, and lets him loose among the sheep. The proprietor of the sheep and all his shepherds remonstrate strongly, but in vain, against this outrage. When he sees many of his sheep worried and many of them scattered, he cries out imploringly for redress. At length, when no redress is granted, it occurs to him to gather his shepherds together ; they seize the wild beast ; a council of war is held ; some say, ' Kill it and cast it out ' ; the majority resolve merely to muzzle and chain it—(laughter)—thinking that will be sufficient. This is accordingly done ; the sheep rejoice in the deliverance, many of the scattered ones return. But lo ! the strong man comes rushing out in a rage, at the head of a troop of armed servants, and says, ' What ho ! ye shepherds, what dreadful evil have ye done ? ' The shepherds answer, with undeniable reason, ' Ye undertook to guard our sheepfold with the utmost care, else we should have nothing to do with you ; and, instead of that, ye have turned in this furious beast among the sheep, and ye would not, notwithstanding all our remonstrances, take him away. And, therefore, we have tried to cure the evil ourselves, but instead of killing this beast, as we might have done, we have simply put a

277

muzzle on his mouth to prevent his biting and devouring the sheep.' The strong man draws himself up and answers with the utmost gravity :

" ' 1. Ye are greatly mistaken in your ideas ; it is not the beast, but the muzzle, that has done all this mischief —(loud laughter and cheers). If ye had not put on the muzzle no evil would have happened.

" ' 2. This beast has now acquired a " vested right " to be here, and to worry as many sheep as he pleases—(much laughter)—and to meddle with him is a most formidable " attack " on " vested rights."

" ' 3. He is not a beast at all—(laughter)—but a decided advantage to the fold—(laughter)—insomuch that I am not sure if the sheep could live if he were removed—(much laughter).

" ' 4. You are aware that every sheepfold must have an animal such as this at any rate—(a laugh)—and you may as well have this as any other.

" ' And lastly, whether this be a beast or not, whether it is useful or otherwise, whether it has a right to be here or not, one thing I have resolved—and my will is law— I am determined, " firmly " determined, that the beast shall remain here, say what you will—(loud cheers). And moreover, since your shepherds have dared to touch him, I will turn them all about their business, and appoint shepherds of my own, who will take all their instructions from me, and, in particular, will suffer this animal to go at large untouched, and to worry as many sheep and lambs as he pleases.' Such," he concluded this portion of his speech, " is an unexaggerated representation of the kind of argument by which the Cabinet of England in this letter endeavours to justify the unconstitutional encroachments which have been made on the dearly purchased and solemnly guaranteed rights of the Church of our fathers, and by which they attempt to excuse their refusal of redress." [1]

The serious answer by the Commission to the Government's reply was followed by similar unflattering dissections of it on scores of platforms, amid scenes of mingled laughter and indignation. One or two popular orators acquired a fame they could never have aspired to in less hectic days ; and there was a certain impatience with those who could not, or would not, join volubly in the chorus of clamour.

But such gatherings were not the rule, and it should be realized that it was the meetings held under the auspices of the convocation that were general and typical. The demand was widespread for the solemn treatment of grave issues. Of the multitude of reports I have selected the one from Skirling, where Mr. Hanna was minister. "A few weeks ago, the Rev. Mr. Hanna, minister of the parish, called his people together, and gave them an account of the proceedings of the late Convocation, and of the measures which so many of the ministers of the Church of Scotland had considered it to be their duty to adopt. Another meeting of the parishioners was held on Monday evening, which was addressed by the Rev. Messrs. Martin of Bathgate and Pitcairn of Cockpen, a deputation appointed to visit the parishes within the bounds of the Presbytery of Biggar. . . . The declaration of adherence has been signed by every individual in the congregation above sixteen, with the exception of one family, who, however, are by no means unfriendly. . . . A parochial association has been formed for the purpose of raising funds for the support of a free Church." [2]

Such calls to action were more common and more effective than the flamboyant activities of the few whose orations filled the newspapers.

[1] *Witness*, January 25, 1843   [2] *Ibid.*, January 25, 1843

CHAPTER TWENTY

THE FATE OF THE CHAPEL ACT

1834–43

IN the early spring of 1843 there came another serious blow in the shape of the verdict in the Stewarton case ; and since this case was so important in itself, and so determinative in its results, it must be given at least a brief consideration. All the earlier cases had arisen out of the Veto Act. This one arose out of the Chapel Act ; and the general effect of the decision was to declare that act also beyond the competence of the Church.

Now, if any Act challenged at the time of its passing had ever acquired stability, this one apparently had. A chapel minister—a Moderate—had sat in the Moderator's chair. Two Acts of Parliament had assumed the parishes *quoad sacra* it had created as quite normal and legal. Leaders of every party, group, and tendency within the Church had welcomed the return of one branch of the Secession to the mother church in 1839, and most of its congregations and ministers came under the scope of the Act. But one of the congregations thus received was in a parish with not a few suspicious heritors. Would there not, if not now, at least ultimately, be a raid on their unexhausted teinds to support this new charge ?

This congregation was located at Stewarton in Ayrshire, in a district in which the Secession cause was relatively strong. The minister was the Rev. James Clelland, and Stewarton was a thriving little town with a growing population and a wide country district round it.

In accordance with the directions of the General Assembly of 1839, Mr. Clelland, with the bulk of his Kirk Session and members, applied to the Presbytery of Irvine at its first meeting thereafter to be admitted as an integral part of the Church of Scotland. They were admitted, and Mr. Clelland at once took his seat as a regular member of the Presbytery.

The next step, in accordance with the provisions of the Chapel Act, was to assign to the new congregation a territorial district from within the old parish of Stewarton. It appeared, from the outset of the process, that the minister of the parish objected, so far at least as related to losing any of the landward part of his parish. It may be admitted that it was calculated to put a severe strain on a parish minister to have to receive as a colleague on an equal footing one who for some time had been a not unsuccessful rival. This difficulty, however, would not have been found incapable of adjustment had it not been for the action of the patron, supported by a considerable body of the heritors. When they heard of what was afoot they protested to the Presbytery through an agent that it was beyond the power of the Presbytery to allocate a parochial district to Mr. Clelland, and to admit him to a seat and vote in the Presbytery. The Presbytery referred the matter to the General Assembly, which through the Commission decided that they should " proceed according to the laws of the Church, instructing them at the same time to insert express words in the deliverance by which they allocate a territorial district to the Church in question, limiting the effect of the same to matters of spiritual jurisdiction and discipline, which alone are implied in, or would be affected by, such allocation under the existing laws of the Church ; and also to insert the reservation, *likewise implied*, to heritors and their tenants in the part of the parish which may be set apart for the new church, having legal right to the sittings in the original church, to continue, in their option, members of the congregation thereof." [1]

Meanwhile, the patron and the dissatisfied heritors had gone to the Court of Session for an interdict against the Presbytery of Irvine " from innovating upon the present parochial state of the parish of Stewarton as regards pastoral superintendence, its kirk-session, and jurisdiction and discipline belonging thereto," [2] and against Mr. Clelland " from sitting, acting, and voting as a member of the Presbytery of Irvine." [3] The Presbytery, however, proceeded to designate and assign a territorial district to the new congregation.

It might well seem that in all this there was no footing for a civil action. The religious resources of the Church of Scotland in the parish of Stewarton had been increased, without any additional burden, present or prospective, on the heritors. But in their action for suspension and interdict they averred that " any illegal alteration of the statutory constitution of the courts of the Established Church, and any new ecclesiastical arrangement of the parishes of the Church, if illegal and inconsistent with the statutes, might be prevented by the Supreme Civil Court." [4] " The Court of Session was the only court which could afford the remedy sought." [5]

They found the Court of Session ready to afford the remedy. By eight to five the Lords of Session decided in favour of the heritors and against the Presbytery. The most striking thing apparent in reading the verdicts of the thirteen is that not one of them shows any indecision. Not one adopts the tone, " I rather think the law is

---

[1] *Report of the Stewarton Case*, p. 3   [2] *Ibid.*, p. 3   [3] *Ibid.*, p. 2
[4] *Ibid.*, p. 7   [5] *Ibid.*, p. 7

with the Church on this point, and against it on that," or, " On the whole, taking all things into consideration, balancing this statute against that, I incline to this opinion." Eight of them unhesitatingly brand the Church as having exceeded her statutory power ; five as unhesitatingly justify her in her action. And the thirteen in doing so are surveying the same statutes. The longest verdict and the most erudite is the unfavourable one of Lord Medwyn ; the second longest and the most powerful is the favourable one of Lord Moncrieff. Both are an education in Church History and in ecclesiastical law. From what source do their totally opposed conclusions spring ? Does each depend simply upon a selected catena of statutes seen through the eyes of a partisan ? No, the difference goes deeper than the contents of statutes ; it concerns the whole relation of these statutes to the Church's jurisdiction. Lord Medwyn's basic idea is that the Church of Scotland owes its whole jurisdiction to the statutes, and beyond what is definitely prescribed in some unrepealed statute, she cannot trespass. Lord Moncrieff's basic idea is that when the State recognized and confirmed the jurisdiction of the Church, it was dealing with an institution which already had a history, which had already in 1567 been operating efficiently and smoothly through its regular Church courts, and that its spiritual jurisdiction is only trammelled where statute law has prescribed definite limits. " Fifteen General Assemblies were successively convened and held before there was the least notice either of such an institution or of any system for the government of the Church in any act of Parliament. In those various Assemblies, the most important acts, both of judgment and of legislation, were exercised by the body so assembled ; and though all was done openly and in public, there was no complaint, and no surmise that these Assemblies were usurping powers that did not belong to them." [1] " As the Church itself was adopted, its jurisdiction ecclesiastical, as previously exercised and existing, was declared sole and exclusive in the broadest and strongest terms." [2] To Lord Medwyn ecclesiastical jurisdiction as vested in the Kirk is specifically conferred by the State, and is confined to points specified in statutes, among which will certainly not be found the authority to erect new parishes in any sense of that word. To Lord Moncreiff the Church has an inherent and legally recognized ecclesiastical jurisdiction which it may freely exercise for the spiritual good of the land, so long as it does not come into conflict with some definite statutory limitation. Thus precisely the same statutes are found to bear totally different implications. A careful reading and comparison of the two verdicts will demonstrate, to most people to-day, the historical soundness of Lord Moncrieff. The Church had a right to take this step in Stewarton, and her reception of members of the Associate Synod was " calculated to do much good, without the possibility of injury to any one." [3]

But the verdict was otherwise. Its effect was to declare the Chapel Act illegal. The Church had no right to further its work by erecting that unheard-of evasion, a parish *quoad sacra*. It must either revert to the anomaly of Chapels of Ease, with ministers without a Kirk Session and with no seat in the Presbytery, or obtain the sanction of the Court of Teinds, having first received the assent of seventy-five per cent. of the heritors, to a new parish *quoad omnia*. This wrought two mischiefs : it sapped the foundations of the whole great Church Extension scheme, and it entailed this, that in the judgment of the Court of Session, the majority of the Presbyteries of the Church

[1] *Report of the Stewarton Case*, p. 94   [2] *Ibid.*, p. 101   [3] *Ibid.*, p. 87

were wrongly constituted, having unwarrantably admitted to their ranks the ministers and representative elders of these congregations and their pseudo-Kirk Sessions.

A few days after the decision there was a special meeting of the Commission of the General Assembly. After an explanation by the Moderator of the urgent reasons for calling the meeting, Dr. Cook drew attention to the decision in the Stewarton case, and asked that the names of all *quoad sacra* ministers be withdrawn from the roll of the Commission. His motion was rejected by 115 votes to 25. Whereupon he and his supporters left the meeting. This was the beginning of definite division, and was a foretaste of the additional troubles that were fast thickening round the Church.

The Commission went on to adopt a final appeal to Parliament. This petition was laid before the House of Commons on the 10th of February by Mr. Fox Maule, the member for Perth. The 7th of March was fixed for a debate on the relevant motion which he submitted, viz. that the House should resolve itself into a committee to take into consideration the grievances of which the Church of Scotland complained. There followed a debate not unworthy of the best traditions of the House of Commons. Friends of the Church did their utmost, but the whole weight of the government was thrown against them. After the Prime Minister's express and emphatic repudiation of the Church's claims, there could be no doubt of the result. By a majority of about three to one, the Church's petition was totally rejected. It is not irrelevant to note, however, that of the Scottish members, 37 took part in the division ; 25 voted for Mr. Maule's motion, and 12 against. Thus, just as the Claim of Right was adopted by the General Assembly by a majority of over two to one, a similar proportion of the

Scottish members recorded their sense of the real grievances of the National Church. By 8 to 5 the interpreters
of Scots law had created a situation that by 25 to 12 the
Scots who had been sent to Parliament to make law strove
in vain to rectify. Though there was a subsidiary debate
later in the House of Lords on a similar motion and with
a similar result, it was this failure of the valiant attempt
to rouse the House of Commons to legislative intervention
that made the Disruption appear inevitable and imminent.

During all this political activity, Dr. Chalmers had
not been much in evidence. He had certainly used what
influence he had with friends in the Tory party, and he
had lifted up his voice in the special January meeting
of the Commission. But he had been more deeply
immersed in practical plans. His financial schemes for
the future had received a definite welcome at the Convocation, though there had been a reluctance to make any
effort to put them into operation. It seemed like taking
to the life-boat while the ship was not in imminent
danger of sinking. He was himself, however, so impressed
with a sense of urgency that he resolved to give a lead.
He was now living in the parish of Morningside. It was
laid on him, he felt, to do pioneer work within its bounds,
and that without delay. So before the end of 1842 he had
formed a local association, which began systematically
to collect for the support of the future ministry, and to
secure donations for the churches that would have to be
built. This lead was followed in a few localities during
January. The decision in the Stewarton case quickened
the tempo.

Following on an impressive gathering of representative
elders in Edinburgh on 1st February, a provisional
committee was set up to deal with practical matters of
preparation. There were three distinct sub-committees,

on finance, on architecture, and on statistics. Dr. Chalmers was made convener of the first of these ; and he threw himself into the work with an enthusiasm unequalled in any part of his career. Circulars, personal letters, interviews filled his days. Within a fortnight, he was able to announce to an influential gathering in Edinburgh : " The money has come in upon us like a set rain at the rate of £1,000 a day ; "[1] and it was to that same gathering that he spoke words referred to earlier.[2] He had been saying that he now hoped that it was within the distinct range of possibility that not only would provision be made for the outgoing ministers, but that the whole land would have the blessing of Christian instruction. " When we come to that—and I think it may be soon—I shall feel myself in my old element, at my old work of Church Extension in Scotland. . . . For Church Extension I knocked at the door of a Whig ministry, and they refused to endow. I then knocked at the door of a Tory ministry, but they offered to enslave. I now therefore turn aside from both, and knock at the door of the general population." [3]

The main practical point of his speech was its emphasis on the necessity of a thorough organization. An extensive and intensive campaign for new local associations followed. By the end of April there were over five hundred on the model of Morningside, and Dr. Chalmers expressed himself hopefully in a letter to a friend that " by the meeting of the General Assembly the country will be half organized, and we look for a great additional impulse from the Disruption when it actually takes place." [4]

Devoting himself to this, he seems to have left other

[1] *Witness*, February 18, 1843   [2] Page 146   [3] *Witness*, February 18, 1843
[4] Hanna, vol. iv, p. 333

forms of preparation in other hands. How precisely was the Disruption to be accomplished? What procedure was to be adopted in leaving the Establishment in which they could no longer conscientiously labour? Dr. Bryce attributes to the leaders of the party a " grand design " of going out under a vote of the General Assembly like the one which had approved of the Claim of Right.[1] And he gives the credit for the frustration of this to the Presbytery of Fordyce which, he claims, was the first to meet in conclave, " uncontaminated by the illegality " of the presence of *quoad sacra* ministers, to nominate representatives to the General Assembly—a move, he adds, " altogether unexpected by the dominant party in the Church." Later, however, Dr. Donald MacLeod put forward rival claims for his brother Norman. He was then minister of Loudoun Parish, in the same Presbytery as Stewarton. On the strength of an article in the *Presbyterian Review* he was evidently convinced that the prevailing party planned to gain a definite majority in the Assembly, to utilize that majority for declaring the connection between Church and State at an end, and " moreover, to excommunicate those who remained in the Church as by law established." [2] As Moderator of the Presbytery, he proceeded on that conviction. When the election of commissioners was due, holding " that as the decision of the Court of Session satisfied him that the ministers of Chapels *quoad sacra* had no legal position in the Ecclesiastical Court, he declared his determination not to admit their votes, and intimated that, should they insist on retaining their seats at the meeting of Presbytery, he would then separate, and

[1] Bryce, *Ten Years of the Church of Scotland*, vol. ii, p. 354
[2] Donald MacLeod, *Memoir of Norman MacLeod*, 1878 one-volume edition, p. 120

constitute the court from a roll purged of the names of all not legally qualified." [1] " He accordingly," adds his brother and biographer, " separated with those who adhered to him, and the first split in the Church took place." [2] Two sets of nominations were sent up to the Assembly from the Presbytery of Irvine, and as the same thing had happened in many Presbyteries which had *quoad sacra* or even Parliamentary ministers on their rolls, it was evident that the task of sifting the commissions to the Assembly of 1843 would present almost insurmountable difficulties.

Still, this action can hardly have come as a surprise. From the moment that Dr. Cook had asked for the purging of the roll of the Commission within a week of the Stewarton decision, and had withdrawn from it on the rejection of his motion, this move must have been anticipated and provided for. There is no trace of any drastic change of plan in the biographies or correspondence of the leaders ; or any sense of disappointment at the actual manner of the exodus in the biographies of those most remote from the centre, who must have been indulging in forecasts of the event. The only hint that some other way may have been contemplated is that Dr. Chalmers and Principal MacFarlane had each their own following as prospective moderators, but this may simply have been a foreshadowing of the inevitable separation.

[1] Donald MacLeod, *Memoir of Norman MacLeod*, 1878 one-volume edition, p. 120   [2] *Ibid.*, p. 121

Chapter Twenty-one

THE DECISIVE WEEK

1843

THE general lines of proposed action in the matter of the Assembly of 1843 having been prepared by the Provisional Committee, and having been communicated to known sympathizers throughout the land, it was resolved to make the final adjustments, both of documents and procedure, at a mass meeting in Edinburgh on the earlier days of the week in which the Assembly was to meet. In addition to the private advance intimations, there was this notice in the *Witness* and other newspapers : " We are authorized to state that a meeting of ministers adhering to the Convocation resolutions, and of elders approving of these resolutions, will be held on the evening of Monday, the 15th, at 7 o'clock in St. Luke's Church, Young Street. *Admission is to be only by tickets*, which will be issued to the parties applying *personally* at No. 7 North St. Andrew Street on *Monday forenoon*." On the Wednesday following, the *Witness* carried this report : " Consultation meetings of the ministers and elders favourable to the erection of the Free Church have been held on Monday and yesterday in St. Luke's Church, very numerously attended. We cannot, of course, state what was transacted, but this much we can affirm, that the greatest harmony has prevailed among them as to the course of duty which they are called upon to follow."

From none of the standard authorities on the Disruption period do we have any light whatsoever on those private gatherings in St. Luke's. The unfriendly, being excluded, had to depend on hearsay ; the friendly felt that their lips were sealed, and contented themselves with some paraphrase and amplification of the approved report in the *Witness*, as quoted above. Nor did these gatherings enter largely into the reminiscences of any who took part ; their happenings, important as they were, were immediately eclipsed by the more momentous and decisive events that followed, which upset the even tenour of their careers and left their mark for ever on their lives. But a generation after, in 1877, Dr. Norman Walker, in his life of the historian of the Ten Years' Conflict, made public the brief and hurried correspondence which Dr. Buchanan found time to send to his wife in Glasgow. He did not arrive in Edinburgh until the Tuesday, having missed, in consequence, the first of the meetings. But his friends were full of it. And this is what he writes for the eyes of his wife alone.[1]

" There had been a meeting last night—the first for consultation—Dr. Chalmers in the chair, who made an admirable statement. In the course of the evening Dr. Gordon made a most powerful and impressive speech, which was received with the utmost enthusiasm and unanimity. It is most encouraging to see so much decision and so much of one mind among our ministers and elders. It augurs well."

On the Wednesday, he continued thus :

" It is quite wonderful to see the perfect unanimity which prevails. Men seem fully to have made up their minds, and to be quite prepared for the great crisis of

[1] N. L. Walker, *Dr. Robert Buchanan, an Ecclesiastical Biography*, pp. 219ff.

to-morrow. It is also comforting to observe the entire mutual confidence and affection which prevail among the ministers and elders who have assembled. All seem to feel like brethren, and to be deeply impressed with the conviction that God has some great work for us to do, since He has been so evidently and so wonderfully preparing the hearts and minds of all to encounter, calmly and cheerfully, the events that are before us. I forget if I told you that the Protest we are to give in to-morrow to the Assembly is prepared, and was read over several times yesterday at the meetings and unanimously approved. It is a most admirable document, drawn up with great precision and beauty, and very solemn at the close. Dunlop, to whose pen we are so much indebted, drew it up. We meet at one o'clock to-day for the purpose of signing it, and finally arranging about the way of tabling it to-morrow. Probably there will only be a brief statement made by Dr. Welsh, and then the Protest given in at once."

On the same evening at half-past seven he added this :

" We had the signing of the Protest this forenoon. It has been resolved that on leaving the *Old* Assembly to-morrow, we should go, not to the New Church in Lothian Road, but to the great building at Canonmills. The impossibility of finding room for the multitude of elders and others who wish to be admitted is the reason for this change. It is truly a most eventful time ; and it is most comforting to see how men's minds seem to be prepared for it. We are all to go to the levee to-morrow, and to be quite respectful to the Queen's representative— *all the more* that we mean to leave him in the Assembly."

His final note was written on Thursday forenoon.

" The eventful day has at last come—a day that will be memorable in the annals of the kingdom and of the Christian world. All the preparations are now made. The signing of the Protest was continued last night, and was resumed this morning, and will go on till twelve o'clock. Between three and four hundred ministers had signed by the time I left St. Luke's Church last night : the entire number of signatures will not be ascertained till midday. The meeting last night was like all that preceded it—full of harmony and mutual love ; while there was much solemnity, there was at the same time the greatest cheerfulness. Men seemed to be enjoying the calm consciousness of discharging a high and sacred duty. It is finally agreed we are not to say a word in the Assembly. Everything is to be done by the Moderator, Dr. Welsh."

From these letters and a few similar remains [1] various things are apparent. Firstly, this gathering of ministers and elders, to which entry was only obtained by personal application for a ticket of admission, was marked by a harmony and unanimity throughout much more complete than that of the Convocation of ministers in the preceding November.

Secondly, the Protest—a document already prepared by Mr. Dunlop and approved by the Provisional Committee—was finally adjusted in the earlier sessions after repeated readings.

[1] The most detailed is an MS. account by the Rev. James Smith, Dumbarton, now in New College Library, which incorporated so many extra details that only the shortage of paper prevented the writer issuing it in a planned volume of Disruption documents.

Thirdly, in the later sessions, signatures were appended. The original document was signed only by those who had been duly commissioned as members of Assembly ; but there were other copies for all ministers and elders who were willing to set down their names to it. The ministers numbered 400 as against the 354 who had subscribed to both resolutions of the convocation. The result was noteworthy, in view of the fact that the Government was still receiving assurances that there would, at the last moment, be a general withdrawal at the very brink of the abyss, and that only a handful would separate, the rest in their wisdom sitting tight, appalled by the prospect of the loss of security and of a comfortable living in familiar surroundings. One of these many assurances deserves to be recorded. It was that of Dr. Cumming of Crown Court Chapel, London—the divine who later became acclaimed as an expert in prophecy through his detailed delineation of the future of history and the end of the world on the basis of an ingenious handling of biblical Apocalyptic, and who was so severely castigated by George Eliot in her essay on *Evangelical Teaching*. The budding prophet was, in the early months of 1843, as far out in his calculations as he was to prove later in the field that brought him fame. His pamphlet on the subject contains some definite but inconsistent forecasts as to the numbers who will abandon the Establishment. The most pessimistic is the second : " If Government is firm, I venture from fairly accurate information to assert that less than one hundred will cover the whole secession." But at one point he seems to feel that he has been over-liberal in this estimate. " The *few* manses and pulpits likely to be vacated will be filled with good and holy ministers." And, finally, he comes to the conclusion that the outlook is less gloomy even than that. " I am no satisfied that any will secede." [1] The numbers of the signatories made it evident that the constant rumours about the success of the " forty " which encouraged the Government to refrain from action, and created disquiet and perturbation in many a country manse, were greatly exaggerated.

Fourthly, there was a final decision as to the exact procedure to be followed. It is evident that Dr. Buchanan did not himself expect that the Moderator alone would speak in the unbroken Assembly. He would have liked to hear an oration from Chalmers or Candlish or Gordon or Cunningham before the withdrawal.

Fifthly, there was one considerable readjustment of plan made at the last moment. The Provisional Committee had selected, as the seat of the Protesting General Assembly, a new church which had just been completed in Lothian Road to house Dr. Candlish and the departing congregation of St. George's, but had also planned some great public gatherings at Tanfield Hall. The new church had over 1,000 sittings, and the *Witness* as late as the Wednesday had published a plan of the building, in order that those at a distance might be able to visualize the proceedings of the Assembly. It was a good and central meeting-place for such a gathering, but its dimensions were not adequate to accommodate all those who wanted to be present, and felt that they had a right to be present. At the eleventh hour, therefore, it was decided to abandon the proposal, and to transfer to Tanfield Hall, which could seat about three times the number.

On the 18th of May the Assembly opened, as it does to-day, with public worship in St. Giles. The sermon was preached by the retiring Moderator, Dr. Welsh.

[1] J. Cumming, *Present State of the Church of Scotland*, pp. 10, 16

From the text, " Let every man be fully persuaded in his own mind," he delivered the most memorable sermon of his career. But it must have been the tension of the situation which made this able and somewhat arid discussion on *The Limits and Extent of the Right of Private Judgment* so moving and heart-searching as many hearers found it to be. For even the application of the doctrine was, in itself, devoid of any fervour of appeal. No-one could complain that the retiring Moderator misused his position to rouse his own party. The discourse was apposite, dignified, and solemn, but not inflammatory.

The opening diet of worship ended, the members made their way to St. Andrew's Church. Dr. Welsh took the Moderator's chair, and opened the proceedings with prayer. Then, at the close, amid a tense silence, he spoke these words : " According to the usual form of procedure, this is the time for making up the roll ; but in consequence of certain proceedings affecting our rights and privileges, proceedings which have been sanctioned by Her Majesty's Government, and by the Legislature of the country, and, more especially, in respect that there has been an infringement on the liberties of our constitution, so that we could not now constitute this court without a violation of the terms of the union between Church and State in this land, as now authoritatively declared, I must protest against our proceeding further. The reasons that have led me to come to this conclusion are fully set forth in the document which I hold in my hand, and which, with the permission of the House, I shall now proceed to read." [1]

He then, despite his obvious weakness, read in a firm and unfaltering tone the Protest which had been finally

[1] *Proceedings of the General Assembly of the Free Church of Scotland, May 1843,* pp. 4-5

adopted two nights before. The first part of the document particularizes the disabilities under which the whole Church and its General Assembly labour ; [1] the second part makes a protest against a General Assembly being constituted at all in terms of the recent decisions of the civil courts.

It concludes thus :

"And, finally ... WE PROTEST, that in the circumstances in which we are placed, it is and shall be lawful for us, and such other commissioners chosen to the Assembly appointed to have been this day holden, as may concur with us, to withdraw to a separate place of meeting, for the purpose of taking steps for ourselves and all who adhere to us—maintaining with us the Confession of Faith and Standards of the Church of Scotland, as heretofore understood—for separating in an orderly way from the Establishment ; and thereupon adopting such measures as may be competent to us, in humble dependence on God's grace and the aid of the Holy Spirit, for the advancement of His glory, the extension of the Gospel of our Lord and Saviour, and the administration of the affairs of Christ's house, according to His Holy word ; and we do now, for the purpose foresaid, withdraw accordingly, humbly and solemnly acknowledging the hand of the Lord in the things which have come upon us, because of our manifold sins, and the sins of this Church and nation ; but, at the same time, with an assured conviction that we are not responsible for any consequences which may follow from this our enforced separation from an Establishment

---

[1] The first five particulars are among the grievances in the Claim of Right ; the last three relate to cases decided since its adoption by the Assembly, especially the Stewarton Case and the Second and Third Auchterarder Cases.

which we loved and prized—through interference with conscience, the dishonour done to Christ's crown, and the rejection of His sole and supreme authority as King in his Church." [1]

Having read this document, Dr. Welsh laid it on the table, and bowing to the Queen's representative, left the chair, and accompanied by Dr. Chalmers and Dr. Gordon and the other 200 Commissioners who had signed the tabled protest, proceeded out of the church, followed by an even greater number not commissioned who had signed as adhering with them to it. That was the dramatic and crucial moment of the Disruption.[2] The decisive step had been taken. Fully persuaded in their own minds, for conscience' sake over 400 ministers had abandoned the churches they loved and positions they had prized.

From that hour there were two General Assemblies in Scotland, the first and only time since 1652, when Resolutioners and Protesters met in rival camps.

[1] *Proceedings of the General Assembly of the Free Church of Scotland, May 1843* p. 14.　　　　　　[2] Cf., however, p. 350

CHAPTER TWENTY-TWO

THE TWO ASSEMBLIES

1843

A COMPARISON of the two General Assemblies of 1843 is, manifestly, no fair criterion by which to estimate the prospects of the now separated Churches. Both found themselves in uncharted waters ; both had crucial decisions to make, and tremendous problems to face. The one Assembly went on its way, very conscious of depleted numbers and the loss of leaders whom it had been accustomed to revere if not to follow, and without a definite united policy. It was composed of three main groups uneasily yoked together—the old Moderates, whose dearest wish was to return to the conditions of the peaceful days before 1834; the new Middle Party, which promises of government measures to an obedient Church had induced to remain behind; and a smaller group which had normally voted with the Evangelicals and still held to the Evangelical ideals but did not think the questions at issue important enough for them to take the extreme step of separation. The other Assembly faced its daunting task of building up from the foundation a national organization of evangelical witness and Christian usefulness in the first flush of a flaming enthusiasm. The biographies of Free Churchmen and the histories they sponsored are full of the inspiration of that first Assembly ; similar works from the Church of Scotland side pass over their critical General Assembly in a significant silence, and jump at once to later stages of that Church's marvellous recovery.

No clearer light has been left on the feelings of the Assembly in St. Andrew's Church than the correspondence of Norman MacLeod. His letters to his sister in the manse of Loudoun lay bare the perturbations and misgivings of a clouded week.

Early on Thursday morning he wrote : " The day has come, beautiful in the physical world, but thundery and ominous in the moral one. All the ' Convocationists ' are going out. They have been unanimous. No vote is to be taken on any point. They lodge a protest and walk.[1] The excitement is prodigious. I am very sad, but in no way frightened." [2]

That same evening he continued : " They are off. Four hundred and fifty ministers and elders, one hundred and fifty members. . . . Everything in their conduct was dignified. God bless all the serious among them. The row is only beginning. I am to protest against the Strathbogies. I am lighter than in the morning, but very dowie. I think we MAY, by God's blessing, survive. . . . I take my stand for Constitutional Reform. *We are at our worst.* IF we survive this week, we shall swim. How my soul rises against these men, who have left us to rectify their blunderings, and then laugh at our inability to do so." [3]

On the Tuesday following there was this short note : " I have but five minutes. The Strathbogie case is over, thank God ! I think we may swim. It was to me a terrible night. I spoke until half-past twelve p.m. [He must have meant a.m.] I voted twice yesterday against my old friends. I could not help it. I followed my own

[1] Either this was a shrewd guess, or it indicates that the pledge of secrecy was not kept inviolate.
[2] D. MacLeod, *Memoir of Norman MacLeod* (one-vol. ed.), p. 128
[3] *Ibid.*, pp. 128–29

judgment. Great gloom, but not despair. Four hundred and fifty have this day for ever abandoned the Church." [1]

Finally, on the second Thursday, he wrote : " We are going ahead slowly ; our disagreeable work is nearly over. We yesterday reached zero. . . . I wait in hope and with patience. I am ashamed at the cowardice and terror of many of our ministers. I feel the secession deeply, but I am possessed with a most chivalrous and firm determination to live and die fighting for this bulwark of Protestantism, this ark of righteousness, this conservator of social order and religious liberty, the dear old Kirk. . . . I trust that posterity will vindicate our doings. It is for future generations we are now suffering." [2]

What created in Norman MacLeod's mind these violent alternations of feeling ? It was not so much the magnitude of the loss as the heterogeneity of the crew that remained to man the ship. Nowhere was this more manifest than over the case of the seven deposed ministers of Strathbogie. There were those in the Assembly who held that they had never been legally deposed, and who, acting on that conviction, had held ministerial communion with them. These had no difficulty in recognizing those commissioned by them to the General Assembly, and even themselves, as fellow members. But there were others who held that, however unjust the sentences might have been, they had been solemnly deposed. The sentence must now be as solemnly rescinded. But would this rescindment legalize acts of theirs before their rein-statement ? Could their commissions to the General Assembly be sustained ? No fewer than three motions on the subject were put to the vote. The one that ultimately carried was that of Dr. Mearns : "That,

[1] D. MacLeod, *Memoir of Norman MacLeod*, p. 129. The reference is to the Deed of Demission. [2] *Ibid.*, p. 130

whereas sentences of suspension and deposition from the office of the holy ministry were, in the years 1840 and 1841, pronounced against seven ministers [naming them] of the Presbytery of Strathbogie ; which sentences, proceeding on incompetent grounds, and being passed by the General Assembly in excess of its jurisdiction, were *ab initio* null and void ; the General Assembly do declare that the said ministers are still in possession of their ministerial state, rights, and privileges, as if no such sentence had been pronounced ; and that those of the said ministers, now surviving, have right to meet in Presbytery, and that the commissions of the Presbytery referred to the Assembly should be sustained." [1]

To this finding no fewer than three separate sets of reasons of dissent were tabled, and one independent protest. The last was by Norman MacLeod. It was in the form of an alternative motion, not persisted in, to the effect that " the seven ministers of Strathbogie having been deposed on improper grounds by the Assembly, and deprived of their status and privileges as ministers of this Church, this Assembly, in consideration of the peculiar circumstances of the case, and with a view of restoring the peace and good order of the Church, hereby rescind the said sentence, and restore them to the exercise of these powers and privileges of which they have been deprived." [2]

In support of this motion he said this : " We cannot but admit the fact that these Strathbogie ministers are deposed men. . . . For myself, I cannot but hold these ministers as deposed. Unreprehensibly, it may be, in the sight of God ; unconstitutionally, it may be, in the eye of the law ; but this, if true, only makes the act of the Church a greater sin. That act was passed in solemn

[1] *Proceedings of the General Assembly*, p. 204   [2] *Witness*, May 24, 1843

Assembly. *This* Assembly may ecclesiastically undo it, but I cannot but hold it as having been ecclesiastically done. If they are by this House received this evening as ministers, I cannot help it. I may protest, and shall, against this method of doing it, and against their commissions as invalid, but I see no reason for leaving the Church or the Assembly on this account. . . . I *may* be doing wrong in sitting here with men having bad commissions, but I have *no doubt* I would do much wrong were I to desert my beloved Church or this Assembly in their hour of trouble and danger. . . . I shall not, with so many motions upon your table, press this one upon the House, but satisfy myself with a dissent and protest in my own name, and in the name of many in the Church, against recognizing these ministers until reponed as ministers of this Church." [1]

This decision and the protests are characteristic of this Assembly. Neither the Veto Act nor the Chapel Act was rescinded. They were treated as though they had never been. The courts of the land had declared them *ultra vires*, and the Church must simply accept that verdict. Back to 1833 was the watchword.

But there was also this young forward-looking group to stem the tide of pure reaction. When a kind of middle group had suggested a consultation with Her Majesty's Government as to what steps might be taken to improve the position, Dr. Bryce desired the insertion of the words " if any," [2]—*i.e.* What steps, if any. He and his stalwarts were quite content with the position as laid down by the civil courts. In view, however, of the vigour of the protest against their insertion, the words were not persisted in ; and the Middle Party was able to continue its conversations with representatives of the Government

[1] *Witness*, May 24, 1843   [2] *Ibid.*

as to the utmost modifications it would prepare and Parliament would enact to ease the pressure on the Church of the series of hostile verdicts. Before another Assembly came, Lord Aberdeen's Act, slightly amended, had given the people some standing in vetoing a presentee,[1] and Sir James Graham's Act, instituting *quoad sacra* parishes, had dealt, at least in part, with the disparity of presbyters which the Chapel Act was designed to remedy.

It was fortunate for the future of religion in Scotland that there was no formal answer to the protest approved by this Assembly, or the Commission to which it had finally remitted it. Free Churchmen were accustomed to claim that this failure meant that the protest was unanswerable. The claim was thoroughly justified, if all that they meant was that it was beyond the range of a united answer. Each separate group, however, could have prepared a distinct answer which, to its own members, would have been adequate. And if there had been competing answers the other votes show that in this Assembly one embodying extreme Moderate, and indeed Erastian, principles would have carried the day. The complicated series of events which prevented an official answer saved the Church from committing itself to positions which it would have regretted within a generation.

Neither the legislation nor the debates of this Assembly were fitted to stir enthusiasm. The most promising

---

[1] It was not welcomed by all, *e.g.* Rev. Wm. Pirie, afterwards Principal Pirie of Aberdeen, wrote in his diary at the end of June 1843 : " Lord Aberdeen's Bill is passing with some amendments, but I doubt if it will do much good. If a change is to be made, I really think Patronage should be done away with altogether. I am willing to give the Bill a fair trial, but I am in principle a popular election man." *Memorial of Principal Pirie*, p. 53

feature was the emergence of two big men, not as yet united in policy, but equally filled with a genuine longing to restore the Church of Scotland to the traditions of its best days as an instrument of spiritual and social well-being. Both of them at the moment were ministers in country places. One was the Rev. James Robertson of Ellon, who had already attracted attention as one of the junior spokesmen and pamphleteers on the Moderate side, but with an emphasis of his own. The other was the Rev. Norman MacLeod of Loudoun, whose characteristic productions were, from the beginning, more literary and popular. Both, within the year, were transferred to more important spheres of labour, Robertson to the Chair of Church History in the University of Edinburgh vacated by Dr. Welsh, and MacLeod to the parish of Dalkeith.

With this brief glance at the significant doings of the one Assembly, it will be well now to pass over to the other. Tanfield Hall having been hurriedly prepared to receive the departing members and those who adhered to them, the Assembly at once, in unfamiliar surroundings, confronted the new conditions. After opening the proceedings with prayer, Dr. Welsh at once nominated Dr. Chalmers as the one man " in the eyes of all Christendom " [1] called upon to occupy the chair as Moderator. His words were few, but the closing sentences deserve reproduction. " Surely it is a good omen, or, I should rather say, a token for good from the Great Disposer of all events, and the alone Head of the Church, that I can propose to hold this office an individual who, by the efforts of his genius and his virtues, is destined to hold so conspicuous a place in the eyes of all posterity. But this I feel is taking but a low view of the subject. His genius has been devoted to the service of his heavenly Master,

[1] *Proceedings of the General Assembly of the Free Church of Scotland*, p. 9

and his is the high honour promised to those who, having laboured successfully in their Master's cause, and turned many to righteousness, are to ' shine as the stars for ever and ever.' " [1]

In his opening address, after some fine and adequate words on the significance and solemnity of the occasion, congratulating the members on the fact that, " in the issue of the contest between a sacrifice of principle and a sacrifice of their worldly possessions, they had resolved upon the latter," [2] and a call both to humility and to courage, Dr. Chalmers went on to a statement of the meaning of the occasion, which, marked as it is by stresses and emphases all his own, was to become a centre of conflict in later debates, and even in much later legal decisions.[3] Dealing with the danger which faced the Church of simply shaking itself free of one kind of subjection, only to fall into another, he said this : " The Voluntaries mistake us, if they conceive us to be Voluntaries. We hold by the duty of Government to give of their resources and their means for the maintenance of a gospel ministry in the land ; and we pray that their eyes may be opened, so that they may learn how to acquit themselves as the protectors of the Church, and not as its corruptors or its tyrants. . . . That is to say, though we quit the Establishment, we go out on the Establishment principle ; we quit a vitiated Establishment, but would rejoice in returning to a pure one. To express it otherwise—we are the advocates for a national recognition and national support of religion—and we are not Voluntaries." [4]

[1] *Proceedings of the General Assembly of the Free Church of Scotland*, p. 9
[2] *Ibid.*, p. 10
[3] Particularly in the House of Lords in 1904, in the Free Church Appeal. *Cf.* R. L. Orr, *Free Church of Scotland Appeals*, pp. 566ff
[4] *Proceedings of the General Assembly of the Free Church of Scotland*, p. 12

It is too often forgotten that this passage does not stand alone in this connection, that there was another and a greater danger against which Dr. Chalmers continued his warning. "If we thus openly proclaim our differences with men who, under the guise of principle—and of this principle we question not the honesty—refuse in the affairs of the Church to have any participation with the Government, still more resolutely do we disclaim all fellowship with men who, under the guise of direct and declared opposition, lift a menacing front against 'the powers that be,' or disdaining government, and impatient of restraint, manifest a spirit of contention and defiance. . . . If on the flag of your truly free and constitutional Church you are willing to inscribe that you are no Voluntaries, then still more will there be an utter absence of sympathy on your part with the demagogue and agitator of the day—so that in golden characters may be seen and read of all men this other inscription, that you are no anarchists." [1]

These are the words as they appeared in the amended form of the address edited for publication. They certainly convey the substance of the address as delivered. But they do run more smoothly; and omitted from the edited version are the two passages which seem to have evoked the most spontaneous and unrestrained applause. "Like the Apostles of old, they would be accused of 'turning the world upside down.' But they were for peace, law, and order—not tumult, turbulence, and confusion." "They must not seek for freedom in the applause of the multitude. Still more galling than the tyranny of the State was the tyranny of the multitude." [2]

Immediately after this address the Assembly set about

[1] *Proceedings of the General Assembly of the Free Church of Scotland*, p. 12
[2] *Witness*, May 19, 1843

its business with precision and dispatch. The roll was made up, not only of those commissioners to the General Assembly of the Church of Scotland who had signed the Protest, but of all ministers adhering to it, and one elder from each Kirk Session adhering. Various committees were named to deal with phases of the overwhelming task that faced the Church ; the first one to take into consideration in what manner the separation from the Establishment should be effected and completed. The result of its work was the preparation of an Act of Separation and Deed of Demission, which was read and re-read to the Assembly on the Monday evening. The forenoon sederunt of Tuesday was devoted to its signing —a session without speeches—which was to prove in many memories one of the most notable of all.

This impressive instrument, fully legal in form, and consequently most involved in structure, was designed to make the act of renunciation of State benefits decisive, and to emphasize afresh the grounds of this separation. Through its content and their appended signatures they made it plain what it was they were giving up, and equally plain what they claimed to retain. The terms of the central paragraph are that they " hereby do, for themselves and all who adhere to them, separate from and abandon the present subsisting Establishment in Scotland, and did, and hereby do, abdicate and renounce the status and privileges derived to them, or any of them, as parochial ministers and elders, from the said Establishment, through its connection with the State, and all rights and emoluments pertaining to them, or any of them, by virtue thereof : Declaring, that they hereby in no degree abandon or impair the rights belonging to them as ministers of Christ's gospel, and pastors and elders of particular congregations, to perform freely and fully the functions of their offices towards their respective congregations, or such portions thereof as may adhere to them ; and that they are and shall be free to exercise government and discipline in their several judicatories, separate from the Establishment, according to God's word, and the constitution and standards of the Church of Scotland, as heretofore understood." [1]

One cannot look at this document without feeling in close contact with a deed without parallel in the history of the Christian Church. At various times in various lands—in Scotland notably in 1661—a comparable proportion of the national clergy have been ejected from their livings. They could, of course, have retained them at a price. Individually, in the solitude of their isolated manses, or after local consultations, they had to make their choice ; and not infrequently they have saved the Christian future through their loyalty. But this renunciation had features peculiarly its own. Even after the Protest and the withdrawal the Government did not expect this further step. Sir James Graham said, in reply to a question by a Scottish member, " I cannot collect from the Protest a declaration of absolute withdrawal from the Church : I collect from it only a secession from the General Assembly." [2] For the greater part of a week the Government seems to have anticipated the kind of situation of the Commonwealth period, when the Resolutioners and Protesters had their rival ecclesiastical courts, but all stuck like limpets to their respective parishes, and succeeded, in most cases, in retaining their livings. Sir James Graham saw in front of him a time of increased confusion, with a multitude of new legal

---

[1] The original document is in the Register House, Edinburgh ; the official duplicate in the archives of the Church of Scotland in the Tolbooth.

[2] *Witness*, May 25, 1843

issues, as varied as the permutations of the possible views of patrons and congregations might permit.

In one speech in the Assembly there is a hint that in a few quarters such an expedient had been suggested. The Speaker was Dr. Gordon.

" Sir, it is a most miserable subterfuge I have heard pled, that we might have remained in the Established Church, and there retained intact our theoretical opinions, and that we might have there risen solemnly to protest as often as the civil courts actually interfered with ecclesiastical procedure, and that in this way our consciences might have been satisfied : yes, that subterfuge is one that I tremble to think of a Christian man allowing himself for a single moment to entertain. Why, the very fact of our drawing our stipends after the declaration that the State has made is, on our part, a solemn promise, as honest men, to the State, that we will never make such a declaration, and is an acquiescence in the principle ; and a protest after that would be a dishonest, a hypocritical protest. There is no other alternative. The conscience of everyone has shut us up on both sides. On the one side, if we had remained in the Establishment, and held by our principles, to protest would have been dealing falsely and dishonestly with the State. We would have been taking the benefit on a totally different ground from that on which the State said it would give it. On the other hand, if we had remained in the Establishment, and submitted, we must have abandoned our allegiance to the great Head of the Church." [1]

So, although the fathers of the Secession had felt that, in all honesty, they could occupy their churches and

[1] *Proceedings of the General Assembly of the Free Church of Scotland*, p. 31

manses and draw their stipends while constituted into a separate Presbytery, and did in fact occupy them for the seven years that passed before they were actually deposed, no such possibility occurred to the sensitive consciences of the fathers of the Disruption. There could be no half-way house for them ; and the more dramatic and clean-cut their renunciation, the greater hope for Christ's Kingdom in Scotland. It was an immense sacrifice, and it was made honourably, humbly, and hopefully. Every loyal member of the Church of Scotland to-day, whatever his own ecclesiastical ancestry, must look back on this unique episode with a feeling of the deepest admiration and genuine pride. And far beyond Scotland, throughout the world-wide Church, wherever " earthly power or authority " has threatened what the Norwegian bishops, in a phrase very like the old Scots one, have called " the Mastership of Jesus Christ in His Church," [1] this deed of theirs stands high as a beacon to hearten and to guide.

As one reads the full record of the transactions and proceedings of that first General Assembly certain broad impressions remain.

One cannot fail to be impressed with the high religious level on which the whole business was conceived and maintained. This is due not only to the number of sessions or parts of sessions given over to devotional exercises, but to the frequency with which a spirit of high dedication finds unforced and spiritual expression in the midst of prosaic deliberations. The loose tagging of a hallowed word on to some minor ecclesiastical duty on the lips of an imperfectly consecrated man can always give a jar. Few General Assemblies are immune from this experience, but never once does it intrude in all the many pages of these reports. The impression left is of

[1] *Pastoral Letter*, Easter, 1942

the high exaltation of a great deliverance finding its natural expression in high resolve.

Another is the sheer courage of the venture. There, in Tanfield Hall, are gathered some 450 ministers who have as yet no churches to preach in, no manses to live in, no colleges to train their students, no constituted Kirk Sessions to back them, no definite communion rolls, facing a task which embraces all Scotland and stretches far beyond its shores. Typical of the gallant determination which pervaded their ranks are these introductory words of Dr. Keith, in speaking to his report on the young Jewish Mission. " We meet under different circumstances, and in a different place than heretofore, and the question often asked at me and at my fathers and brethren is this : " What are we to do with these schemes ? My answer has invariably been, and I trust that to it you will warmly respond—CARRY THEM ON— more vigorously than ever." [1]

But along with this, and to a certain extent qualifying it, there is the unmistakable evidence of wise and careful planning. This came chiefly to the fore when Dr. Chalmers submitted the report of the financial section of the Provisional Committee. The external voluntaryism he had commended so vigorously was now a very sturdy tree. The local societies were doing valiantly, not for their local needs, but for the great central funds. With greater extension and better organization they would build all the new churches needed in a simple way, and provide a steady nucleus for the support of the ministry. While the Sustentation Fund may have owed its shape to Dr. Chalmers' personal desire to be delivered from his pet aversion " internal voluntaryism," the fluctuations of a purely local provision, his energy,

[1] *Proceedings of the General Assembly of the Free Church of Scotland*, p. 86

enthusiasm and driving force had already ensured also its success. The applause with which the Assembly greeted the announcement of one princely gift after another was more than equalled when Dr. Chalmers gave samples of the cumulative power of " littles." Already there were 687 local associations, and Dr. Chalmers, after referring to the fact that at the Convocation he had been called a Utopian, added, "At the hazard of being regarded as a Utopian this second time, and at this new stage of our advance, I will make as confident an avowal now as I made then, that if only we make a proper use of the summer that is before us in stirring up, I don't say the people of Scotland, but that portion of them who are the friends of our Protesting Church—if we do what we might, and what we ought, we will not only be able to repair the whole disruption [*i.e.* in so far as it has taken away financial support], but will get landed in the great and glorious work of Church Extension." [1]

A fourth and final impression is of the prominence of the œcumenical note. The separation did not make them separatists. Numerous contacts, actual and planned, with other Churches, punctuate the record of the proceedings. Whatever may have been the case among lesser men outside, few bitter things were said in the Assembly about any fellow-Christians. The most obvious jarring note is in a speech by one who was not given to offending in this respect, Dr. Candlish, when he said : " It is clear to me that no faithful member of this Free Protesting Church of Scotland can give any countenance to the worship of God in connection with the Establishment. . . . They have laid the Establishment prostrate at the feet of the civil power, and annulled

---

[1] *Proceedings of the General Assembly of the Free Church of Scotland*, p. 47

every vestige of liberty in the Church of Christ, if they be a Church of Christ." [1] But the prevailing note is that of a Church which means not only to be nationally adequate and efficient, but to march and fight with the world-wide regiments of one great army until the final victory and consummation. [2] Typical of this Assembly are these words from the closing address of the Moderator : " The deliberations, for I cannot call them the debates, of the Assembly are now terminated. We have reason to bless God for a harmony that has been quite marvellous. Let us rejoice in it as a token for good : and may He who turneth the spirits of men whithersoever He will, turn this common enthusiasm on behalf of great and high objects into an instrument for the growth of charity and cordial affection among all Christians—that they may at length rally around one and the same standard, and go forth with one heart and one hand on the mighty enterprise of spreading the Gospel everywhere, and achieving, both at home and abroad, the farther triumphs of our faith." [3]

It was a good thing for the realization of one instalment of his hope that the Assembly over which he presided was so united, and an equally good thing that the other Assembly was not.

---

[1] *Proceedings of the General Assembly of the Free Church of Scotland*, p. 177
[2] Since practically all the foreign missionaries adhered, it undertook at once work as widespread and various abroad as had been supported by the undivided Church of Scotland.
[3] *Proceedings of the General Assembly of the Free Church of Scotland*, p. 181

CHAPTER TWENTY-THREE

THE "OUTWARD BUSINESS OF THE HOUSE OF GOD"

1843–47

ON October 17, 1843, at the gathering of the second General Assembly of the Free Church, Dr. Chalmers, as retiring Moderator, preached the opening sermon. He used an odd text, Nehemiah xi. 16, " And Shabbethai and Jozabad, of the chief of the Levites, had the oversight of the outward business of the house of God." No-one has ever claimed for it a place among his greater sermons ; there are no traces in Disruption literature of any deep impressions left by it ; yet its timeliness is beyond question, and for sober practical wisdom it was typical of one side of the preacher. The exaltation of the moment of liberation, he contended, must now be succeeded by deliberate wisdom, in the practical planning of the external embodiments and guarantees of the life of freedom, and of the machinery for expansion into the neglected areas of Scotland, and beyond. In two sentences we may find its essence distilled. " It was an inward and a right spirit, we hope, which animated the devotions and the doings of the first General Assembly." [1] " But the inward principle should not prevent, nay, the very strength of it will prompt us onward to the outward business of the House of God." [2]

Part of the application was devoted to a plea for the

[1] *A Sermon preached at the Opening of the General Assembly, etc.*, p. 5
[2] *Ibid.*, p. 6

general revival of the office of Deacon in their ecclesiastical policy. It was not that outward things were unworthy of the attention of the most godly and devoted ministers, or that he had in contemplation a ministry which, from serener heights, would look down on these activities, but simply that their energies might be more exclusively and effectively devoted to spiritual ends. The revived order would release the latent energy of both minister and elders. " It is well known," he said, " that the cessation of deacons in our Church, by the transference of their duties to office-bearers of a higher degree, has secularized the work of the eldership. And, let us not undervalue even the spiritual importance of outward things, seeing that the restoration of this ancient order, and the reassumption by them of their proper and original duties, might emancipate the higher functionaries for their higher labours, so that elders might become what they were in purer and better days—fellow-workers with their pastors in the cure of souls, and important helps in the ministry of the Gospel." [1] It was this Assembly that took the first effective steps towards their reinstitution as in all the early Reformed books of discipline.

But, as though to minimize and even to obliterate what he had said about higher and lower, one of his own main interests in these closing years was just this outward business of the House of God. It found one main outlet, the support of the ministry, and one secondary one, the housing of the congregations.

As we have already noted, when other men's minds were so entirely occupied with principles, he had astounded the convocation with practical proposals for the support of a non-endowed Church. He had personally set the example of inaugurating, in his own district of Morning-

---

[1] *A Sermon preached on the Opening of the General Assembly*, pp. 13–14

side, a contributory association to meet the needs of the future. He had presided over the financial section of the Provisional Committee ; he had drafted and issued the appeals for support, and for the formation of local associations everywhere ; he had laid down the lines of ingathering and administration of the fund which was to be the basis of the Church's finances ; he had found for it a name which it was to bear during the whole separate history of the Free Church—the Sustentation Fund.

To its success and to its organization he was to devote the bulk of his labours, outside his more immediate task of training students, during the remaining four years of his life. His main writings of the period deal with it. They are, nominally, four in number, though the fourth is only a revised edition of the third intended for a wider circle. They are, *Considerations on the Economics and Platform of the Free Church of Scotland (1843) ; Considerations on the Economics of the Free Church for 1844 ; The Economics of the Free Church of Scotland (1845) ; Earnest Appeal to the Free Church of Scotland on the Subject of its Economics (1846).*

Before we can adequately appreciate the merits of the Sustentation Fund—his lasting monument in the realm of Church finance—or understand fully his own amendments on the original scheme, there are some facts that have to be borne in mind.

First of all, the problem was a new one—immediate provision for a Church of some 600 actual and 800 potential congregations. Many of these congregations possessed within their membership financial resources more than sufficient for their own needs, even when denuded of endowments and buildings. More, however, had no prospect of survival, if left to their own resources. The Secession in 1740 had begun its separate career with eight self-supporting congregations, and only added to the number of regularly sanctioned charges where there was a definite promise of stipend, and a reasonable prospect of self-support. And never, even in the days of its most rapid increase, had it to face a problem at all commensurate with that which the Free Church faced at the outset. It was not, however, the magnitude and immediacy of the task alone that removed it most completely from all previous separations : it was the programme of the " new " Church. It recognized from the beginning that it had a national responsibility. It would, in separation from the State, continue its nation-wide activities, and see to it that the " true " Church of Scotland had its churches, schools, ministers, and teachers in every corner of the land. It must carry on the great work of Church Extension to which its leaders had devoted themselves within the Establishment.

The second thing that we have to remember is the conviction fundamental in Chalmers' own thinking, of the inadequacy of Voluntaryism. It is true that his arguments were mainly directed against what he called internal Voluntaryism, trusting to the demand for religious instruction creating the supply ; he had given a somewhat tepid approval to what he called external Voluntaryism. A church without endowments is forced, whether it approves of it or not, to resort to some form of Voluntaryism. Nothing else than the external form, in which the place of stable endowments was taken by some other form of support from outside, drawn from the free-will offerings of the sympathetic elsewhere, was ever contemplated as possible. The practice of other Churches, including all the earlier Scottish separate communions, was to let each individual congregation pledge itself to do its utmost in the first place and then, if necessary, to supplement its efforts out of a special fund raised by the wealthier congregations. For the programme which the Free Church envisaged, this was manifestly inadequate ; and to Dr. Chalmers' mind it would, even though adequate, have been undesirable, since the minister thus received his salary directly from his congregation, who would expect him to become their mouthpiece, rather than the faithful witness of God in their midst. To supply every district of Scotland with a ministry really free, free to declare the whole counsel of God, the minister's subsistence must not depend on the goodwill of his own people. A faithful minister must not be subjected to the possible penalty of starvation for his faithfulness.

Bearing in mind, then, the magnitude and immediacy of the task, the nation-wide programme, and Dr. Chalmers' profound distrust of internal Voluntaryism, we are in a position to appreciate his scheme, for it was his scheme before it ever had the benediction of the Church, some time indeed before there was a Church to give it a benediction.

There were three main points made in the initial appeal of February 1843 which are thus stated in that document.

Firstly, " there should be a General Fund, supported by contributions from all parts of the Church, and made available for the benefit of all the adhering congregations, by means of an *equal* dividend towards the support of each Minister."

Next, " room should be left in some way for the supplementary efforts of each Congregation on behalf of their own Minister."

Finally, " this equal dividend, being always one and the same to each Minister of the Church, and so increasing with every increase of the General Fund, should not, however, increase to more than a certain point, even though beyond and, it is to be hoped, greatly beyond, this point the Fund itself should continue to increase. What, then, it may be asked, should be done with the surplus ? This surplus, which it is our earnest prayer might be made as large as possible, should not go to the increase of any Minister's stipend, but should go to the increase of the number of Ministers or Missionaries—to the increase, not of ministerial income, but of ministerial service." [1]

Each minister of the Free Church, therefore, according to the scheme, was to receive a sure and equal minimum income from the Central Fund irrespective of the contribution of his own congregation or local association to that fund—a minimum which might be supplemented by such further provision as they might undertake and decide to supply. Since the first equal dividend was £105,[2] every minister received that sum from headquarters, with, in addition, directly from local sources a supplement, ranging from some hundreds in a few great city charges, down to tens, and even to sporadic gratuitous services like carting, in some remote villages and rural districts.

The scheme of this first pre-natal circular determined the lines of Free Church finance for ministerial support during its whole history, and while it did not accomplish all of which its author dreamt at its launching, was much more triumphant than his later forebodings on the subject. He had builded better than he knew.

For a great scheme of this nature it is obvious that very much hinged on the principles and methods of in-

[1] *Circular under the Authority of the Financial Committee*, etc., No. 1, p. 1
[2] £105, on one method of calculation, would equal £240 in 1939.

gathering. Local associations had to be formed of friends of the Free Church, and a whole staff of voluntary workers had to be enrolled to make regular calls for the promised contributions. Weekly calls were from the first Dr. Chalmers' ideal method. He was fascinated with the power of littles. He was always reckoning up precisely what a penny a week from the members of the associations would total up to. Leakage would be less with weekly calls than when 4d. fell to be collected each month, or 1s. 1d. every quarter. The greatest difficulty the scheme would have to overcome was just " the insensibility of most minds to the power of littles." The natural inertia of humanity will make deacons and collectors ask, " What is the use of going round weekly for a few pence per household, when it might be as easily collected in the form of a few shillings quarterly ? " He could see no symptoms of a lack of cheerful giving, but after two years he did see signs of a falling off of conscientious collecting. In March 1845 he told a great audience—of collectors— in the Free Tron Church in Glasgow, " The great want is the want of a regular, practical, thorough-going agency." " There is an apathy, a sluggishness, an indifference, a listlessness of disposition, which prevents many from plying their rounds with that regularity which they ought to do." " We never make it a matter of remonstrance with a man that he does not give a farthing to the cause ; but we have good reason to remonstrate with one who will not stir a footstep in the cause." [1]

In the first days local associations were formed in every corner of the land which housed a group of sympathisers, however small ; but the tendency was for those groups which saw no immediate prospect of a Free Church ministry within their range to drop off, and within a few

[1] *Sustentation Fund of the Free Church, Address in the Free Tron Church, etc.*, p. 3

years all the local associations were congregational associations, and that new court of the Church, the deacons' court, in most districts kept before the eyes of every voluntary agent by precept and example the ideal diligence for which Dr. Chalmers pled. The steady rise of the total contributions year after year bears testimony to their faithfulness.

As soon as associations became generally identified with congregations it became apparent that there were two main groups among them, the aid-giving which contributed more to the General Fund than they drew from it, and the aid-receiving which contributed less. It was an analysis of the relations of these two, once the facts were before him in black and white, that was to lead to modifications in the scheme to the effecting of which Dr. Chalmers devoted his final writings on the subject. In these pamphlets, though there was at first a reluctance to admit the fact, he gave up the principle of the equal dividend. In the second he says explicitly, " Whatever reason might be alleged for an equal dividend among the first ministers of the Disruption, its continuance with all the succeeding ministers would be absolutely ruinous." [1] It must be asked, therefore, what scheme he proposed to substitute for it, and why ?

Let us begin with the why. He was perfectly satisfied that the scheme, if fully worked, would be quite adequate for the present and future support of the Free Church, if it was willing to be simply the largest agent outside the Establishment, co-operating with it in the religious instruction of Scotland. But there must be a much larger sum available if the Free Church was to be the really national Church of his life-long planning. Account must be taken not only of the increased number of ministers,

[1] *On the Economics of the Free Church of Scotland*, 1845, p. 15

from 470 to 650, and of the congregations already in being
waiting for ministers among the students in training, but
" above all, of the vast extent of the land which remains
to be possessed, and from every part of which we receive the most unbounded assurances of welcome—so that
with but an adequate enlargement of means there lies
before us the magnificent enterprise of covering the whole
of yet unreclaimed Scotland with our churches and our
schools ; and thus to fill up every deficiency, whether in
the amount of Christian or of common education for all
the families." [1]

How, then, was the fund to reach such a state of
affluence that this programme would come within the
realm of practical politics ? Into the minor suggestions
made, in the shape of closer relations between headquarters and the local associations, it is not necessary to
enter. It is his drastic amendment of fundamental
principle in the light of two years' working that remains
important. He had grown depressed by the way in which
many of the aid-receiving congregations rested on their
oars, apparently devoting their whole attention to their
local needs, confident that if only they sent up some £20
or £40 to Edinburgh, their minister was secure. He
would receive the equal dividend. Every such congregation drew £85 or £65 from the fund. If every aid-
receiving congregation were conscientious in its givings,
and realized its responsibility, the possibilities of the fund
would be multiplied. But how was this sense of responsibility to be stimulated ? The soundest way was by
instituting a new rule—the rule of one-half more, or of
one and a half. That is to say, if a congregation sent up
£20 this did not ensure the payment of the equal dividend,
it only meant a payment of £30 from the fund ; if £40,

[1] *Earnest Appeal, etc.*, p. 13

£60, and so on. The obvious reply to this proposal was that no minister of a poor congregation could subsist on £30 or £60, plus whatever supplement his congregation might or could pay directly. But, Dr. Chalmers would have retorted, human nature being what it is, no minister would be asked to do so. " The strong and natural, yet somewhat selfish, preference for their own minister *versus* the Christian good of all Scotland would, instead of working as now against our Associations, be enlisted upon their side," [1] *i.e.* the obvious way now of securing a more adequate stipend for their own minister was to contribute more largely to the fund. " The influence would tell over the whole length and breadth of the Church ; and in the consequent mighty enlargement of our resources we should soon get the better of all our difficulties and of all our fears." [2] Further, no new association was to be accepted as a congregational unit until it had reached the contribution of £50.

So potent was the spell of the equal dividend that this proposal was received with alarm and consternation ; but so potent was the spell of the old man eloquent that it was resolved to give it a trial. The experiment, how-every, lasted no longer than a year after his death. In 1848 a special commission of investigation at the close of a weighty report gave its conclusion that " for a permanent arrangement the equal dividend presents fewest objections." [3] So against his later mind the original plan of Dr. Chalmers' remained ; and with various checks and sliding scales adopted from time to time in later years, it was the basis of the stable finance of the Free Church during the fifty-seven years of its separate history.

---

[1] *Considerations on the Economics of the Free Church for 1844,* p. 7
[2] *Ibid,* p. 7
[3] *Report of Select Committee on Sustentation Fund,* 1848, p. 2

The name of Thomas Chalmers may not stand so high as he hoped in the ranks of economic theorists, but no name stands higher as a practical economist in the whole region of modern ecclesiastical finance.

The other main aspect of his concernment with practical affairs calls for a brief notice. It arose from the exceedingly difficult problem of provision, both temporary and permanent, for the worship of the outgoing people left without a church.

While the main aspects of the problem were left to other leaders, in every detail of it which came under his notice Dr. Chalmers showed the profoundest interest, and not infrequently gave wise guidance. But there was only one, apart from the housing of the College, which affected him personally. His own parish church of Morningside had to be vacated. Some temporary accommodation had to be found. No suitable place was immediately available. So Dr. Chalmers threw open his own house to the congregation. We catch a glimpse of those days in a letter to an American correspondent. " The Moderates are carrying it with a high hand. In my own parish they have ejected the minister from his *quoad sacra* church, and the service has been carried on in my own home for three Sabbaths to a congregation one day of towards 400 people. . . . We are to have a tent during autumn, and expect to have our church built by the beginning of winter." [1] How such a congregation was crammed into even a largish house is difficult to picture, but Dr. Hanna speaks of his father-in-law, planted midway up the staircase, preaching to " a disjointed congregation scattered into different rooms, all of whom could hear, but not half of whom could see " [2] the preacher.

[1] *Correspondence*, p. 432   [2] Hanna, vol. iv, pp. 357–58

Of the multitude of local difficulties there is a very full—perhaps over-full—compendium in Dr. Thomas Brown's *Annals of the Disruption*. Towards the solution of any one of them Dr. Chalmers was always ready to intervene where he could be of any service. Bit by bit in most quarters local adjustments were arrived at.[1] But as the months passed, and the years, it was evident that there was going to be a residuum of places where there was a Free Church congregation and no possibility of a church, since all the land round about belonged to one landowner, who refused on any terms to allow a Free Church building to be erected on his estate. No good purpose is to be served by recalling the names of these " die-hards."

It became evident to the Free Church that some form of parliamentary action was imperative. After more than one vain attempt to move it to a sense of its responsibility, the House of Commons was induced in March 1847 to set up a Commission " to enquire whether, and in what parts of Scotland, and under what circumstances, large numbers of Her Majesty's subjects have been deprived of the means of religious worship by the refusal of certain proprietors to grant them sites for the erection of churches." [2]

The examination of the earliest witnesses displayed an intention on the part of some members of the Commission to cross-examine along the line that the principles at stake were of such minor importance, and the language habitually used by Free Churchmen about their opponents was so violent and unpardonable, that any self-respecting landowner was justified in refusing to aid and

[1] Reports to the General Assembly of 1844 disclose that 470 churches were already completed, and about 230 in process of erection.

[2] Hanna, vol. iv, pp. 497–98

abet a schism so uncalled-for and so destructive of community life. It was therefore felt that it would be essential to an adequate presentation of the Free Church case that Dr. Chalmers himself should go to London and be examined as a witness.

It was for this purpose that he made his last journey to London, a month before his death. No other witness was subjected to such a gruelling examination, for his earlier answers to questions designed to elicit information were so damaging to the Government, its action and inaction alike, that Sir James Graham, who had intimated his intention to refrain from putting questions, changed his mind. He left the building, and returning with a great array of printed documents, newspapers, and the like, set himself to retrieve the position by involving Dr. Chalmers in contradictions and inconsistencies. The record of the questions and answers was speedily issued as a separate publication. One Edinburgh periodical makes this comment : " Dr. Chalmers seems to have looked upon the Committee as his pupils (either of the Free Kirk College or of Assembly), whom he was bound to indoctrinate with his own peculiar views on ecclesiastical matters. Occasionally his manner towards Sir James Graham reminds one of the manner which, we are told, he frequently assumed towards his young aspiring brother, Dr. Candlish. On the other hand, though the Baronet was faithful and strict as an examinator, yet he showed unusual kindness and reverence towards the venerable theologian and orator who stood before him." [1]

This is far from the impression most readers will take from the evidence. It is rather that of an acute and expert advocate using every trick of Parliament House

[1] MacPhail's *Edinburgh Ecclesiastical Journal*, September 1847, p. 89

to discredit the aged leader and, incidentally, to vindicate himself. Some sentences from Dr. Chalmers' journal-letter for the day confirm and focus this other picture. " Armed with documents, he fell upon me for an hour. . . . My only regret is that it was . . . the last hour, when, a good deal exhausted, I was scarcely able mentally to frame or orally to articulate a reply. . . . In his hands the examination did at length degenerate into twaddle, and the best answer from me would have been that it was twaddle. . . . We kept our ground, however, and I was at perfect ease throughout." [1]

As was to be expected, while his vindication of the basic principles of the Disruption satisfied the most militant of his brethren, no less trenchant was his dealing with the accusation of wild and unchristian language so often attributed to them. " I should say that never was a great change effected in a country with less violence on the part of those who suffered by the change ; and speaking generally, I think that there has been upon the whole a very noble exemplification on the part of the Free Church, and of its friends, of the charity which endureth all things." [2]

He was well aware, from newspaper controversy, that one such definite charge would be brought against himself. He had said in the General Assembly of 1839, and he had repeated it, always by way of reminiscence, in post-Disruption speeches, that an Assembly acquiescing in bondage would be a " moral nuisance," and that " an Erastian Establishment should be swept off the face of the country." He was ready for the charge, having already dealt with it in at least one provincial newspaper. When Sir James Graham confronted him with these words he

[1] Hanna, vol. iv, pp. 501–502
[2] *Refusal of Sites : Evidence of the Rev. Dr. Thomas Chalmers*, p. 25

was ready with this answer. " When I first gave utterance to that expression there was no such idea in our own heads as a disruption. We certainly had no other object in contemplation than that we should remain in the Establishment. If the 470 who have signalized themselves so much by their opposition to the encroachments of the civil court . . . had turned round upon their own principles, when they saw that their emoluments were threatened—I say that a Church with 470 recusants in it, who had so glaringly trampled upon their professions for years back—such a Church would have scandalized the whole community; it would have been a 'nuisance.' I do not think a 'nuisance' would be too strong an expression. In like manner, had we done what it was alleged we would do; had we returned to the Church, the expression of a 'nuisance' would have been alike applicable. I do not say that it is equally applicable now. I am not very fond of substituting one name for another; I do not like to give names unless there is a call for it. I do not consider that it is an appropriate designation now, that of 'nuisance.' A nuisance implies a certain power and virulence of positive mischief, which I do not think the Established Church of Scotland possesses. I think that the Established Church of Scotland has become, comparatively speaking, effete and impotent, either as to good or evil; and I would rather denominate it a nullity than a nuisance. I do so without any desire to stigmatize the Church; but I do it under the impulse of a deep conviction, that if this vitiating flaw be suffered to adhere to the Established Church of Scotland, it will never be an efficient Church in our country." [1]

The Commission's report was so favourable that no

[1] *Refusal of Sites: Evidence of the Rev. Dr. Thomas Chalmers*, p. 26

legislation was thought necessary. It was felt that its recommendation might prove sufficient to break down the last walls of resistance. And so it proved. It was not long till every congregation had its church, however plain. Dr. Chalmers' final intervention in outward business had been by no means fruitless.

CHAPTER TWENTY-FOUR

THE SUNSET OF HIS LABOURS

1843–47

In the majority of the publications that he issued after the Disruption, Dr. Chalmers is described as Principal and Professor of Divinity in the New College, Edinburgh. From 1843 to 1847 his main occupation was the training of Divinity students, and this was his official designation. He never taught within the walls of the present college, though he laid the foundation-stone and saw the building taking shape. The rooms at 80 George Street, with their annexes near and far, were all the college that he ever knew. For any public function like the opening lecture, recourse had to be made to other Free Church buildings, mainly to Dr. Candlish's church in Lothian Road.

As the Disruption drew near, it was evident that the Free Church would have no lack of students eager to begin or to complete their training for its ministry. At one time it seemed likely that there would also be a plethora of professors. Finally, however, there were only three who signed the Deed of Demission—Drs. Chalmers and Welsh in Edinburgh, and Dr. Black in Aberdeen. At the outset only one college was contemplated, and Edinburgh was chosen as its site. For some reason, it was decided that Dr. Black should remain in Aberdeen in the meantime, and take charge of students who could not change their plans and come to Edinburgh. So Edinburgh was left with two professors, who could provide adequately for Divinity and Church History in

331

the makeshift first year. But it was necessary to secure another, who would be responsible for Hebrew ; and in " Rabbi " Duncan, late missionary to the Jews, the Church had at its disposal one with " unrivalled attainments in Hebrew and Oriental Literature," [1] and with general approval he was designated to that Chair. A fourth professor, Dr. William Cunningham, was given leave of absence to proceed on a delegation to America. In temporary premises and with a staff of three, New College began its not undistinguished career.

By the time of Dr. Chalmers' last session there were eight professors and at least one lecturer, and the scope of the curriculum had been extended to include certain philosophic and scientific disciplines which normally belong to the Faculty of Arts. The fullest training, however, of future ministers remained its goal. As Dr. Chalmers said when he laid the foundation-stone in June 1846, " Let us not imagine that the edifice whose foundation is now being laid, shortly to arise in graceful superstructure to delight the eye, we hope, of admiring citizens, is only to serve as an idle decoration for the metropolis of our land. Let it be our endeavour and our prayer that it shall become a fountainhead, where the waters of life might issue forth, for the healing of our families—a well of moral and spiritual life to our beloved common people, and to be prolific far and wide of that richest blessing, the blessing of well-filled pulpits and well-served parishes." [2]

For the assessment of his work as principal and professor there is an abundance of material. There are not only the recorded reminiscences of many of his

---

[1] *Proceedings of the General Assembly of the Free Church of Scotland, October 1843*, p. 62

[2] *Report of the New College, 1846*, Appendix, p. 34

enthusiastic students, most of whom regarded him with a reverence not far short of idolatry ; there are the three volumes [1] of his posthumous works, in which Dr. Hanna has gathered up every scrap of his teaching that he regarded as in any way fit for publication. Two of these volumes are devoted to the *Institutes of Theology*, in which his set lectures are incorporated in a condensed form ; the third contains the less formal notes that he prepared for the " questionary or conversational course " [2] on the text-books of the class, which were three in number, Butler's *Analogy*, Paley's *Evidences*, and Hill's *Lectures in Divinity*.

In the contents of these three volumes there is nothing specially distinctive. Their teaching is the orthodox Calvinism of his day, though not expressed in the orthodox vocabulary nor tied down to the orthodox scheme. He never ceased to manifest a suspicion of those whom he called the ultra-orthodox, and, in these later years, his dislike of anything suggesting a dead traditionalism appears with growing frequency in his private journal. " Let me not be the slave of human authority, but clear my way through all creeds and confessions to Thine own original revelation." [3] " Deliver me from the narrowing influence of human lessons, and more especially of human systems of theology. Teach me directly out of the fulness and freeness of Thine own word." [4] But while there is in his journal this outspoken impatience with the second-hand and the derivative, it is not easy to catch to-day, in the portly pages of his posthumous papers, an explanation of the spell that Dr. Chalmers cast upon his students in the crowded benches of 80 George Street, but there is enough to explain the considered

---

[1] Vols. vii, viii, and ix   [2] *Posthumous Works*, vol. ix, p. xix
[3] *Horæ Sabbaticæ*, vol. i, pp. 69–70   [4] *Ibid.*, p. 350

verdict of an anonymous student of 1852. "Whether or not, as Professor of Theology, he has materially advanced sacred science, it is quite certain that from his chair he did render a service to his country which was incomparably of higher importance and value, inasmuch as he sent forth over its surface a body of men who, if they turn not aside from the path whereon he set them forward, may, and with God's help will, bring about the Christian regeneration of Scotland." [1] Despite his early dreams of literary eminence, no verdict on his work would have given more pleasure to Chalmers the Professor.

A marked characteristic of New College from the beginning was the cosmopolitan character of the students in attendance. Round about a fourth or fifth part of the students were from other lands and other communions drawn by the fame of Dr. Chalmers, and one of the effects of the Disruption upon him was greatly to increase his appreciation of other Churches, and to develop his œcumenical spirit. It had been in evidence before. The record of his preaching engagements outside Scotland showed that he moved in no narrow groove. But it was the world-wide messages of sympathy and cheer which poured in from so many organizations in so many lands during the summer of 1843 which definitely deepened his sense of Christian solidarity.

It was in the midst of these demonstrations of brotherly feeling that he was invited to address a public gathering to commemorate the bicentenary of the Westminster Assembly. The occasion seemed to call for the unfurling of the Presbyterian and Calvinist flags ; but he devoted his whole attention to Christian union. He began by adverting to a slogan which, he said, had been

[1] J. Dods, *Thomas Chalmers*, p. 184

fathered on himself : " Co-operation without incorporation," and asked that it be amended to a formula—more
cumbrous, perhaps, but better in every other way—
" Co-operation now, and this with the view, as soon as
may be, to incorporation afterwards." [1] It is true that
he was as confident as the Westminster divines that the
resultant incorporation would be found in some form of
Presbyterianism. Two sentences will give the whole
flavour of the speech. " The Congregationalists among
us can tell whether they are very sanguine of ever bringing
down even the best and holiest men of Episcopacy to
the level of their own platform ; and the Episcopalians
can, in like manner, tell whether they ever cherish the
fond imagination that, in opposition to a bias strong as
that of gravitation itself, they will be able to draw up
Congregationalism to their towering heights of Episcopacy
—(great laughter). We, on the other hand, are sanguine
enough to believe it not impossible that we should both
bring down the one and draw up the other to the intermediate place which we ourselves occupy " [2]—(great
cheering).

In the following year he wrote the prefatory essay to a
volume on Christian Union, and not long after he took
part in the initiation of a practical step towards that end.
This was an invitation, sponsored by a layman of the
United Secession and signed by Scottish ministers and
laymen of every denomination, to selected brethren of
all the Churches in England to meet at Liverpool, in
October 1845, to consider the formation of an Evangelical
Alliance. The conference duly met, and resolved to
proceed, in a remarkable spirit of harmony. It drew up
a constitution for the new Alliance, the first considerable
manifestation of the œcumenical spirit in the English-

[1] *Christian Union : Address, etc.*, p. 2   [2] *Ibid.*, pp. 4, 5

speaking world for many a generation, and it laid down certain lines for future proceedings. The published reports of the meeting and the verbal accounts of his colleagues awoke in Chalmers' mind a great hope and not a little disquiet. The aim was unimpeachable, the whole spirit most laudable, but were the proposed activities those best calculated to secure permanent results ? So, in 1846, he gave forth to the world an important pamphlet : *On the Evangelical Alliance, its Design, its Difficulties, its Proceedings, and its Prospects. With Practical Suggestions.* His main point was that co-operation was the immediate duty. That was agreed. But how was it to find expression ? Its main outlet should be in a Universal Home Mission, each denomination through all its local congregations co-operating for the evangelization of their respective neighbourhoods. To the objection that thus we would be conferring a licence on all sorts of error and false theology to range abroad as they may in the work of an indiscriminate proselytism, he gives this counter, " Where is the man, and what is his denomination, who can hold up his face to the declaration, that he would rather have the millions of our hitherto neglected population not to be Christians at all, than to be Christians minus their [own] peculiarity ? " [1]

It is for this Universal Home Mission, with its own periodicals and its own pamphlets, along the lines of the publicity methods of the great Foreign Missionary societies that he pleads with special insistence and power. The new Alliance, however, must not rest content with this. It must always keep alive the goal of a fuller unity. To this end he makes the further practical suggestion " that committees should be formed of members taken from various denominations, and this for the express design

[1] *On the Evangelical Alliance, etc.*, p. 51

336

of treating on the subject of their respective differences, with a view to one or other of the following conclusions : (1) Whether the differences might not be so adjusted as that Churches of various name and now aloof from each other could merge into one and the same body; (2) *If not*, what bond of affinity or mutual recognition could be devised, which might make it apparent to the world that, under their subsisting diversity of name and form, they are one in substance and principle—or one in Christ Jesus ? " [1]

It is not unfitting that this particular campaign of Chalmers should have its historic beginning in a commemoration of the Westminster Assembly, for it was thoroughly in harmony with the programme of one of its leading spirits, Alexander Henderson, who had explicitly declared that any reformation and unity " must be brought to passe by common consent. We are not to conceave that they [*i.e.* England and Ireland] will embrace our Forme ; but a new Forme must be sett downe for us all, and in my opinion some men sett apairt sometime for that worke." [2] Thomas Chalmers was a true successor to Alexander Henderson both in his attachment to Presbyterianism and in his œcumenical vision.

The work, however, which lay nearest to Dr. Chalmers' heart in his closing years was a practical experiment of his own to demonstrate the nature, meaning, and probable effect of a Universal Home Mission. On the road from his own house in Churchill to the temporary abode of the Free Church College there lay, between the West Port and the Grassmarket, a district almost untouched by all the manifold Christian activities of Edinburgh. It had come into the public eye as one of the haunts of Burke

[1] *On the Evangelical Alliance*, etc., pp. 67–68   [2] Baillie's *Letters*, vol. ii, p. 2

and Hare and of their victims. There were 2,000 people in the area with only some ten per cent. attached in any way to any Protestant communion. Twenty-five per cent. were paupers on the poor-roll of the city. Twenty-five per cent. were street beggars, thieves, or prostitutes. How far these two classes overlapped is not clear from any of the statements.

The spiritual destitution and material degradation of this district laid ever more powerful tentacles on his conscience. Something must be done, and he himself must see that it was done. While many to whom Chalmers opened his heart took it upon themselves to dissuade him from such a hopeless proposition, he could not decline the challenge. He saw it every day more clearly as a specially needful " outfield," ready to respond to constant and wise attention and most fitted to demonstrate the saving power of the gospel.

It was not long before he had gathered round him a zealous group of men and women whom he had infected with his own sense of urgency. To them he expounded his plans. They were based on his experience in Glasgow. The foundation was to be assiduous visitation. There were to be twenty distinct districts, in each of which there were about twenty households. One official visitor was appointed for each district. He or she was to distribute on the first visit a leaflet, explaining the enterprise of which the visit was a herald. When the early visits revealed that some seventy-five per cent. of the children were growing up without any education whatsoever, it was agreed that the first steps would be towards the general and the religious education of the children. Dr. Chalmers insisted that the bait of a free education was not to be used, but that all who desired education for their children were to make a small weekly contribution (2d.) towards it. Only when they made some sacrifice for it would parents really appreciate the boon.

In the heart of the district, at the end of the very close made notorious by the murders, there was a disused tan-loft, reached by an outside wooden stair. Here the school began in November 1844. The numbers, small at the outset, gradually increased until, within a year, more than half of the neglected children of the West Port were enrolled.

Within six weeks of the opening of the school a weekly service was inaugurated. One who was present says that, despite the assiduity of the visitors, there were barely a dozen adults from the district present. It was an unpromising beginning. But before long Dr. Chalmers found a most acceptable and pertinacious agent in the Rev. William Tasker, under whom the growth of the worshippers began to keep pace with the growth in the number of schools. In the December of that year, Dr. Chalmers was able to give a hopeful report to a public meeting of the citizens of Edinburgh. His address was published immediately thereafter under the title *Churches and Schools for the Working Classes*.

In this address he gave a full and vivid account of the results thus far achieved. The time had come for a definite advance. The old tan-loft had served its day for worship. A church was needed in the heart of the district. " For this purpose," he continued, " I must throw myself on the liberality of the Christian public. I have not been very troublesome in this way hitherto. To be sure I have been a great wholesale beggar in my time. I headed the enterprise of Church Extension, by which 200 new churches were erected, at an expense of £800,000; but I am not sure that I ever headed an enterprise before for a special or local object. But if this local object is fulfilled, if I succeed in this, and if it is followed up, as it might be, by other imitations of it—I shall be the head of a far more important enterprise than I have ever been engaged in throughout the whole course of my life." [1] As the speech went on, Dr. Chalmers pictured parallel enterprises in the other neglected corners of the city and, answering an unspoken objection that he was trying to foist a denominational enterprise on the general Christian community, he said : " Some people say, ' Oh ! this is all a scheme of the Free Church.' Now, I say this is a mistake. Who cares about the Free Church compared with the Christian good of the people of Scotland ? Who cares for any Church, but as an instrument of Christian good ? For, be assured that the moral and religious well-being of the population is infinitely of higher importance than the advancement of any sect. For myself, I should rejoice if the ministers of every evangelical denomination would go and do likewise. There would be a far greater likelihood of our coming to a closer union, if we were engaged together in such missionary work, than by meeting in Committees, and drawing up articles which give rise to interminable controversies." [2]

It is quite fascinating to watch in the leader of the Free Church the fusion of his early enthusiasm for the transplanting of the virtues of the parochial system of the Church of Scotland into the larger cities, with the new enthusiasm for a Universal Home Mission, which would be the nursery of a larger union.

For one last look at the West Port enterprise and its place in the mind of its originator we cannot do better than transcribe part of a letter which he wrote to an American correspondent, just three months before his

[1] *Churches and Schools for the Working Classes*, pp. 12–13   [2] *Ibid.*, p. 21

death. " I wish to communicate what to me is the most joyful event of my life. I have been intent for thirty years on the completion of a territorial experiment, and I have now to bless God for the consummation of it. Our church was opened on the 19th of February, and in one month my anxieties respecting an attendance have been set at rest. Five-sixths of the sittings have been let; but the best part of it is, that three-fourths of these are from the West Port, a locality which, two years ago, had not one in ten churchgoers from the whole population. I presided myself, on Sabbath last, over its first sacrament. There were 132 communicants, and 100 of them from the West Port." [1] The evangelization of Edinburgh's western slum was a glorious sunset to his labours.

It might seem from this chapter and the last that Dr. Chalmers' life in these closing years was quite as thronged with public activities as it was at the height of his strength. This was far from being the case. Though his interests were so manifold, he had more frequent intervals of comparative leisure. These he employed in his study. About one half of them he devoted to preparing his *Institutes of Theology* for publication. In much of the other half he was engaged in a very different task. In 1841 he began two sets of MSS. volumes. In one set entries were made on week-days ; in the other in the greater quiet of the Sundays. Neither set was ever intended to be made public. In the daily journal he wrote down reflections arising from the daily Bible reading, until he had made comments, largely devotional, on the whole Bible. To this certain of his friends had free access. Many people knew of its existence, and after his death there was a desire expressed for its publication. This was duly done, and the *Horæ Biblicæ*

[1] Hanna, vol. iv, p. 411

Quotidianæ form the first three volumes of his posthumous works.

The Sabbath series had a character of its own. With the text of the passage before him he allowed his mind to roam more widely. The message would relate itself to his private problems, and from the conjunction of the two his spirit would rise to private and intimate devotions. No-one, during his lifetime, was permitted to read these volumes. But his family, after his death, felt that they would be so stimulating to the devotional life of others that it would exhibit undue reticence to withhold them from the Christian public. So as the *Horæ Biblicæ Sabbaticæ* they form the fourth and fifth volumes of his posthumous works.

No-one can wonder at the esteem in which they have been held by choice spirits in later generations. They have been kept, in many a household, when the other seven volumes have been parted with long since. They are far more intimate than the most affectionate of the private letters that have survived. They have hardly a parallel in the whole of Christian literature. The historian is apt to read them very much through their dates, and to try to fit them into the particular problem with which he was faced at the moment. Thus used they possess distinctive value, but read simply without any reference to, or even knowledge of, these problems, the two volumes stand very high indeed in the ranks of the classics of experimental religion.

In order to illustrate their quality and to indicate the added value their dating gives to their contents, let me quote a part of one of the earliest entries. The passage before him was the tenth chapter of Matthew— Our Lord's commission to the twelve—and the date was December 1841.

"The time, perhaps, is coming when the work of Christianization must begin anew over the face of a land desolated of its wonted provision for the ministry of the Gospel. Prepare me and counsel me aright for such a time, O God. My own preference should be for an organization to raise the requisite supplies ; and for the keeping up of a parochial system. It is clear that apart from these there is a method distinct from either of them, by which the missionaries of the present day might go forth as did the Apostles of old—providing nothing beforehand, and instead of fixing themselves anywhere, making the place of their ministrations depend upon the reception they met with. But is there aught in our economics adverse to the spirit of these instructions, and might we not in consistency therewith imitate substantially these first teachers of Christianity, by walking in the footsteps of their faith and self-denial and wisdom and harmlessness ? Let it not be in our own wisdom, O God, that we devise for Thy glory and the good of our Redeemer's kingdom, but in the wisdom which Thou givest." [1]

The historian naturally turns with especial avidity to the Sunday following the Disruption. The course of his reading found him that day in the gospel of John, at the nineteenth chapter, the story of the Crucifixion. Only towards the end when his thoughts were dwelling on Joseph of Arimathea and Nicodemus is there any distinct reflection of the situation. " Thou gavest Him and His cause to have favour with one, at least, of the rich in this world. . . . Not many rich, not many noble are on our side—yet Thou canst turn the hearts of men whithersoever Thou wilt ; and we desire to bless Thee, O God, for the measure of countenance vouchsafed to our Church even by the affluent and the noble of our day, and by the

[1] *Horæ Sabbaticæ*, vol. i, pp. 16-17

great bulk of the common people. But we desire to look beyond men, regarding them but in the light of instruments and secondary causes ; and directly to Thee, O God, would we refer everything that befalls us—if prosperous, receiving it with all gratitude as a kindness from heaven—if adverse, submitting to it as to one of heaven's wise and righteous visitations ! " [1]

These are not fair samples, however, from which to deduce the devotional depth of the Sabbath readings. In dealing with the impact of great contemporary events upon the artistic temperament, G. K. Chesterton says, " Bewick's birds have the air of being singularly unaffected by the French Revolution." The same is true of these readings. Only at rare intervals can one detect such plain reflections of the problems of the day. The soul of the writer has, like a bird, escaped into the upper air.

It was at the time of the Assembly of 1847, during the very night before his second report on the work of the College Committee was eagerly awaited by the Supreme Court, that Dr. Chalmers, suddenly and unexpectedly, slipped peacefully away. The Assembly was stunned as it seldom has been in its history. At the first shock of the news there was dominant a devastating sense of loss ; but gratitude to Almighty God for the gift of such a man found expression in the simple solemnities of a public funeral in which the heart of the city was profoundly stirred, and of which a contemporary newspaper thus chronicles its impression. " It was the dust of a Presbyterian clergyman that the coffin contained ; and yet they were burying him amid the tears of a nation, and with more than kingly honours." [2]

[1] *Horæ Sabbaticæ*, vol. i, p. 144   [2] *Witness*, June 5, 1847

Chapter Twenty-five

RETROSPECT

ONE striking sequel to the death of Thomas Chalmers was a veritable spate of funeral orations. In addition to the hundreds that were printed, by way of excerpt or summary, in city and provincial newspapers, there were scores that found separate publication in full or augmented form. The bulk were from Scotland and from the Free Church, but other lands and Churches joined in to swell the tribute. No other Scottish churchman had ever such a coronach. While an Argus-eyed critic might see in all this "an indulgence of authorcraft rather than of grief," [1] and while only in a minority of cases is any fresh contribution made to the understanding of the man or his work, nevertheless their mere volume makes its own appeal, and one finds oneself concurring in the verdict of his colleague, Dr. James Buchanan, who, in opening the next session in New College, said : "These tokens of a universal interest and common sympathy . . . which have flowed in one unbroken current since the announcement of his departure . . . show more eloquently than words can tell that the master-mind of the Free Church, the veteran hero of the Disruption, tenacious to the last of his peculiar principles, and testifying for them with his latest breath before rulers and nations,[2] was still recognized and honoured the world over, as the greatest representa-

[1] MacPhail's *Edinburgh Ecclesiastical Journal*, 1847, p. 201
[2] Referring to the evidence before the Parliamentary Committee on the Refusal of Sites.
(336)

23

tive and noblest specimen of living, large-hearted, catholic-minded Christianity." [1]

The deepest impression that remains from this mass of reading—and this seems to sum up Scotland's immediate reaction—is the prevalence of the note, even in those most closely associated with him, of veneration as from a distance. Dr. Chalmers is treated as though he belonged to another order of being, to a race of supermen. For this impression the Scripture texts, on which the tributes were founded, may be held partly responsible, but only partly. The analogies of Moses and Abraham and Paul would not have been pushed so far with other leaders. For one who mingled so much and so constantly with his fellow men of all classes and conditions, there seems to have been something about him remote and inaccessible. Even the most outstanding of his brethren looked on him as one who habitually moved on heights too lofty for them to feel quite at home in his company. When the protagonist of any worthy cause is removed from the scene of his earthly warfare this note is never altogether absent in tributes paid to his memory. But in Chalmers' case it was the all-pervading note. Love and grief for the comrade-in-arms is swallowed up in veneration for the exalted personality. The uncommon man has almost blotted out the common humanity. It is no matter for astonishment that, in the situation he had left behind, there were keen watchful eyes in the land which saw in all this the incipient stages of idolatry.

Nor did this marked veneration cease with the contemporary pulpit tributes. It is quite as emphatic in later verdicts of men of distinction who had known and heard him. Dr. John Brown, with memories rekindled by the *Posthumous Works*, coined for his description a

[1] J. Buchanan, *A Tribute to the Memory of Dr. Chalmers, etc.*, pp. 4–5

phrase which is significant. A *solar* man he termed him,
" drawing after him his own firmament of planets." [1]
To Professor David Masson as he looked back on the days
of his youth, there were great Scottish figures in many
walks of life, but the brightest luminary was Chalmers.
" He had met no human being in the world," he was
never tired of saying, " that he would call greater than
Chalmers." [2] Even Thomas Carlyle, who, in a crabbed
mood of disagreement, could cavil at him as " ill-read,"
was constrained to say, " No preacher ever went so into
one's heart. I suppose there will never again be such
a preacher in any Christian Church " [3] ; and later, on
hearing of his death, " I believe that there is not
in Scotland, or all Europe, any such Christian priest
left." [4]

If that impression waned the reason is not far to seek.
He became associated in men's minds with a sectional
interest, strong and flourishing indeed, but still sectional.
Lesser men outside felt that to indulge in praise of
Chalmers was to increase the prestige of the Free Church,
at the expense, perhaps, of their own. A bigger man like
Norman MacLeod regretted that his Assembly took no
notice of the death, and a little later spoke of him to a
gathering of the laymen of the Church of Scotland as one
" whose noble character, lofty enthusiasm, and patriotic
views will rear themselves before the eyes of posterity like
Alpine peaks, long after the narrow valleys which have
for a brief period divided us are lost in the far distance
of past history." [5] To-day, liberated from this inhibition,
all may freely join in the homage paid by the men of his
generation. Over thirty years ago a leading churchman

[1] *Horæ Subsecivæ*, 2nd series, p. 62   [2] A. Philip, *Thomas Chalmers*, p. 20
[3] D. A. Wilson, *Thomas Carlyle*, vol. i, p. 134   [4] *Ibid.*, vol. iii, p. 376
[5] D. MacLeod, *Life of Norman MacLeod*, one-volume edition, p. 176.

said, " Chalmers belongs to us all." [1] His words have their force multiplied now.

If we were to seek, from among the manifold activities recorded in the earlier pages, one phrase which might sum up the ideals of this devoted spirit, there are many who would choose " the Christian good of Scotland " as *the* watchword of his life. A Scotland regenerated in every part, religiously, morally, economically, and socially was his aim throughout. He burned to see a people evangelized and evangelizing, steadfast in good and for good, industrious, and reaping the rewards of industry. Scotland was to be a vineyard of the Lord, with the weeds of poverty, crime, and irreligion banished by an efficient Christian culture.

But at no point in his career were the boundaries of Scotland his horizon. From the very moment of his evangelical rebirth at Kilmany it was the world-wide Christian enterprise that held his allegiance and drew forth his devotion. At the height of his social experiment he was campaigning for the Moravians. It was while he was commending to the public the lessons of that experiment that he was kindling the choicest spirits to serve their Lord in India. In his later years the phrase " the Christian good of Scotland " almost vanished from his vocabulary. It had been replaced by the " Universal Home Mission," to which the West Port was more a personal than a denominational contribution. He yearned to see the organized religious resources of every branch of the Christian Church united in a co-ordinated attack on heathenism, destitution, and ignorance. It was as a defender of the Christian faith that he won his theological spurs ; in the Church's practical concerns

[1] Dr. Robertson Nicoll, in addressing the Theological Society of Edinburgh University, *British Weekly*, October 27, 1910.

he was the exponent of a vigorous and continuous united offensive on a world-wide front. Remembered by many as the author of division, he was much more markedly the apostle of union. No more catholic-minded man was ever driven by circumstances into being the founder of a separate denomination. For it was simply and solely because the Church of Scotland, established and endowed, was to him the obvious instrument for the Christian good of the part of the world nearest to his hand, that he sought to make it efficient. Just as he had counted release from the antiquated machinery for dealing with poverty in Glasgow necessary for coping with poverty in St. John's, there must, he felt, be a similar release from the accumulated deadweight of a *laissez-faire* ecclesiastical past, before the Church of Scotland could fully accomplish its task of dealing with a changed and changing world. In no spirit of challenge to the State, but simply and solely for the welfare of its citizens, he embarked on that course of reform which was to end in the Disruption.

In a retrospect on the Disruption itself it is not unnecessary to recall the primary intention of the term. It is too often taken for granted that it meant a disruption *of* the Church, and that it was adopted by the " Free Protesting Church " to emphasize its magnitude, as being too extensive to be called a Secession merely, and in reality, " a rending in twain," to quote Dr. J. R. Fleming's description.[1] And when Anglican divines heard in Scottish churches phrases like " the glorious Disruption," particularly in prayers of thanksgiving, they wondered into what Bedlam they had strayed. But there was no suggestion of schism in the word. It was not a disruption *of*, it was a disruption *from* ; not even a disruption from their brethren who remained behind,

[1] *The Church in Scotland, 1843–74,* p. 19

but a disruption from the Establishment. And by the Establishment they meant the whole privileges, emoluments, status, and obligations as then interpreted of the State relation. It was a word used by Dr. Chalmers in various connections throughout his whole career. It appears early in his journal and letters, applied to very diverse separations, such as from excessive addiction to secular studies and the Parish of Kilmany. His own life had seen a " disruption " from these. In its ecclesiastical application it appears first, so far as one has observed, in his speech in the Assembly of 1839, where " the calamity of a disruption " manifestly refers to a disruption from the State. In later speeches it is equated with " a clear, and an honourable, and withal a Christian outgoing," and " a withdrawal from the intolerable position forced upon us." The language of the Protest and of the Deed of Demission bears the same implication ; and the mere fact that the latter was sent to the Government suggests that it was its signing and transmission, which not only completed but constituted the decisive disruptive act. Disruption took place when the " true " Church of Scotland thus severed itself from the State.[1] Tanfield Hall was its scene, not St. Andrew's Church, where the severance of brethren took place. It was this implication which led the Established Church, at first at least, pointedly to avoid the term. What was a " glorious Disruption " to the one Church, was to the other a " lamentable Secession." [2] But, into its

---

[1] A typical example of the inscriptions on the original Free Churches is to be found in this one from Dumfriesshire : " The People of Glencairn / aided by the Central Fund / built this house for the worship of God / When for adhering to her old standards and the / Testimony of the Martyrs / On behalf of / Christ as King of Sion / the Church of Scotland was severed from the State."

[2] Henry Cowan, *The Scottish Church in Christendom*, p. 195.

original use and fundamental meaning, the thought of a split in the Church did not enter. The Disruption would have remained a Disruption, indeed it would have been all the greater a Disruption, had it been unanimous.

In point of fact, however, it did entail a " rending in twain," which in turn led to consequences both good and bad. On the credit side must be entered the awakening of the Christian people of every church in Scotland to their responsibility for the religious welfare of every corner of the land and the multiplied provision, in some quarters excessive, for the worship of God and the education of the children. In the larger centres a healthier emulation in good works displaced traditional inertia and superseded less wholesome ancient feuds. To all this there must be added the distinctive denominational contribution of the Free Church, which, from its initial plans through its subsequent achievements, alike in evangelism and education, at home and abroad, through its great teachers and leaders and missionaries, evoked the admiration of Christendom, as a living branch of the Church Universal abundant in blossom and equally abundant in fruit.

On the debit side must be placed, particularly in places with declining population, overlappings of agencies, and the consequent animosities. Men tended to be esteemed religious in proportion to the strenuousness and effectiveness of their activities against the other side. Ecclesiastical allegiance became a first consideration in local secular appointments, ruling even the granting of leases and the engagement of shepherds and ploughmen. And that hateful temper, *Schadenfreude*—for which the Germans alone have the word, but from which no people is immune —insinuated itself too often into the hearts of rival churchmen. There was, unquestionably, a sombre lining to the glory of the Disruption.

An adequate assessment of the responsibility for this catastrophic element would entail a recapitulation of the whole ground already covered. But, undoubtedly, in the critical final stages the onus rests on the Government of the day. When it refused to give its mind to " that massive and magnificent state-paper, the Claim, Declaration, and Protest of 1842," [1] and instead took the opportunity of roundly rebuking the Church for its swollen pretensions and continued contumacy, the die was cast.

It has been frequently asserted, however, in exculpation that had it foreseen the magnitude of the withdrawal it would have acted otherwise ; that, misled by its own particular Scottish correspondents, it decided that a final demonstration of firmness would ensure a widespread, almost universal, retreat from the positions the Church had taken up. In confirmation, it is pointed out that, in later life, nearly all the statesmen involved, in one way or another, expressed their great regret at what had happened. Sir James Graham, in particular, is recorded as saying that " he would never cease to regard it with the deepest regret and sorrow, as the saddest event of his life, that he should have had any hand in that most fatal act." [2] His first biographer, going even further, asserts that he " was convinced, when too late, of the error into which, in deference to the judgment of others, he had fallen." [3]

That he and the others did regret the sequel to their decision is unquestionable, but that he or they ever came

---

[1] A. Taylor Innes, *Studies in Scottish History*, p. 134
[2] N. L. Walker, *Robert Buchanan, D.D.*, p. 208
[3] Torrens, *Life of Sir James Graham*, vol. ii, p. 233

to regard the decision as an error in policy is very doubt-ful.[1] The attempt to represent them later as a group of penitents in white sheets has no substantial basis. They were, and remained, consistent Erastians, ready to smother any assertion of her autonomy on the part of the Church. They would have held up their hands in genuine horror at the release of the Church of Scotland from the yoke of patronage in 1874, a release, opposed indeed by the Free Church, but hastened by the con-tiguity of its system of popular election, and the failure of Lord Aberdeen's Act. And no words would be adequate to describe their consternation had they been confronted with the spectacle of the Church of Scotland presenting to their successors in 1921 as articles lawful for her to enact, those contained in the schedule to the Enabling Bill, in especial Article IV.[2] No! Misinforma-tion may have led them to scamp consideration, and to act more peremptorily than they might have done ; but sound information would not have altered their decision.[3] They were convinced adherents of what Dr. Figgis has called " the concession theory of corporate life " [4] : the conception of an independent ecclesiastical authority in the commonwealth was, to them, a noxious weed to be ruthlessly extirpated. It stands to the credit

---

[1] C. S. Parker, *Life and Letters of Sir James Graham*, vol. i, pp. 395-96

[2] *Vide* p. 356

[3] Even the Duke of Wellington, who, in his letter to Lord Aberdeen in the heart of the conflict, suggested a solution similar in method to that of 1921, " that the kirk should state clearly the rule which it is pro-posed to adopt, and that that rule should be made the subject of an Act of Parliament," and who was praised by Dr. Buchanan (*Ten Years' Conflict*, vol. ii, p. 124) for his " almost intuitive sagacity " in mastering " the true theory of the Church and State system of Scotland," might well have found himself precluded from giving his support to the measure when confronted with its contents.

[4] J. N. Figgis, *Churches in the Modern State*, p. 25

of the British Government of 1921 that, just when totalitarian states were beginning to assume new forms and were on the eve of a fresh prevalence, it should so handsomely and unreservedly recognize the historic claims of the Scottish Church.[1]

It was, indeed, a historic claim on which this recognition set its seal. It had been blazoned on the Church's banner from the beginning. Scotland for Christ through a Church free from civil domination in the ordering of its own spiritual affairs under Him sums up the witness of almost four centuries. For Scotland's main contribution to Reformed Theology has been within this domain of the Erastian Controversy. Dr. William Cunningham put the matter in his simplest language when he wrote: " Of all Protestant countries, England is the one where the claim of civil supremacy over the Church was most openly put forth, most fully conceded, and most injuriously exercised ; while our own beloved land is that in which it has all along been most strenuously and successfully resisted." [2] No century has been without its conflict, and none without its literary defence. The events that issued in the Disruption constituted the most subtle and penetrating of them all. When the struggle reached its culmination in the spring of 1843 it looked as though the Erastian forces had been following a plan. The new outworks constructed by the Church were first to be levelled with the ground, and then, by infiltration, the central citadel was to be taken from the rear. For it was no mere question of jurisdiction that was finally at stake. There are to be found scattered throughout the opinions of even the majority judges,

[1] *Vide* Sir C. G. Robertson, *Religion and the Totalitarian State*
[2] Cunningham, *Historical Theology*, vol. ii, p. 568

ample acknowledgment of the validity and finality of the Church's jurisdiction—within the limits conceded or prescribed by statute. Even Sir Robert Peel in the House of Commons could speak of the exclusive jurisdiction of the Church in spiritual matters, though what was left of it after the decisions of 1842–43 was microscopic. There are, of course, many apparent exceptions, like the declaration of Lord Wood in the Stewarton Case that the Court of Session had a two-fold duty to " declare what the Church is bound to do, and enjoin performance, and what it is bound not to do, . . . and enforce the restriction." [1] Even this, in its historical context, is less drastic than it sounds apart from it.

The final quarrel of the courts and legislature was not with the fact of the Church's jurisdiction, but with her claim as to the source of that jurisdiction. It was the high anti-Erastian doctrine of the Westminster Confession that was once more challenged that " The Lord Jesus, as King and Head of His Church, has therein appointed a government in the hands of Church officers, distinct from the Civil Magistrate "—a doctrine reasserted in the Resolution of 1838, with the explanatory amplification " that in all matters touching the doctrine, government, and discipline of this Church, her judicatories possess an exclusive jurisdiction founded on the Word of God "—a doctrine which was to be still further defined in the fifth question of the formula of questions put to all probationers and ministers of the Free Church that that government is " distinct from, and not subordinate in its own province to, civil government, and that the civil magistrate does not possess jurisdiction, or authoritative control, over the regulation of the affairs of Christ's Church "—all of which and more came to be embodied

[1] *Stewarton Case*, p. 73

in the United Free Church Act anent Spiritual Independence (1906) and then in the Articles Declaratory of the Constitution of the Church of Scotland in Matters Spiritual (1926), which together constitute the basis of the constitution of the re-united Church in this matter. It is well at this point to incorporate Article IV that it may be read in the light of the central points at issue in 1843.

" IV. This Church, as part of the Universal Church wherein the Lord Jesus Christ has appointed a government in the hands of Church office-bearers, receives from Him, its Divine King and Head, and from Him alone, the right and power subject to no civil authority to legislate, and to adjudicate finally, in all matters of doctrine, worship, government, and discipline in the Church, including the right to determine all questions concerning membership and office in the Church, the constitution and membership of its Courts, and the mode of election of its office-bearers, and to define the boundaries of the spheres of labour of its ministers and other office-bearers. Recognition by civil authority of the separate and independent government and jurisdiction of this Church in matters spiritual, in whatever manner such recognition be expressed, does not in any way affect the character of this government and jurisdiction as derived from the Divine Head of the Church alone, or give to the civil authority any right of interference with the proceedings or judgments of the Church within the sphere of its spiritual government and jurisdiction."

It was this historic claim that was the focus of attack

and the centre of resistance in the Disruption conflict. The Lord Justice Clerk specifically denied the possibility of any jurisdiction which "*not being derived from the State*, cannot be subjected to the control of the judgment of the Courts appointed to enforce the laws made by the State." [1] And many scornful words were directed against the pretensions of Churchmen—their doctrine of the Headship of Christ—and any independent jurisdiction or legislative authority flowing therefrom.

Within this generation a brilliant outside observer, Professor Laski, in language remote from the terminology of the struggle, thus states its essential meaning. " The Presbyterians of 1843 were fighting the notion of a unitary state. To them it seemed obvious that the society to which they belonged was no mere cog-wheel in the machinery of the State, destined only to work in harmony with its motions. They felt the strength of a personality which, as they urged, was complete and self-sufficient, just as the mediæval state asserted its right to independence when it was strong enough not merely to resent, but even to repudiate, the tutelage of the ecclesiastical power. They were fighting a State which had taken over bodily the principles and ideals of the mediæval theocracy. They urged the essential federalism of society, the impossibility of confining sovereignty to any one of its constituent parts." [2]

Illuminating as this reading of their action is, the men of the Disruption were not pre-occupied with questions of political theory. They faced a concrete issue. And while it can be clearly seen to-day that these fundamental problems were involved, that was not how they presented themselves to those who had to make a decision which would shape the future of their land and church. Leaving

[1] *Stewarton Case*, p. 56   [2] H. J. Laski, *The Problem of Sovereignty*, p. 65

out of account those who were moved by considerations of personal security or of personal popularity, the best of the men of 1843 found themselves confronted with the old choice of the priority of principle or institution.

To Chalmers and the like-minded, principle was paramount. An essential element in the Church's witness had been denied. Every attempt to attain its recognition had failed. Full loyalty to the Headship of Christ was impossible within the now fettered institution. Let us abandon the Establishment, they said, and continue and deepen our witness to the principle, even if it be without the gate. Denuded as we will then be of what we have valued, we may do much, perhaps more than ever, to hold and to win Scotland for Christ.

The best on the other side stood by the institution. True, the Headship of Christ had been sadly impaired, but that doctrine had suffered hard knocks before. Let us, they said, accept the present limitations as transitory, and, even though some brethren seem content with them, let us work persistently for their removal. A better day will dawn when we will be able to fly the confessional banner in the face of all the world. Within a century a better day did dawn, but it was the Disruption that had made it possible.

. . . .

The historical survey here comes to an end. But a final word may be permitted in another vein, containing things *sermoni propiora*, "properer for a sermon" as Charles Lamb translated it. It needed but little imagination, on that 2nd of October 1929, in the huge hall of reunion, to see the radiant figure of Thomas Chalmers, dwarfing all other intrusions from the past, raising those speaking hands of his in benediction, and calling on the great assembly to join, to the tune Scarborough or Devizes,[1] in the familiar lines of the 147th Psalm :

> God doth build up Jerusalem ;
>   And He it is alone
> That the dispers'd of Israel
>   Doth gather into one.

Have we lived up to that fine hour, the culmination of many a struggle and the fruit of many a sacrifice ? Is the reunited Church doing all that it might for the Christian good of Scotland, and in the Universal Home Mission ? With institution and principle now reintegrated does the glow persist ? And will it brighten ? " Pray ye, therefore, the Lord of the harvest."

[1] Dr. Chalmers' two favourite tunes, *vide* Hanna, vol. ii, p. 291

INDEX

Aberdeen, Earl of, 199f, 203f, 222, 223, 228, 233, 240, 243, 304, 353
Alison, Dr. W. P., 224
Anderson, James, 36
Argyll, Duke of, 228, 240, 242

Balfour, Dr. Robert, 28
Ballantyne, Rev. J., 97
Begg, Dr. James, 106, 107n., 277f
Black, Dr. Alexander, 331
Brougham, Lord, 141, 173, 175, 199, 265
Brown, Rev. C. J., 138, 139
Brown, Dr. James, 16
Brown, Dr. John, 50n., 346
Brown, Dr. Thomas, 84, 85
Brown, Rev. Dr. Thomas, 326
Bryce, Dr. James, vii, 124, 177, 212, 233, 268, 270, 288, 303
Buchanan, Dr. James, 345
Buchanan, Dr. Robert, vii, 171, 222, 291, 295
Burns, Rev. Robert, 48n.
Bute, Marquis of, 245

Campbell, Mr., of Monzie, 242, 263
Campbell, John, afterwards Lord Campbell, 15
Campbell, William, 151
Candlish, Dr. R. S., 196, 220, 224, 228, 232, 249, 266, 268n., 270, 295, 313, 327
Carey, William, 16
Carlyle, Thomas, 225, 347
Chalmers, Alexander, brother of Thomas, 34, 35
Chalmers, Grace, wife, 40, 67
Chalmers, James, brother, 19
Chalmers, Jane, sister, 35
Chalmers, John, father, 13, 21, 22, 24
Charlotte, Princess, 46
Clark, Rev. Thomas, 183, 184, 186

Clelland, Rev. James, 280, 281, 282
Cockburn, Lord, 5n., 188, 273
Collins, William, 143
Cook, Dr. George, 10, 127, 136, 139, 179, 182, 185, 195, 202, 212, 213, 219, 229, 246, 254, 285, 289
Cottenham, Lord, 173, 175, 199
Cumming, Dr. John, 294
Cunningham, Dr. William, 196, 250, 253, 295, 332, 354

Dalhousie, Earl of, 182
Denney, Prof. James, 35
Duff, Alexander, 77, 149
Duncan, Dr. Henry, 212
Duncan, Dr. John, 332
Dunlop, Alexander Murray, 198, 213, 243, 248, 268n., 292, 293

Edouart, M. August, vi, 50n.
Edwards, Rev. John, 207ff, 215ff
Edwards, Jonathan, 17
Eliot, George, 294
Erskine, Rev. Ebenezer, 190, 191

Figgis, Dr. J. N., 353
Fleming, Dr. J. R., 349
Foster, Rev. John, 12
Fox, Charles, 227
Fuller, Rev. Andrew, 50

Gladstone, W. E., 112
Gordon, Dr. Robert, 211, 222, 291, 295, 298, 310,
Graham, Sir James, 107, 223, 273, 276, 304, 309, 327, 328, 352
Gray, Rev. Andrew, 138
Gurney, J. J., 93

Hamilton, Sir William, 84
Hanna, Dr. William, vii, viii, 22, 27, 267, 279, 325, 333